M000301296

NORAH LINDSAY

THE LIFE AND ART OF A GARDEN DESIGNER

NORAH LINDSAY

THE LIFE AND ART
OF A GARDEN DESIGNER

Allyson Hayward

F

FRANCES LINCOLN LIMITED

PUBLISHERS

Frances Lincoln Ltd
4 Torriano Mews
Torriano Avenue
London NW5 2RZ
www.franceslincoln.com

Norah Lindsay: The Life and Art of a Garden Designer
Copyright © Frances Lincoln Ltd 2007
Text copyright © Allyson Hayward 2007

First Frances Lincoln edition: 2007

Allyson Hayward has asserted her moral right to be
identified as the author of this work in accordance with the
Copyright, Designs and Patents Act 1988 (UK)

All rights reserved. No part of this publication may be
reproduced, stored in a retrieval system transmitted in
any form, or by any means, electronic, mechanical,
photocopying, recording or otherwise, without either
permission in writing from the publisher or a licence
permitting restricted copying. In the United Kingdom such
licences are issued by the Copyright Licensing Agency,
Saffron House, 6–10 Kirby Street, London EC1N 8TS.

British Library Cataloguing in Publication Data
A catalogue record for this book is available from
the British Library.

ISBN 978-0-7112-2524-4

Designed by Anne Wilson

Printed and bound in Singapore

9 8 7 6 5 4 3 2 1

Contents

INTRODUCTION

ORAH LINDSAY, NÉE BOURKE, socialite and garden designer, was the charming and beautiful daughter of an upper-class family who lived her entire life among England's country-house elite. She lunched with Winston Churchill, gardened for the Prince of Wales, holidayed with Edith Wharton, and hobnobbed with Hollywood's Merle Oberon, David Niven, and Vivien Leigh. She was beautiful, musical, artistically talented, high spirited, and a great conversationalist. A brilliant hostess, she mingled with the political and social luminaries of the era, all of whom were captivated by her clever repartee and quick wit. In 1904 her home, the Manor House of Sutton Courtenay, overflowed with garden beds filled with flowers, guest room beds filled with friends, and rowing boats on the Thames filled with the handsome youth of the day – many of them the young men of Oxford University. Weekends spent in the company of Norah Lindsay were always filled with laughter and music, glorious meals, and non-stop outdoor activities.

In 1924, at the age of 51, with her marriage having fallen apart and with her financial situation dire, she put her garden design skills to use and embarked upon a garden design career that continued for the next two decades. Her commissions ranged from manor houses on the country lanes of England, and grand aristocratic estates, to royal gardens on the Continent. Her client base consisted of royalty, English nobility, and American expatriates.

Some of Norah Lindsay's gardens are intact and maintained. These treasured gardens abound with an informal scramble of flowering plants, accented with elegant topiary – a trademark of her original design style. Some of the properties are now under the careful guidance and preservation of The National Trust. Some of the estates are vigilantly guarded through private ownership, a few have been modified or simplified, and some are now the dilapidated and run-down shells of their original selves. In all, the spirit of Norah Lindsay's brilliance and consummate skill still lingers.

When I first came upon an essay more than a decade ago about Norah Lindsay, I was captivated by her story. There was something about her that intrigued me. I was fascinated by the plants she chose for her gardens, by the people she chose for her circle of friends, and for some peculiar reason, by the fact that she died in the year I was born. A curious connection at best, but that short essay got me going.

The Norah Lindsay that I first encountered in that essay and during the early months of my research was famous for her happy carefree life, flitting from one grand country house to another, without a care in the world. Every article that chronicled her life proclaimed that she lived an untroubled existence; that she sat at the dinner tables of the rich and the famous; and that she was more interested in her social standing than in taking the time to write a

OPPOSITE A doorway into the garden at Sutton Courtenay. ABOVE Norah Bourke.

book about the gardens she was so brilliantly planting. Everywhere the descriptive words for Norah's character were 'elusive, social butterfly, gadfly'. Nothing could have been farther from the truth about this woman and her life than these assumptions. To earn her modest wages, Norah toiled for long hours in her clients' gardens. She was known to wake at dawn to meet the head gardener in order to direct the plantings, or help with the staking and transplanting. Having no money for a car of her own, she had to rely on public transport, so the physical labour that she put into her gardens often followed closely on the heels of uncomfortably hot or tediously slow and damp train travel connections. Only when she was especially fortunate did one of her clients send their own personal car to transport her to her next assignment. This was not an 'elusive, social butterfly' mode of existence. Norah expressed her feelings in a letter to her sister as she described a day of work at Port Lympne with Sir Philip Sassoon. 'I got up at cock crow on Friday and spent the day at Philip's in broiling sun walking about the whole of his place with his gardener. In the late afternoon caught a train back to Sutton … What a busy life – what with music and garden and now other people's gardens! Well, it's all to the good, as it prevents moping, which a lonely woman who only likes a crowd of loving humans round her is inclined of course, to do.'[1] Norah tried to put an uplifting ending to the letter, but in the autumn of 1926 she wrote of her true feelings, 'I am a tired and cold business woman! I used to adore lying in bed in a hot bedroom and having nothing to do.'[2] Norah Lindsay's life was not frivolous or easy. Her life was productive and filled with gifted creativity.

In the course of tracing the life of Norah Lindsay, I chose physically to follow her steps as closely as possible. I travelled throughout England on numerous occasions, sometimes accompanied by a friend or relative acting as my navigator; and sometimes alone, with only a map and the spirit of Norah riding at my side. I visited and stayed overnight in the grand homes where Norah had once been. I experienced first-hand what life might have been like at Cliveden, now a private hotel where the traditions of Norah's era still lurk. With copies of her letters describing

her gardens at Cliveden, I walked the property, observing and comparing the small vestiges of Norah's mark on the gardens from the descriptions that I held in my hand. I continued my garden-hopping searches for about four years. As I was led on tours of the many gardens by their owners or head gardeners, I realized that they all held a special admiration for Norah's talents.

I visited the beautiful home of Sir James and Lady Scott at Rotherfield Park in Hampshire. There, I was treated to a private tour of the gardens by Lady Scott, followed by a sumptuous family lunch with Sir James and Lady Scott and their two children, during which we traded stories about Norah and the gardens. After lunch, with enthusiasm at a heightened state for 'all things Norah', together we trooped up the front staircase of the house, which had been made famous as the set backdrop for a wedding scene in the 1994 film *Four Weddings and a Funeral*. From there we retired to the archives where, sitting on the floor while poring over scrapbooks and carefully protected documents, we read out from pages written in Norah's hand of her planting schemes for the property. We marvelled over the invoice that indicated that she charged only £5 5s for a professional day of gardening.

I sped from one county's Public Record Office to another, poring over the archives of the people Norah Lindsay worked for and socialized with. I remember very vividly one day spent in the Hertfordshire Archives and Local Studies Office, with my navigator friend seated at the table beside me. We read certain passages out loud to each other and cried over the soulful condolence letters in the Grenfell Family Archives which Ettie, Lady Desborough, received when she lost her two sons during World War I. One distraught letter after another, from one grieving mother to another, made us so clearly aware of a mother's misery during wartime and of the great loss of England's cherished youth during that era. Norah wrote a series of letters to her friend Ettie after the death of Ettie's second son: 'He is now with his dear boy beyond all the cheering and the fighting. I can picture those two beloved golden heads always waiting and watching over you. Till that happy day when you are again together, as in the sunny hours at Taplow. My heart trembles and aches for you and my sky is so clouded – all the time I am thinking of you and the pain of it all. Your sorrowful, Norah.'[3] Ettie responded with her heartfelt thanks and wrote, 'No mourning was worn for either Billy or Julian, but of course you couldn't fail those boys, it would be like mourning the death of a Meteor.'[4] My navigator friend and I had trouble recovering from that day in the records office. We returned to our rooms at Cliveden and quietly floated on the Thames in one of the hotel's vintage boats and talked long into the evening of Norah and of the historic times and of the people with whom her life had been intertwined.

Norah Lindsay was a prolific letter writer. During my research, I located volumes of her correspondence. As I sifted through the hundreds of letters that she wrote to family and friends, I was able to uncover the drama and exciting story of a life that was thought, until now, to be lost for ever.

A visit to Sam and Jane Whitbread of Southill Park in Bedfordshire was consistently the highlight of each of my trips to England and the basis for a large portion of the primary source research that went into this book. The Whitbread family has owned this grand estate since 1795. Norah's sister Madeline married a Whitbread and Sam is the great-nephew of Norah Lindsay, or Aunt Nornie[5] as she was called by her family members. In addition to providing me with food and lodging for weeks on end, I was allowed unrestricted access to their family archives which were filled with the letters and journals of Norah, her siblings, her parents, and other relatives. At meal times, we would sit together in the dining room, as Sam recalled stories of his grandmother Madeline and his Aunt Nornie while she lived at Southill Park during World War II. After dinner, I would retire to my bedroom – the room that

RIGHT ABOVE Norah's letter of comfort to her dear friend, Lady Desborough, undated.

RIGHT BELOW Writing with her distinctive scrawling script, Norah frequently used bright green ink that seemed to leak off the edges of the pages.

Norah had lived in during the war years. Jane and I liked to joke that I was trying to channel her energy each night from within the four walls she had known so well during those years. Each evening when I closed the door of Norah's bedroom, and sat down to a final hour or two of reading her letters before retiring, I marvelled that I was sitting in the very room where she wrote those letters, and maybe her energy wasn't that far away from me. Something was certainly keeping me going with this story.

I travelled to London to meet Penelope Dare, the granddaughter of Anne Burroughes, Norah's elder sister. She shared with me her memories of her Aunt Nornie and the early journals of her grandmother's life. She remembered Norah as 'very amusing and funny, eccentric and wonderful. Norah talked to the children in the family as if she were talking to an adult, often entertaining them with impersonations of the famous people she associated with, or by taking them to the movies and afterwards gossiping about the actors she knew. Norah acted in a very modern way. She was very unlike her older sister Anne, who was straight, stern and bossy. Norah always had a

The Manor House of Sutton Courtenay, current view.

painted face, lots of lipstick and pinched curls across her forehead. She dressed in exotic orange or purple pyjamas [fashionable daywear in the 1920s and 1930s] topped with white fur or blouses of some kind topped with layers of jewellery. Norah wore many rings, and when she sat down to play the piano she pulled off the rings, made a pile of them on top of the piano, and began to play. When she played the piano it was utter enchantment. Conversations with Norah were about the arts, the war and politics, who married who, and who was unhappy with whom, gossip, gossip, and endless talk of gardening.'[6] The family journals provide the basis for much of the story of Norah's early life. A major portion of the family photographs used throughout this book are from Mrs. Dare's family collection.

This whole story could not have been told without a few trips to the Manor House of Sutton Courtenay. The Hon. David Astor, who purchased the property from Norah's only son, Peter, allowed me to tour the house and grounds on many occasions, view the family scrapbooks, compare current garden plans to older plans, and spend hours with the head gardener Keith Deane, a helpful and knowledgeable source from which some of the garden's details used in the text of this book are derived.

Collectively, what I found in the research surprised me. Much of the early information I had read about Norah Lindsay before my research trips to England was not correct. While some bits and pieces of information have been accurately written about Norah Lindsay, there has been no single book that has documented the full story of this talented and well-connected garden designer. I hope to untangle the myths and distortions surrounding her name. This book clarifies Norah Lindsay's long and productive career and traces the legacy of her extraordinary talent. The book is not meant to be a scholarly analysis of her garden designs or a studied description of her flowerbeds. It is an overview of Norah Lindsay, the person. The story follows a cultural and social history of pre-World War II England, with the strong and independent Norah Lindsay surrounded by the political and social decision makers and trendsetters of the era.

This book is dedicated to David Lindsay, Norah's grandson, who so generously encouraged my search and provided me with a home base when I needed it during my travels. David never met his grandmother. I hope through the pages of this book that he comes to know her and to understand the details of the fascinating life she led.

'It's Miss Norah Bourke'

THE EARLY YEARS 1873–1895

Madras, India

NORAH MARY MADELINE BOURKE was born on April 26, 1873, in the family's cosy stone bungalow in Ootacamund, India. Norah was welcomed into the world by her doting parents and her ten-month-old sister, Anne. Anne, strong and splendid, was clearly her father's child; while Norah was her mother's, endowed with real loveliness and a gift for music at an early age.

Norah's father, Major Edward Roden Bourke, one of five brothers, was an imposing, handsome man – six feet four inches, bursting with energy. He had wavy brown hair, a thick chestnut moustache, and large twinkling eyes. He possessed the Irish gift of storytelling, an unabashed sense of humour, and a devotion to his family that never wavered. He had been educated at Westminster, where he excelled at rowing. A natural sportsman and an accomplished shot, he had entered the army by joining the Inniskilling Dragoons. Edward dedicated himself to a career in the military and was posted to Ootacamund ('Ooty'), the famous hill station near the junction of Tamil Nadu, Kerala and Karnataka in the Nilgiris Hills of India. Edward's military assignment was secure while he served as military secretary and postmaster general under the leadership of his older brother, Richard Southwell Bourke, 6th Earl of Mayo, Viceroy and Governor-General of India.

Norah's mother, Emmie, had been born in 1855 in India to General Hatch and his delicate wife Minnie Fraser. After five years of living in the hot plains of India, she was sent off to boarding school in Brussels. Emmie was 'lovely, really lovely, with a little perfect oval white face, a turned-up nose, wide green hazel eyes, black brows and lashes, and narrow hands and perfect feet and legs. She was

Volume N/2/54   Folio 73

These are to Certify that the Secretary of State for Foreign and Commonwealth Affairs has in his custody a Register of **Baptisms** at Ootacamund AD 1873; in which Register there is an entry of which the following is a true copy:

Serial Number or No.	
When Baptized	Year 1873 Month May Day 25th
Said to be Born	Year 1873 Month April Day 26th
Child's Christian Name	Norah Mary Madeline
Sex	Daughter of
Parent's Names Christian Surname	Edward Roden and Emma Mary Augusta Bourke
Abode of Parents	Ootacamund
Quality, Trade, or Profession of Father	Post Master General
Signature, Designation or Name of Priest or Minister or person by whom the Ceremony was performed Baptized Name Designation Signature	J. B. Sayers L.L.D. Chaplain

In witness whereof I have hereunto set my hand, at 96 Euston Road, London, NW1, this Eighteenth day of October in the year of our Lord Two thousand.

Hadley Sutton

IN FC12   *Foreign and Commonwealth Office*

ABOVE Norah's baptismal record (which served as a birth certificate in colonial India).
OPPOSITE Sketch of Norah Bourke by Violet Granby.

small, but carried herself with great dignity. Added to this delightful equipment she had charm, which bewitched people, and a contralto voice, which turned your heart right over. She had had an excellent education and was the loveliest music maker. She studied at the Brussels Conservatoire and played the piano like a professional, with a touch that sucked the music from her finger tips.[7] The gifts of talent, beauty, and privilege, which had been bestowed upon her from birth, shaped her overly spoiled and flirtatious ways; traits which she displayed throughout her life.

In addition to Norah's older sister, Anne Kathleen Julia Bourke, who was born on June 9, 1872, the family grew when Cecil Richard, 'Little Dick', the longed-for son, appeared on September 29, 1875, 'being fair, loving and serene'.[8]

The family spent their stay in Ooty enjoying the glorious scenery, cool soft breezes, and the retinue of servants who made their daily life one of total comfort and privilege. The children became out-of-doors spirits, playing under the grateful shade of the margosa trees. They learned to appreciate the flower gardens filled with sweetpeas, verbena, cornflowers, and hollyhocks. To lovers of nature, the fine, stately trees of India were of great interest, especially to Norah, who perhaps stored these subtle memories away to be unearthed and used in her future career. Anne and Norah grew strong little limbs, playing daily in the gardens under the watchful eye of several attendants, while Little Dick remained cosseted inside with the Ayah, his nanny, hovering over him.

Edward's posting became less secure when his brother, Viceroy since 1868, was assassinated in February 1872. During the ensuing few years, without the support of his brother, Edward Bourke's prospects in India were seriously impaired and uncertain. In 1875 he moved the family back to England. Again he attached himself to the success of one of his brothers, this time his brother Harry, the successful founder of the investment company, Brunton, Bourke & Company on Finch Lane in London, Edward embarked upon a financial career.

London

Edward, 'Pupsy' as his children called him, found 'a tiny house in London on Montagu Square where rents were small, and began at the bottom of the ladder at Brunton, Bourke & Company to earn something for his lovely Emmie and his adored children'.[9] Four years later, on May 28, 1878, Madeline Emmie Louisa Bourke joined the brood. Life for the Bourke girls was active and happy, filled with friends and parties, although they never quite understood why their brother played alone in his nursery with his tiny families of china cats and dogs, or why his 'fair soft hair got rubbed away from the back of his head from always lying down'.[10] On November 30, 1884, the girls were taken to the nursery, where shadowy anxiety-ridden figures seemed to float around the bed, and Little Dick was propped up on his pillows, so thin and frail. It was time to say goodbye. While thinking themselves quite grown up,

OPPOSITE CLOCKWISE FROM TOP LEFT Norah's father, Edward Roden Bourke; Norah's mother, born Emma Mary Augusta Hatch; Edward and Emmie Bourke shortly after moving into their home in Montagu Square; Norah Mary Madeline Bourke was born in 1873 in Ootacamund, Madras, India.

ABOVE Norah Bourke as a toddler.

who died when he was 9

the three girls, aged six to twelve, never recovered from the overwhelming sensation of seeing their dying brother of nine, lying so soft and cold in that quiet nursery.

The family, having grown too large for the cramped quarters on Montagu Square, and in need of putting the sadness of Little Dick's death behind them, moved to 25 Great Cumberland Place, a dignified house with Adam fanlights, and a grand entry hall with red and black mosaic marble – a house with plenty of room for the family to grow into. And grow it did. The birth of the Bourkes' fifth child, a son, Nigel Edward Jocelyn Bourke took place on August 21, 1886. As Nigel matured he became the apple of his mother's eye, with his rugged good looks and a disarming charm.

For the children, in addition to daily piano and French lessons, at which Norah excelled, there was the matter of the daily walk in the Park. Norah, now in her teens, had many friends and wished to be out and among them often. She had a schoolgirl's penchant for gossip, as did other young, blossoming girls who were attracting their fair share of attention from the opposite sex. Norah was a beautiful young woman, and as the merry band of friends would troop down Rotten Row, 'murmurs of admiration would follow her from the occupants of the green painted chairs, and now and then a recognizing voice, "It's Miss Norah Bourke."'[11] This admiration for Norah filled her sisters with great satisfaction and pride, and did not go unnoticed by the coquettish Norah, always quick to flash a sparkling glance at the young men.

Emmie dressed her children and herself as beautifully as she dressed her home. The Bourkes were always turned out in the loveliest of clothes, and had perfectly shaped figures, and quiet, gentle manners. Their friends included aristocrats and royalty. The Bourke children grew up in a socially well-connected family,

ABOVE Cecil Richard Bourke, 'Little Dick', Norah's younger brother who died at the age of nine.
RIGHT Fraulein Durr, the strict governess hired to watch over the Bourke children.
OPPOSITE CLOCKWISE FROM TOP LEFT Norah, Little Dick, Anne. 1879. London; noted London photographers, Elliott and Fry took this photograph in 1886 of Norah, age thirteen, and Anne, age fifteen; Nigel Edward Bourke dressed for Norah's wedding, April 1895; Emmie and Nigel, 1886, in the drawing room at 26 Great Cumberland Place; Madeline Emmie Louisa Bourke, age six, 1884.

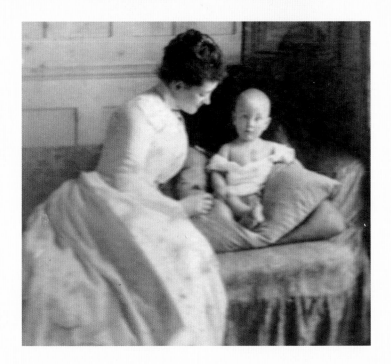

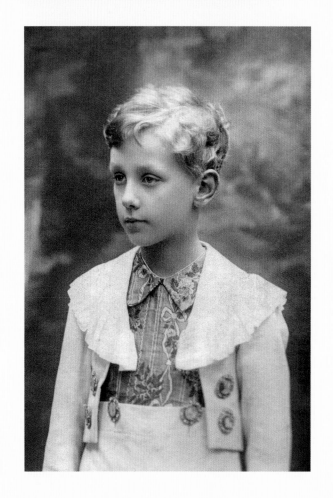

Photographs of the young Norah:
TOP ROW LEFT TO RIGHT At thirteen, in 1886; two pictures
of sixteen-year-old Norah, in 1889; at seventeen, in 1890.
BOTTOM ROW LEFT TO RIGHT Norah Bourke, shortly after
her engagement in 1894; Norah, now Mrs Harry Lindsay;
Norah shortly after her marriage in 1895.

spending frequent long weekends with the family of Percy and Madeline Wyndham, both important patrons of the arts, staying at their notable Arts-and-Crafts house, Clouds, in Wiltshire, and at Petworth House, the Wyndham family mansion in West Sussex. They walked with the Wyndham sisters around the serpentine lake laid out by Capability Brown[12] and flirted with the handsome male houseguests on the benches under the shelter of the Doric Temple. They played tennis on the lawns at Taplow Court in Maidenhead with Ettie, Lady Desborough, and her children Julian and Monica Grenfell; and sat at the fireside of Belvoir Castle with the beautiful Violet, Marchioness of Granby, later Duchess of Rutland.

Life was a social whirlwind revolving around lawn parties, Ascot week, tennis matches, hunt weekends, balls, and plenty of shopping. The families and friends that the Bourkes socialized with during Norah's youth became the families and friends that eventually kept her in business when she most needed work to survive in her later years. They were a constant source of referrals and commissions.

LEFT ABOVE Uncle Percy and Aunt Madeline Wyndham at Petworth.

LEFT BELOW Norah's uncle, Richard Southwell Bourke, 6th Earl of Mayo, Viceroy and Governor-General of India.

OPPOSITE ABOVE Taplow Court, c.1889. Standing left to right: Lord H., Pamela Wyndham, Queenie Grosvenor, Norah Bourke, Mr Grosvenor, Willie Grenfell, Maurice Bourke, Lord Ampthill, Lord Chesterfield, Evan Charteris, Charlie Adeane, Sir Richard Graham. Seated left to right: Emmie Bourke, Nigel Bourke, Monica Grenfell, Madeline Adeane, Lady Cynthia Grahame, Ettie Grenfell (Lady Desborough) with Billy Grenfell on her lap.

OPPOSITE BELOW The Bourke family at Millburn, 1886. Standing left to right: Algy Bourke, George Bourke, Madeline Bourke, Bob Bourke, Flora Bourke, Harry Bourke, Anne Bourke, Lily Lambert, Connie Bourke, Charles Bourke. Seated, left to right: Mary Bourke, Norah Bourke, John Bourke, Blanche Mayo, Emmie Bourke (Norah's mother). Seated in front: Wyndham-Quin and Eva Wyndham-Quin.

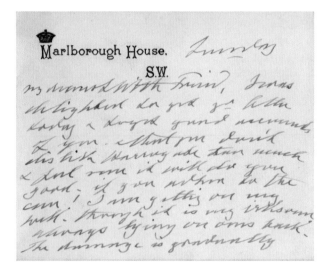

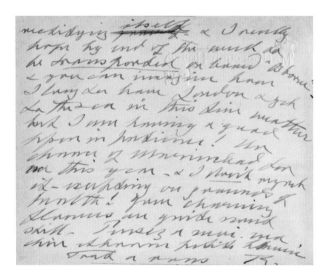

LEFT ABOVE The beautiful Emma Bourke who caught the eye
of a king.

ABOVE Edward VII at Marienbad, 1907; Emmie kept this
photograph of the King in her scrapbook.

LEFT One of several letters from Edward VII to Emmie
Bourke. He referred to her in his letters as 'Mrs. Eddy' or
'My Dearest Little Friend'.

OPPOSITE Violet, Marchioness of Granby, by J. J. Shannon
from *The Book of Beauty, a collection of beautiful portraits
with literary, artistic, and musical contributions, of men and
women of the day.*

Mother's Friendship with the King

Norah's mother, Emmie, could almost be characterized as calculating. She cultivated the friendships that secured her place in society. She loved being included in all the best parties and with all the best people. On one occasion, in the winter months of 1899, while Emmie and Madeline were on a short holiday in France, she met Edward VII, then Prince of Wales. They exchanged letters, met for teas and lunches, and remained friends for years to come. Edward, both as Prince of Wales and King of England, wrote to Emmie from Marlborough House, Sandringham, Balmoral, and Windsor Castle. He thought of her when he was on holiday and wrote to her from Cannes and Paris. Edward addressed her as 'Mrs. Eddy.' or his 'Dear Little Friend'. His letters were filled with invitations to dine together, and occasionally included Eddie and Madeline in the request. The requests were probably more of a summons.

Eddie Bourke showed no concern for the King's interest in his wife. He trusted in his relationship with Emmie and was proud that his beautiful wife had caught the eye of the Monarch. He saw it almost as a compliment – his wife was so extraordinary that even a king would covet her.

Norah Comes of Age

The beautiful and talented Violet Granby, Marchioness of Granby, had long been friends with Norah's mother, Emmie. Violet, married to Henry Manners, Marquess of Granby and subsequently, in 1906, 8th Duke of Rutland, was an aesthete whose whole life was governed by art and beauty, whereas her husband was the ultimate sportsman and agriculturist. The Bourkes often weekended at their ancestral home, Belvoir Castle, also the home of the Belvoir Hunt (one of the oldest and most famous in England). The guest lists for these weekends included a coterie of high-minded friends interested in beauty, mixed with high-spirited men anxious for a rollicking good hunt. At the core of these guest lists were the members of a group known as The Souls – the Asquiths, Charterises,

Grenfells, Listers, Horners, Tennants, Herberts and Wyndhams. The group seemed to take shape sometime in the late 1880s with their shared tastes for art, music, literature, and dignified sports such as golf and tennis. Violet's daughter described them as a 'group of intelligent, cultured men and women, who knew how to live and love and serve and savour the best.'[13]

with malaria. He lived in what he called his 'talipot house', a lean-to made from the gigantic leaves of the tall talipot palms. This hut-like structure was situated in a remote hunting camp in the jungles of central Ceylon. The severity of his sickness forced him to move back to the coast, to a suite of rooms in the capital city of Colombo, where he wearily fought off the debilitating disease. When he was well enough to travel, Harry returned to England proudly sporting trophies from his big-game hunting trip. He returned with a scrapbook of photographs illustrating the story of his hunt and with artefacts made from various animal parts, evidence of the elephants and water buffalo that he had so proudly conquered. He also returned with malaria, the infectious disease that would recur throughout his life.

Lacking any serious direction or interest in business, Harry entered the military in 1892 as a member of the First Battalion of the Gordon Highlanders. Harry honoured himself and his regiment with his tireless commitment to his battalion and its post in India.

At the time that he met Norah Bourke, Harry had three years remaining in the army to complete his current tour of duty. He returned to India for a brief time after the initial meeting with Norah at Belvoir Castle, and by some stroke of luck, managed to get himself sent back to England to complete the remainder of his military

OPPOSITE ABOVE The adventurous Harry Lindsay, pearl fishing off the coast of Ceylon, 1891.

OPPOSITE BELOW Harry Lindsay (seated) surrounded by the local hunters in his hut made of talipot palm leaves.

LEFT ABOVE May 1891; Harry contracted malaria when on his hunting adventures in Ceylon. He moved into the city of Colombo while recuperating after his first bad bout of the disease.

LEFT CENTRE Many of these Singhalese trophy horns would make their way to the walls of the Manor House of Sutton Courtenay.

LEFT BELOW Cooking dinner in the jungles of Ceylon. Harry Lindsay seated in middle, 1891.

commitment so that he could pursue Norah in earnest. Harry worked very hard to capture and maintain Norah's attentions. He visited Great Cumberland Place for tea and played hours of games of bezique, Norah's favourite card game. He danced with her at the balls during Ascot week, and travelled with the Bourke sisters and their friends as they followed the social scene from one great country-house dance to another. By the end of the season, the dejected Harry Lindsay was preparing to return to his regiment, this time stationed in Aberdeen, as his leave had ended. Anne wrote in her journal, 'I think Harry is rather sad about Norah. He sees she does not care for him and he is too gentlemanly and nice to say anything. He really is a very nice, good man.'[17] Norah seemed to be oblivious of Harry's attentions, and busied herself with other suitors, most notably George Frederick Paston Cooper, the thirty-one-year-old son of the 3rd Baronet Cooper of Gadebridge. Like Harry Lindsay, George Paston Cooper was a fixture on the social scene when not serving his country in the 4th Battalion, the Bedfordshire Regiment.

Throughout the courtships and the attentions of the two men Norah remained quite fickle. When she realized that Harry was possibly giving up his pursuit of her, she became 'dreadfully down in the dumps pining for Harry Lindsay.'[18] All of this was a great worry to Emmie. Norah was attracting the attentions of all the young men, and Anne, the older sister, was barely making a wave in the sea of eligibility. Knowing that the plain sister, Anne, needed to be engaged and married before the charismatic younger sister, Norah, or there might be the problem of a spinster in the family, Emmie organized a six-month trip to Egypt for Eddie, Norah and herself to get the distraction of Norah out of London for a few months. They would leave Anne at Great Cumberland Place and rent the house to their close friends, the Maddisons.[19] These friends were then called upon to chaperone Anne and to see that she was invited to and attended all the winter balls. The younger children, Madeline and Nigel, were sent off to another friend's home for the winter. The ever careful and calculating mother even invited Harry Lindsay to come visit them in Egypt to pursue Norah during the winter months while Anne was back in London working on her own future. In late November 1892, before the December departure, Emmie and Harry Lindsay had one final talk in the living room of Great Cumberland Place that Norah's sister, Anne recorded in her journal. Harry complained to Emmie that he didn't think he could capture Norah's undivided attention, especially with Mr. Cooper in the picture. 'He was very nice and reasonable about Norah and said he quite agreed about not keeping up a regular correspondence and that he would think it very odd if Norah did it with any other man (Mr. Cooper) and that he didn't think he would be able to go to Egypt. He wrote a very nice note to Mother afterwards saying it was very kind of her taking such an interest in him and that he would always remember how kind she had been to him.'[20]

In late December, Harry talked his brother Charles into accompanying him to Egypt to see Norah. Both families were ever hopeful and excited. Anne and Violet, Marchioness of Granby, who were both in London for the New Year's Eve celebrations, had a long talk together about Harry and Norah. Anne wrote, 'Violet and I had a long talk. How I wish Harry were very rich. I

OPPOSITE Emmie and Edward riding camels in Egypt.

am sure he would make Norah such a good husband. He is one of the few really nice chivalrous, honest, and clever men I know.'[21] So went the winter. As Norah and her parents set sail to Luxor, Egypt, they found that they were being accompanied by two attentive suitors. The family fully expected Harry and his brother Charles to be on board, but were surprised to find George Paston Cooper also among the passenger list. Meanwhile, Anne was in London attending all the dances. While all thoughts were on the ever popular and outgoing Norah, Anne, the quiet sister, fell in love with her future husband, George Burroughes.

It took quite a few months, but finally, with the encouragement of her sisters and mother, Norah chose Harry Lindsay to be her future husband over George Paston Cooper. Emmie supported Harry over George because of her close, personal relationship with Violet, Marchioness of Granby. Emmie knew Harry's family more intimately than that of the Paston Coopers and felt secure in pushing Norah toward a positive decision about Harry. After one final brief stint in 1894 with his regiment in India, Harry returned home to ask Norah's father for her hand in marriage.

Harry's life until this time had played out at the whim of his own carefree, impulsive desires. He thrived on the excitement of his own life and his own interests, yet he knew that was all about to change. Captivated by Norah's charms, twenty-nine-year-old Harry had now committed himself to settling down, becoming a family man, and sharing a life of domesticity with Norah. Lt. Harry Lindsay took half-pay and transferred to the reserve list of the Gordon Highlanders on March 20, 1895.[22] With the reputation of a responsible, able soldier, he began at once to plan a future with his new bride.

Harry and Norah were married at the Parish Church of St. George, Hanover Square, Mayfair, London on April 27, 1895, one day after Norah's twenty-second birthday. As Norah's proud parents and siblings sat in the church pews, the couple celebrated their marriage attended by Norah's uncle, George Bourke; Harry's sister, the matchmaker of the marriage, Violet, Marchioness of Granby; William Cavendish-Bentinck, 6th Duke of Portland, a close friend of Harry's, and the Duke's wife, Winifred, Duchess of Portland, who had become one of Norah's closest confidantes. Robert, Lord Wantage of Lockinge, Harry's beloved cousin, rounded out the illustrious bridal party.

ABOVE Harry's cousin, Robert James Loyd-Lindsay, Lord Wantage, also known as Uncle Bob.
RIGHT Harry and Norah's wedding present from Lord Wantage: the Manor House of Sutton Courtenay.

The Wedding Gift – the Manor of Sutton Courtenay

Harry and his cousin, Robert James Loyd-Lindsay, Lord Wantage, had forged a great bond over the years based on the parallels in their lives. Although thirty-four years separated their ages, they were very close, with Harry often looking to Wantage for mentoring advice and guidance. Lady Wantage wrote in a memoir of her husband, 'Every member of the family, young and old, who chanced to stand in need of support or counsel – and there were many – turned instinctively to one who was ever ready to give, not only substantial aid, but, what is rarer and more valuable, the sacrifice of time and labour. He would patiently devote himself to the unravelling of the complicated affairs oft-times entrusted to him, endeavouring to place them on a sound footing and helping those concerned to start afresh. His helping hand was extended to friends and relatives, as well as to many who could urge no claims of kinship or even friendship. Many a man and many a woman in all classes owe their first start in life, or their fresh start after foundering in difficulties, to Lord Wantage's liberal help and wise counsel.'[23] Harry Lindsay was one of those fortunate relatives.

A few weeks prior to the wedding, the generous Lord Wantage bestowed on Harry, the younger cousin he had grown over the years to love, a wedding present, free of rent or any fees, the Manor of Sutton Courtenay.[24] To Harry's new bride, Norah, cousin Bob gave the sum of £5,000.

'A riot of the senses'

LIFE AT SUTTON COURTENAY 1895–1920

Gardening as Pleasure

THE MANOR OF SUTTON COURTENAY was 'situated on fifty-four acres and was comprised of six separate houses nestled in an unspoiled village of old-world charm along the river Thames.'[25] The property in its entirety consisted of: the Tudor Manor House; the Norman Hall, built in the year 1150, with stables and gardens situated on three acres; the Mill House, a Georgian village house with stables and gardens on three acres; Cross Trees, the seventeenth-Century house with stables on one and a quarter acres; the Brookside House, with its small adjoining Tudor Cottage, gardens, and over an acre of orchards; and four other separate pieces of building land suitable for residences or cottages.

Harry and Norah planned to live in the Manor House and chose to use the rent from the other portions of the estate to help renovate and maintain all of the lots, including the Manor House. The legal documents associated with the property indicated that the Manor House was listed as a royal residence in the Domesday survey and that William the Conqueror visited occasionally, and Queen Matilda, wife of Henry I and William's daughter-in-law, stayed there for the birth of her first child. For a period of time the property was jostled from the possession of one king to another, and the Courtenay family was periodically on the receiving end of the fluctuating land grants before it passed from Queen Elizabeth in 1591 to Sir Richard Hyde. Hyde then held the property for a period of sixty years. After that date, the property again passed through many hands and finally to Lord Wantage.

The property included three Tudor guest cottages, enormous old barns, a stable, paddock and rich lush meadows, frontage on the river Thames, and plenty of acreage for the gardens of Norah Lindsay's dreams. The house had a red-tiled roof and lead flats. The south-east face of the manor house, with its five gables, richly carved oak barge boards, leaded glass windows, and stone-flagged walk, greeted the newly wedded couple.

Over the first two decades of Norah's married life, this quaint village would be written about and visited by many of the leading political, social, and literary figures of the era, mainly because of the enchanting Norah Lindsay. She created sumptuous and beautiful gardens and entranced her adoring friends with her music and wit. 'Care sloughed off one's shoulder as one entered the

Norah and Harry Lindsay at the entry gates of the Manor House of Sutton Courtenay, 1904.

BELOW The Manor House of Sutton Courtenay.

OPPOSITE ABOVE LEFT The entrance drive, 1909.

OPPOSITE ABOVE RIGHT A corner of the Sutton Courtenay garden.

OPPOSITE BELOW The front façade and forecourt.

iron gates and walked up to the five gable-roofed house with a stout oak door studded with vast nails and Norah, lovely and picturesque, waiting to welcome one in,' Madeline wrote.[26] Norah held unforgettable parties, inviting not only the family friends she had known for a lifetime, but also their children, many of whom attended Oxford, only nine miles away. 'All the Oxford boys were in love with her and spilt over in her magic garden – such boys! She called them the Olympians. The two brilliant Grenfells, Julian and Billy, Charles Lister, fascinating and gifted beyond most men – Bim Lucas quite unbelievably splendid to look at – Raymond Asquith, Henry Asquith's good looking brilliant son. All sadly killed in the first war – with most of the others of their age.'[27]

'Norah had one unforgettable party which she called an Allegresse. "No one has ever had one before, so no one can say if it's a failure or not," she claimed. She got all the Oxford boys who had excelled in any form of athletics and set them to compete in the water race of crossing the river six times and changing boats eight times, and fleet runners racing fifteen times round the apple tree, and these races competed for with terrific efforts – and Willie Desborough arbiter of all sport, and Henry Asquith [the Liberal Prime Minister, who had a home, The Wharf, next door in Sutton Courtenay] presented the prizes, coloured mops and bright dusters, with brilliant witty speeches, to the exhausted winners. Then in the evening there was a mock trial in the Banqueting Hall. Maurice Baring[28] was prisoner, Raymond Asquith for the Crown and Jasper Ridley for the defence and Henry Asquith was the judge! Gay days before the first war came and shattered all that glorious youth – and brought that epoch to an end for ever.'[29]

RIGHT ABOVE Norah and her guests loved to dress up and act out plays.

RIGHT BELOW Harry as Charles II, with Norah, his Nell Gwynne, at his side, at a Versailles Ball, 1913.

OPPOSITE The Banqueting Hall with Minstrels' Gallery was used for plays, musicals, and indoor dining. Harry's trophies from Ceylon adorned the walls.

most beautiful gardens in all of Berkshire,[35] or for that matter, England. The family shared the comings and goings of the privileged of the era. Weekend parties, for which the Lindsays became well known, followed children's birthday parties, complete with tiny ponies pulling cartloads of squealing imps dressed in their finest frocks.

Norah and her siblings remained close friends after her marriage and they would often visit for a week at a time. The women would walk to the station in nearby Abingdon for a ride into Oxford for a day of shopping or visiting some of their friends. They would 'dress up in picturesque clothes, big black and white hats tied under our chins, which looked nice, but which were quite inconvenient as they blew about frightfully'[36] and go off into the garden to attempt to work. They struck dramatic, staged poses and photographed each other dressed in these unforgettable hats and flowing gowns with sashes of satin wrapped around their waists. They thought themselves riotously funny, but were incapable of making any headway in the garden while dressed in such an affected way.

OPPOSITE ABOVE The front façade of the Manor House with Peter as a toddler.
OPPOSITE BELOW Birthday parties at Sutton Courtenay were happy affairs for young and old.
BELOW LEFT Norah Lindsay posing at the sundial.
BELOW RIGHT Emmie Bourke, Harry, Nancy and Norah Lindsay at the front door, Sutton Courtenay, 1903.

Anne, the eldest sister, a devoted gardener herself, was always a little envious of Norah's successes in the garden, but pushed those thoughts aside when she visited Sutton. She carefully observed what Norah was combining in the garden and took these ideas home to her own flowerbeds. On a visit to Sutton in April 1898 she wrote in her journal, 'Norah and Harry met us at Culham with a large fly, the

BELOW A common means of transport for the Lindsays. They often met their guests at the station and carried them off to Sutton in their pony cart.

OPPOSITE ABOVE Croquet was one of the Lindsays' favourite games. Weekends were filled with hours of croquet, tennis, and swimming in the Thames.

OPPOSITE BELOW LEFT Harry and Norah Lindsay.

OPPOSITE BELOW RIGHT A photograph of Norah, gracefully posed by Harry's brother, Charlie Lindsay, 1898.

pony cart and a luggage cart and we all bounced off to Sutton. The house is looking very lovely, so improved by the new hall which is all panelling and tapestry with old tables covered with antique volumes, gardening books, and ancient leathern chairs. The garden too is gorgeous with great splashes of daffodils and polyanthus and bluebells in the grass and lovely tulips, myosotis and wallflowers in the beds and Regal Crown Imperials all around. Norah looking very pretty and slim. We had a cosy little evening with music and cards. Rather a tragic close, as Norah found three cockroaches in her room and nearly died of fright, sadder still I found only two blankets on my bed and nearly died of cold.'[37] The week continued with gardening, punting on the Thames, spirited games of croquet each afternoon, and music each evening. Norah played the piano while Harry, in his rich deep voice, sang their favourite songs. Anne wrote, 'It rained most of the morning so we stayed in and compiled a list of bulbs and

48

arranged a large basket of roses that came over from Lockinge, such heavenly 'Fortune's Yellow', great fat fellows of most perfect hue and smell.' And after the rain ended, 'A lovely fine warm morning, everything has come out beautifully after the rain. The garden here is lovely. They have so much room and such pretty corners and backgrounds and such soil and also spend a lot on it. It looks perfect just now. But the house is so damp and should only be lived in during fine weather.'[38]

On a visit to Sutton later that summer, Anne, not quite understanding an emerging *laissez faire* style that was developing in Norah, let her jealousies get the better of her when she wrote, 'We found Sutton looking very pretty, masses of roses and poppies and lilies and delphiniums, but all very untidy. I never think they make the most of that lovely garden, it ought to be a blaze of colour, very bright and rather formal, whereas it is always too thin and weedy. But the roses were lovely, the climbing 'Captain Christy' over the pergola with blooms as large as a soufflé plate nearly, the house pretty too, but untidy and rather dirty. Norah looking very well and pretty and very nice. Charlie Lindsay here with us. He did a lot of photos of Norah in Marcus Stone[39] attitudes in a muslin gown and big hat, they ought to be very pretty.'[40]

The work that went into the early gardens at Sutton, until about the time of publication of an article about the Manor House, which appeared in *Country Life* in 1904, could be called Norah's early apprenticeship. She did not employ a professional gardener to assist in the design and layout of the gardens, but rather hired an old man whom she called her head gardener and two young men from Sutton Courtenay. They were paid on a daily basis to help with the heavy work and implement her plans. She had no previous formal training in gardening, but possessed an instinctive, artistic eye. She read the available gardening books and magazine articles that were coming on the market[41] and travelled to local nurseries to study the newest plant specimens. She was a critical observer, and while on holidays abroad with Harry, she judged the merits of the great gardens of Italy and France, took careful notes, and carried home the details that she wanted to include in her own garden. She had an artist's natural command of scale, balance, relationship, and proportion. Her aesthetic development had been strongly influenced by Frances Horner, Violet Rutland (Granby), and Ettie Desborough, who were all part of the coterie of The Souls. Their attention to and discussion of art and beauty obviously rubbed off on the impressionable young Norah.

She combined the naturalistic style of Gertrude Jekyll and William Robinson with the geometry of the clipped trees of Italy, giving her double dug borders solid structural lines. Norah said of her early garden at Sutton, 'this garden has been a lesson in beauty.'[42] She experimented by planting in 'patches', as she called them, and moved plants from one location to another, always in pursuit of the perfect colour combination. In a letter to her sister, Madeline, she wrote of her own personal experience with a common mid-summer gardening problem. Her successful resolution of the problem was based on the guidance of the writings of Gertrude Jekyll. Norah wrote, 'My garden is always gay, but a judicious mixture of early and late things, so I have solved the problem of continuous bloom … it will take me a little time to do, but not very long. Only how I do it is to do one, then see how I could improve it still more, and rub out and do alterations. But really, one can plant (I do) quite comfortably up to the end of March, as nothing stirs till then

LEFT Lady Horner and Norah Lindsay in the garden at Sutton Courtenay. A snapshot by Lady Ottoline Morrell.
ABOVE Lady Horner (top); Lady Desborough (below).

or minds being moved. In fact, Miss Jekyll often moves late herbaceous stuff in mid-summer if there has been a good shower.'[43]

The early gardens of the Manor House of Sutton Courtenay were inspired by a combination of influences that stimulated Norah's aesthetic nature. The herbaceous borders were designed in the style of Gertrude Jekyll, but with Norah's own sense of proportion. Her beds were generally wider than Jekyll recommended. Norah's use of flowers grouped together of varying sizes but of similar colour seemed to give her borders an impression of rolling movement from side to side and front to back. Her style, which some called 'untidy and weedy', suited her personality. She likened the free-growing flowers to her own lifestyle – without restraint or restrictive boundaries.

Her sister Madeline described the garden to her own daughter, Joscelyn:

The garden mostly over, but full of loveliness sunning itself and the overgrown tangle throwing greenery luxuriantly everywhere. I have just eaten tea and wasps in the backyard with Aunt Nornor, and have walked round the garden several times and had each flower explained. I am writing this from Aunt Nornor's with a shocking nib and an enormous pale pink quill pen. It's a notable instrument for writing with, but typical of your Aunt … We went to Oxford yesterday and went to see the wonderful renowned botanical garden of St. John's where a sly and mousey gardener managed to evade giving Aunt Nornor any plants, in spite of her earnest blandishments. They were so funny together – she deluging him in Latin names, and he spraying her with his knowledge of composts and manures … When we returned to Sutton, Humphrey [Madeline's son] had

LEFT ABOVE Norah Lindsay in the garden at Sutton.
LEFT BELOW Norah gardening.
RIGHT ABOVE Harry and Norah in the early years of the garden.
RIGHT BELOW Norah in the River Garden near the well head.

cut down two trees, swept the Courtyard – (a treatment it has been never up till now subjected to, and its clean appearance gives it an unfamiliar look). He has also cut off all the deads from the fuchsias, this operation being attended with loud cries of pain from Aunt Nornor who never *depluches les morts* – but wallows in their decay as in their blossoming.[44]

Norah said it best in one of her later letters when she visited a potential client and explained, 'The gardens are delicious and I really don't see anything for me to do!! Old lawns, low brick walls covered in fig trees, and endless narrow borders all crowded with colour like cottage border annuals – roses – everything mixed up all together which I adore – either a very acute colour scheme or no scheme at all.'[45] Norah adhered to the principles of the followers of William Morris and the Arts and Crafts movement who advocated the fundamental qualities of simplicity, utility, and craft. The Arts and Crafts garden theories exemplified a close collaboration between gardeners and craftsmen. The emphasis on the domestic and vernacular landscape appealed to Norah's sense of creativity, and to her purse. With the help of her three gardeners, she built rustic

OPPOSITE LEFT An early view of the Long Garden at Sutton Courtenay.

OPPOSITE RIGHT An early view of the Persian Garden.

ABOVE Two examples of support structures in the early garden, which were not as refined as those used in the later years.

wooden pergolas, placed at regular intervals along the centre of the Long Garden, and to which were attached swooping sprays of climbing roses. Near the southeastern end of the garden, a bucolic pergola with bench, all tied together with ropes and vines, provided a perfect place for reading or resting. The pergolas and the bench were made from young saplings that were cut and stripped from remote locations on the property.

Norah used design ideas she had witnessed while travelling through Europe, and incorporated them into the garden to give it structure. She planted Irish yews and box, neatly clipped into geometric and fanciful shapes, mixed with pedestals topped with antique terracotta urns brimming with soft mounds of colour and texture. These were the golden happy hours at Sutton.

The family was together, the gardens were bursting, and there was still a little money with which to host the theme parties of their wildest imaginations. But that was all soon to change.

After ten years of total commitment to the gardens and the house, Harry was beginning to grow weary of their everyday life. He continued to take regular hunting weekends at Belvoir and in Scotland and, together, Norah and Harry holidayed in France and Italy. But this was not enough. With all the work that had gone into Sutton, it continued to need constant maintenance and be a financial drain. The problem was compounded when the spring rains of 1903 flooded the River Garden and water seeped into the ground floor of the Manor House. The house was now, more than ever (to Harry), dark, damp, and depressing. Trouble with the marriage began as their travelling trips together turned into trips apart. Norah went off on a social whirl with her many friends, and

OPPOSITE A solicitous Norah
Lindsay tending to her husband,
Harry, at Sutton Courtenay.
RIGHT The allée of trees that were
planted to the river. The same
view, during the flood of 1903
(below).

Harry generally could be found in some hunting lodge, far removed from Norah and her society friends.

In January 1905 the first really troubling signs for the marriage and the Lindsays' finances came to light when Norah left Sutton to stay in London with her sister, the now married Madeline Whitbread. Madeline wrote in her journal: 'Norah is staying with me now. She and Harry are frightfully hard up at present and Norah says that she is going to take a ruined villa in Italy and live there very cheaply and have her friends to stay with her as paying guests. I say she will have them on her hands for months probably with typhoid as the drains in a ruined villa don't sound in any way satisfactory! But Norah's plans are always vague-ish. Though I am bound to say that when she puts what sounds an impossible place like Sutton into paradise, she generally drags it through somehow and even with a show of success!'[46] Harry wasn't interested in hiding from his troubles in some decaying villa in Italy; he had his own decaying mansion to worry about. Instead, he spent more time away from Sutton, leaving Norah with the children to fend for themselves. Harry busied himself with hunt

weekends and eventually returned to active duty in the army. As a result, and to hide from the pain, Norah, now in her early forties, with no money of her own to bring her Italian daydream to fruition, lost herself in her gardens, her teenaged children, and her friends.

Who better can understand the inward problems of a woman than her sister? Madeline, at a heightened level of frustration, wrote, 'Only now and then, when a letter comes from Norah, who seems to have such a happy life, full of moans and groans over her broken heart – and talking to me at the same time about her new flirtations with four men and how much they all love her, then I long to be having fun and flirtations too. But I have what is perhaps even better, a husband who is in love with me. But Norah sometimes vexes me. She is so blind. How can one thoroughly enjoy oneself as she knows she does, and at the same time imagine oneself heartbroken and pining. But I cannot think you can be really heartbroken and be as joyous and gay and interested in heaps of men, clothes, going out, etc. All the glamour goes out of things and one can't be gay and insouciant. However, I am all for Norah being gay, bless her – only her heart is a fraud!!'[47]

Madeline continued her exasperation with, 'Norah is giving all her family a great deal of worry. She is indeed fast bound to the wheel and has a ghastly time in some ways – Flying about – whirling to friends, scintillating at dinners, rushing to Sutton feverishly, and all the time haunting fortune tellers who all tell her she will marry again soon or anyway have the chance very soon. Would she like that? I wonder. I feel she is now so attuned to shining in the great world that she has lost the power of enjoying fully and soberly and thoroughly any great emotion. I think Norah has lost herself completely at present. I have never seen anyone who so honestly has hoodwinked herself as Norah has. She really thinks herself a good, sweet woman loving the country and the simple joys of life beyond anything – a loving, understanding mother and a long-suffering wife. Harry has absolutely no affection for Norah and being as weak as water only cares to appease her and have as little to do with her as possible. He pays the bills. Works a great deal because he has no power of organization and so does much more than he need do. Norah in the meantime goes everywhere and does everything. It's all too extraordinary. She has thousands of men friends and has never lived with a soul except Harry and not with him for the last three years. She is very beautiful. But of course, one can't go on with that and remain quite young. Nature won't allow one to. Poor Norah. The moment she stops whirling, she falls desperately ill. Poor dear, rush bound on the wheel. And yet, the Norah who helped me as a child, who was so religious and so steadily unselfish, can't be dead. And Harry must be dreadfully to blame for his criminal weakness in not having helped her and guided her at first. He said always, "I can't bear seeing her cry" and gave in.'[48] While these journal entries seem harsh, it was Madeline's love for her sister that was prompting these strong words. Years later she wrote, 'I think of Ettie Desborough's flaming health and strength and Maud Cunard's relentless activity, my darling Norah's incurable vitality which burned more vividly as the circle of guests increased and she handled her audience with brilliant audacious certainty, arrows of wit ceaselessly darting to and fro, gay repartee as crisp as the crack of a nutshell, and the whole party sustained and carried on the current of her strong gay personality.'[49]

During the fifteen-year period from the time that Norah married in 1895 until about 1910, more than a few major changes occurred within Norah's immediate family. Her sister Anne, having married George Burroughes, was busy raising her own family at Warren House, Cobham, Surrey. Anne, devoted to her marriage and her children, held the emotional Norah off at a distance, perhaps to protect herself from Norah's hardships. But the two sisters remained close. They visited each other's homes, although infrequently, and continued an extensive letter-writing relationship. Norah's sister Madeline, who had married Howard Whitbread, of the brewery family, in January 1904 and lived between Southill Park and her flat on Montagu Square in London, became Norah's closest confidante and protector. Madeline had the money to care for Norah and her children when the days looked the bleakest. With only a few outbursts that showed

OPPOSITE Norah's younger sister, Madeline Whitbread, as a young woman.
RIGHT Norah's older sister, Anne, and her husband, George Burroughes, at Sutton Courtenay.

her feelings of frustration, she remained steadfast, supportive and proud of Norah.

But it was Norah's mother, Emmie, who really paved the way for Norah's survival and future. One year after Edward Bourke died Emmie married Edward Villiers, 5th Earl of Clarendon. She moved into his home, The Grove, in Watford on the edge of London and lived there until his death in 1914.[50] Known to his close friends as Hydie, he served in Parliament and was Lord-Lieutenant of Hertfordshire. Emmie and Lord Clarendon had enjoyed a close friendship for at least half-a-dozen years, writing letters to each other and spending time together at social engagements. No one in their social circle was surprised when they announced that they would marry. In 1909 when Edward VII visited The Grove Emmie was in her glory as she played hostess to both the King and Clarendon, two men with whom she had conducted long-term letter-writing relationships. Edward VII wrote, 'My dear Lady Clarendon, I have just time before dressing for dinner to thank you for your kind letter. You have invited a very pleasant party to The Grove and sincerely hope it will be fine. I expect to arrive at about 6 or so or after, as I shall be motoring from Sandown as I have a horse running there on Saturday. I was indeed delighted with my visit to your daughter Norah's charming house and lovely garden. I have an old dining engagement or should have made my appearance at the Portlands' dance afterwards as my dancing days are over! Believe me, Yours Very sincerely, Edward R Buckingham Palace Thursday Evening.'[51]

Emmie had long enjoyed more than a few friends in high society in England and abroad. She involved Norah in these friendships, and ultimately it was to these homes of grandeur that Norah fled for pleasurable company and rest. Norah's close relationships with Ettie Desborough at Taplow Court, Maud (Emerald) Cunard, Sybil Colefax,

TOP Emmie Bourke, Norah's mother, who was widowed in 1907.
ABOVE Edward Villiers, 5th Earl of Clarendon, whom Emmie married on August 5, 1908.
OPPOSITE ABOVE The Grove when it was the home of Lord and Lady Clarendon.
OPPOSITE BELOW The Grove as it is today.

Winnie, Duchess of Portland, Lady Frances Horner, and Ian and Jean Hamilton were the direct result of Emmie's friendships with these people and the fact that Norah had been introduced at a very young age into their lives. Norah was always welcome in their homes, often accompanied by her own children. The road to Norah's eventual career was paved by Emmie's introductions to the aristocracy and royalty of England, and by the relationships that Norah herself carefully cultivated under the watchful influence of her mother.

Sutton During the War

The call of war in 1914 had summoned the men of Britain, including Harry. He signed on in 1914 as a Commander in the British Red Cross in France, then became a Staff Captain in the Royal Flying Corps from 1915–1917, a Lieutenant-Colonel in the Royal Air Force from 1917–1919, and finally retired, after the end of the war, from the Gordon Highlanders.

While the war raged on, Norah lived frugally as she gardened at Sutton. Madeline visited her shortly after the war began and wrote, 'Norah's garden almost drowns one's depression caused by the war. The glory and gorgeousness of it are astonishing. We wander about in it all day, tying up and working in it generally for all the gardeners have gone to the war and the result is that everything is growing anyhow and looks lovely.'[52]

Nancy, Norah's daughter, eighteen when the war broke out, who was now a young woman of twenty-two, worked for the war effort in London and lived in a small city flat with two girlfriends. At the beginning of the war Peter, Norah's son, was still too young to enlist in military

LEFT Winnie, Duchess of Portland.
OPPOSITE Norah surrounded by her friends in the garden at Sutton Courtenay. Left to right: Lady Alice Montague, Norah Lindsay, Mr. Ker, Duchess of Portland, Duchess of Manchester.

service, so instead he shuttled between his schoolwork at Eton and his home at Sutton to help his mother. In a letter to Madeline, Norah wrote, 'He (Peter) is at once butler, odd man, gardener, poultry worker and general factotum as he does all the little strange jobs of mending broken seats and wheelbarrows.'[53]

They turned some of the fragrant beautiful beds into vegetable plots, necessary in wartime gardening, designed with Norah's flare for textures and contrasts resulting in edible patches of beauty. 'We live practically on eggs and vegetables. Lucy, our housemaid from town, makes delicious vegetable soups and those with plenty of potatoes and eggs and rice puddings appease Peter's shark-like appetite. Of course he does a workman's day here always out by 7:00 am and carpentering for his hens, so that by 8:30 pm when we all go to bed he is tired out. I don't allow any lights hardly, as our gas is cut off and candles would be such a huge added expense. I never read in bed, but we dine early in the light and when it's dark,

go to bed … I work early and late at the poor decayed garden, looking now very bad after four years of war. Yesterday I had a long consultation with my head gardener (my frail decrepit old gardener) and we decided to give up another big bit of flower garden and mowing as all our attention must be concentrated on the vegetable and potato plots.'[54]

Norah, ever creative at organizing group festivities and putting them to use for her own benefit, invited her friends to come to Sutton to relax. After providing them with a meal, she set them to work in the gardens and on the grounds. In the spring of 1918 she wrote to Madeline:

Eddie Marsh came down Saturday which was a great joy to Peter and I. He said he thought the news a touch better, simply because it was no worse. The difficulty is our having only forty miles between us and the sea at the critical point near Calais, so that we can't go back. Otherwise it wouldn't matter our being pushed back

100 miles as long as we kept our armies intact. How gloriously our men have fought. They have saved the Empire by their heroism and courage. I hardly look at the papers. Just work all day and resolutely believe we shall win. Eddie and I worked in the garden, cutting out dead shrubs and moving them bodily to the back from lunch to dinnertime. The garden is beginning to look lovely. The great excitement is the wild yellow *Tulipa sylvestris* having suddenly come up in a corner under some old trees where only its leaves have shown for years. Many botanists have looked at it with awe, and Dorothy Graham who asked if she might come and paint the Fritillaria will now find a still greater treasure.[55] … Goonie[56] brought Sonnie [sic] Marlborough [the Duke of Marlborough] up as he had motored over from Blenheim (much to everyone's surprise) to have a crack with Squith.[57] He was very charmed with the beauty of this house and garden and made himself very pleasant. The garden is beginning to look gay with anemones and daffodils and fruit blossoms. I'm glad the Wharfites over run it as it's sad no one should be seeing it – and they adore it.[58]

Norah continued to labour in the garden through the summer months, as she wrote early one morning to her mother: 'I go on steadily with my gardening, but as the summer advances and the grasses grow higher and higher – the jungley effect becomes more and more pronounced and I get very depressed feeling the garden will win and return to Virgin Forest.'[59]

In a tearful letter sent to her mother, she wrote, 'I am sure human beings, like flowers, require the sunshine to make them bloom, at least some natures are able to bloom of themselves, but I know mine isn't and unless there is love and gentleness, I feel in the dark and unable to bloom.'[60] A few weeks later on May 30 she wrote to Madeline, 'What enchanting weather. I garden and dig and work hard and Sunday my guests, Jean and Ian Hamilton, did the whole front drive for me – hoed up all the weeds – so grateful was I.'[61]

The troubles with Harry were proving to be almost all-consuming for Norah until one day in late May, when she wrote to Madeline, 'I let the day go by in shameful laziness, as first of all it was gloriously hot and one couldn't come in out of the sun to write and secondly, I had a young man here, so made the most of my golden moments. I can't complain much about life at present as after a black winter of disgust and unhappiness I am soaking in sunshine of Peace here and enjoying every second and realizing my enjoyment.'[62]

That golden afternoon certainly boosted her spirits for the next few months, although it is not known when she was visited again by her young male suitor. A letter written almost a year and a half later during the winter of 1919 confirmed that he was in her life for some period of time and that others knew of him. 'Darling Madeline, Thanks for your delicious letter. I heard of you the other day lunching with <u>my young man,</u> <u>he</u> told me all about it, but <u>you</u> were very mousey and mum. I'm sure you found him far more amusing than Gerry did, and I'm sorry to say he referred to you as "your delicious sister". Altogether a bad case of <u>poaching</u>!'[63]

Throughout the summer of 1918 Norah tended the vegetable garden, and fought off the weeds in the Long Garden. Nancy came home from London at weekends, often in the company of Eddie Marsh and Ivor Novello. They played the piano and Ivor sang divinely in the evenings, after long days in the garden and hours of splashing around on the Thames. Norah observed that Nancy had a very 'comfy delicious relationship with Ivor and Eddie, founded on their numerous Bohemian friends.'[64]

Eddie Marsh appreciated Norah's abilities at the piano and years later wrote in his memoirs of a conversation he recalled in the presence of Winston Churchill: 'John Burns came in to Winston's room in the afternoon, and burst into rhapsody about Norah Lindsay with whom he has been staying for a week at the Ian Hamiltons'. "That fay," he said – "there is no word for her but fay – when she sits at the piano with a few flowers between you and her she shines out of what you call the gloom like a spirit!" Winston agreed with a long contented "H'm, 'm".'[65]

Towards the end of the summer of 1918 Norah's financial situation was dire. She put the house in the hands of several rental agents and was thankful when Lord and Lady Weir stepped forward to rent the Manor for a few months to escape the heat of city living in London. She wrote to Madeline after the Weirs departed, 'All the labour is concentrated now on the vegetable garden, consequently the flower garden is terrible and I am hiring another ancient man to help me dig the borders clean which hasn't been done for four years, and I know it's the beauty of the garden that lets this place well. It certainly was in Lady Weir's case! I believe Lord Weir was always taking people to different places in the garden and saying "now did you ever see a sweeter spot than that" '.[66]

Overcome with the bounty of her garden, she wrote to Anne, 'The garden is in fearful mess, but full of beauty. I feel so languid and lazy this time of year, and have a passionate almost bodily ache for Venice. Everything reminds me of it. My pomegranate is covered with flowers, vines full of bunches of small hard berries, magnolias with lovely buds – all Italy seems here, and it makes me dreamy.'[67]

Many short- and long-term tenants took up residence at Sutton following the success of that first summer rental. When Norah let the house for extended periods, she often spent time in London with Ian and Jean Hamilton, her very close friends. When Jean could no longer provide a temporary home for her, Norah made the difficult decision to take a very inexpensive flat in London, 'a kennel, a cupboard, just for myself and maid.' During the months that she was cast out from Sutton she wrote often to Madeline, 'I pine, I long, I ache for the country (Sutton) and to leave this flat where I thought I'd be so happy. Luckily you have no money worries. I believe verily they are the most frightening.' And again, 'I desperately long for Sutton … and have a great longing to get home and sleep in my own room and see my own garden again.'[68] Her unhappiness continued throughout the winter when she complained that 'Harry never answers my letters, and I often think he sees so very little of me, not more than an hour or so every two months if that, that he has no idea of all I am feeling and enduring.'[69]

The disheartening war, and the condition of the garden, only heightened the sense of loss that she felt as she and Harry settled into a permanent separation. Norah described in a letter to Madeline how they had met on a cold winter night at Madeline's flat in London to 'get something definite arranged' between the two of them. 'But he would not settle a thing. He made me so miserable that I vowed I'd never see him again, but get someone of a business like nature to see him. It was the death scene of all my caring, for I realized he hasn't one spark left for me and I cried so bitterly after he'd gone over his brutal hardness that I had to chuck the opera and go to bed.'[70]

Curiously, especially to women in the 21st century who often have to make personal sacrifices in order to meet a strict family budget, even when money was limited for an Edwardian lady of stature, she always managed to have a little money left over to employ a lady's maid. Norah was a perfect example of this interesting convention. In all the years that she lived at Sutton, and travelled the world, and worked at the great estates during her professional years, she was always accompanied and looked after by her own personal maid. For many years, the ever-faithful Lucy, who was her housemaid at Sutton, tended to her every need while she lived and worked in the gardens at Sutton. During her later years, and until she died, she was accompanied on all of her journeys first by Gladys, then Daisy (Doris) Alston who became her very close friend and confidante for more than a dozen years. These maids helped carry her baggage on her travels, packed and

unpacked her clothing, laundered her blouses, lingerie and gloves each evening, and generally did most of the cooking when a designated cook was not residing at Sutton. Norah was famous for her many wonderful recipes, but was not proficient in the kitchen. She passed her recipes along to her cook, Daisy's mother Annie Gibbon, who prepared the meals, while Norah took great delight in the compliments she received for her wonderful food.

From 1918 until 1920 the Lindsays' marital and financial problems continued to plague Norah. She sold precious plants dug from her own flower gardens to her friends in order to have money to buy heating fuel and, most difficult of all, sold heaps of her beloved books to a man in Reading for £25 to keep the house afloat.[71]

During the spring months of 1919, the house needed maintenance work, the money pot was low, and Harry, Nancy and Peter announced they were all moving into

OPPOSITE Norah Lindsay dressed for travel in her pearls and satin hat.
TOP Annie Gibbon Denton, Norah Lindsay's devoted cook and the mother of Daisy Alston.
ABOVE Daisy Alston with her three-year-old daughter, Norah Janet. Norah Janet was named for Norah Lindsay. When Norah Janet was three years old, Daisy left her husband and daughter to travel and care for Norah full time. Daisy and her daughter were reunited years later after Norah's death.

Sutton for a few weeks to make the needed repairs. Norah, never one for confrontations, or one to miss out on an exciting and fully paid travel opportunity, arranged to travel to the United States to see New York and California with her good friend Ned Lathom. She and Ned had previously travelled together on a trip to Italy and she was assured that he would cover all the expenses on what would be a very exciting adventure. Little is known of the exact details of the entire trip, except that she loved dancing to the band at the Amsterdam Hotel in New York, enjoyed the best food of her life at the restaurants in New York, toured estate gardens on Long Island, and spent a portion of each day in New York in a doctor's office, having her aching feet tended to.[72] The highlight of her American trip was travelling the coast of California, with Ned driving a convertible automobile, as they visited estates and gardens along the way, and 'eating boxes of the darkest chocolates and sipping fine wines all the way to Bel Air!'[73] She wrote to Philip Sassoon, 'I like eating as I go along and think food is as important a part of a motor as a horn. Nut Toffee is the best accompaniment to a Tour[74] … Ned Lathom had a slight cargo of freshly made chocolates lined in Devonshire cream put daily in the motor as we glided from Monterey to Bel Air – it was part and parcel of the Scenery-de-luxe of that vellum bound Land and fattened us a vue de L'Oeuil.'[75]

She returned from the transatlantic trip, full of energy and longing to work in the gardens at Sutton. But the situation at Sutton had not changed in her absence. In August she wrote to Madeline, 'The weather for the first time is changing and cold is upon us. My coal merchant seizes the moment to supply me only with steam coal, which refuses to heat even one bath! The Alpine strawberries raised last February in tarts or in glasses with syrup. Otherwise there is nothing in my garden save the usual late asters, as my bad war gardener let all my dahlias die, which are the mainstay of the garden at this time of year. Have you any cuttings to spare? If so, I beg your gardener to send me some, or to divide old tubers will suit me just as well. The agapanthus have been amazing. Not so the nicotiana which all failed. The outdoor vines are covered with grapes, not eatable, but lovely to look at and to pick for bowls in the house. I ought to have asked for sugar for jam whilst I was in California, I don't have any here. I am sewing cushions, cleaning, and gardening all day.'[76]

Her daily life in September 1919 was carefully described in a letter to her mother. 'I find little time for writing nowadays, nor have I much to say as my life is practically one of a head servant, and I am enjoying it very much, and try not to see the worrying side of things. Both my house maid and parlour maid are departing and I cannot find replacement help though I answer letters and advertisements in the Morning Post daily and spend a small fortune in wires.'[77]

Shortly after the war ended, Harry, who had been recently discharged from the military, attended a shooting party at Haddon Hall, one of the Rutland family homes in Derbyshire. Realizing that a new profession was required now that his military service was behind him, he recognized that he could make money at the amateur craft he had honed over the past two decades. Harry began a gentlemanly, low-key career in antiques and interior restoration. An accomplished photographer, he also pursued a career under the name Hal Linden. Some of his photographs hung in the Embassy Restaurant in London.

Like Sutton, Haddon Hall was a medieval structure complete with banqueting hall and countless oak-panelled rooms and hallways. Haddon Hall had been left almost abandoned for many years as Harry's sister, Violet, and her husband, the Duke of Rutland, chose to live at Belvoir Castle. After the war, Violet's son, John, 9th Duke of Rutland, decided to give Haddon the 'kiss of life, like some sleeping beauty'[78] and vowed to pour money into it to 'modernize and furnish it with the purest taste'[79]. Harry lived at Haddon Hall for many months while he worked on the restoration of the woodwork and furniture. He worked alongside other craftsman who admired his skill, in particular Rex Whistler, who had been hired to paint a portrait of the Duke and his son on the walls of the Renaissance panelled Long Gallery.

From Haddon Hall, Harry's new career took him to the home of Colonel Reginald Cooper, a long-time friend of both Harry and Norah's. Reggie Cooper, an amateur architect who admired Harry's expertise, asked him for advice in antique furniture selection for his home at Cothay Manor in Somerset. Harry worked on interiors in Dorset at Parnham House and Melplash Court and quietly established a following of well-heeled clients. After taking a flat in London, he secured a position at Sindlay's interior design house, where he worked on commission, choosing furniture, paintings, and accessories for the homes of the wealthy. For the next ten years, Norah feverishly tried to encourage her family and friends to shop at Sindlay's so that she could benefit from Harry's commissions.

Harry refinished the woodwork at the Duke and Duchess of Rutland's Haddon Hall in Derbyshire.

'No husband, no money, no home'

A NEW LIFE: GARDENING AS NECESSITY

WITH HARRY LIVING IN A FLAT IN LONDON, and Norah shivering in the cold at Sutton, and money at an all-time low ebb, Harry informed Norah that they would have to sell her beloved Sutton. This startling revelation prompted her to write to Madeline, 'If only all the money my friends had spent on their homes had been done by Sindlay's, I would not be losing my home. In hurting Harry, they have hurt me beyond all repair. But what's the use of talking about it …?'[80]

In the summer of 1920, Harry contacted the London auction house, Hampton & Sons, and listed their home at Sutton Courtenay to be sold at auction at The Golden Cross Hotel in Oxford on July 29, 1920. Throngs of people marched through Sutton that summer. They poked in every corner of the house and garden. Norah was sick at heart and could barely keep up the needed chores in the garden. Portions of the property were sold at auction that summer, but not the Manor House.

To escape the prying eyes of prospective house buyers, Norah slipped off to Taplow Court to the safety of life amidst the Desborough clan. From there, she wrote to her dear friend Jean Hamilton: 'Taplow Court, Sunday, In Bed, My Darling, Just one line to tell you how deeply grateful I am for your perpetual shelter care & hospitality. I never seem to make the most of you when I am in London – but this time you must make great allowance for me, as I have been under such a heavy threatening cloud for so many months that at last the weight has hurt my physical self … what has been undermining me has been the realization of how I stand in Life – No husband, no money, no home. You have all three & they are a refuge to ill health & a constant comfy

ABOVE Norah signed her name in the Visitors Book at the home of Gerald, Lord Berners, at Faringdon. as 'Norah Lindsay of No Address'.

RIGHT The original circular announcing that the Manor of Sutton Courtenay was to be sold at auction at The Golden Cross Hotel in Oxford on July 29, 1920. Portions of the property were sold, but not the Manor House.

BOATING and FISHING in a beautiful and little frequented part of the River Thames.

THE SINGULARLY CHOICE

Freehold Residential Properties

COMPRISING

THE MANOR OF SUTTON COURTENAY

Occupying a delightful and retired position

In the Old~World and unspoilt Village and a backwater of the River Thames,

INCLUDING—

Lot 1 **The XV Century & Elizabethan Manor House** in splendid preservation and full of old oak beams, rafters and panelling. The Guest House, a rare old Tudor building. Enormous old Barns. Motor Garage. A pair of Tudor Cottages. Gardens of an enchanting description. Paddock and rich lush meadows, in all about **32½ acres**, with long frontage to the river.
WITH VACANT POSSESSION.

Lot 2 **NORMAN HALL,** built in the year 1150, with modern residence attached. Stabling and beautiful Gardens of nearly **3 acres.**

Lot 3 **THE MILL HOUSE,** a Georgian Village House with Stabling, Garage and exquisite Grounds and Island of nearly **3 acres.**

Lot 4 **CROSS TREES,** a XVII Century House with Stabling and range of useful Buildings and Gardens of nearly **1¼ acres.**

Lot 6 **BROOKSIDE HOUSE,** a partly modern residence with Tudor Cottage adjoining and Gardens and Orchard of over **1 acre.**
WITH VACANT POSSESSION.

Lots 5 & 7 Two Pieces of Building Land of nearly **4½** and **2¾** acres, suitable for the erection of Gentlemen's residences. **WITH VACANT POSSESSION.**

Lots 8 & 9 Dropshort Cottage and **7 acres** of Land for Cottages.
WITH VACANT POSSESSION.

IN ALL ABOUT **54 ACRES.**

Forming one of the most IMPORTANT, VALUABLE and INTERESTING ESTATES ever offered for Sale in lots.

HAMPTON & SONS

Are favoured with instructions from Lieut.-Col. Harry Lindsay, J.P., O.B.E., to sell the above by Auction at THE GOLDEN CROSS HOTEL, OXFORD,

On THURSDAY, 29TH JULY, 1920,

at 3 o'clock (unless previously disposed of privately).

Solicitors: Messrs. REYNOLDS & SON, The Clock House, 7, Arundel Street, Strand, W.C.2.
Illustrated Particulars, Plan and Conditions of Sale, may be obtained from the Auctioneers—
HAMPTON & SONS, 3, Cockspur Street, Pall Mall, London, S.W.1.

HOWARD & JONES, LTD., PRINTERS, BURY STREET, E.C 3.—56403

background. I think I felt Harry asking for a divorce so bitterly – simply because it left me even more stranded & exposed – as by nature I am a clinging & affectionate creature only asking kindness & care & yet seemingly unable to secure either … The truth is I am dog tired & ache more in my soul than body.'[81]

Many men appreciated Norah, but if she ever had a serious, long-term relationship with any other man after her separation from Harry, it was never made public. She alluded to romantic interests on a number of occasions in

her letters. In 1929 she wrote to her sister, 'I go tomorrow to Cap Ferrat … just 10 days. After that I journey to Paris and stay a night or two with Henriette Davis … B. has now written to say he'd like to meet me in Paris on his way back from Knowsley[82] – he goes there for the Grand National on the 27th – of course when I read that in his letter I was utterly surprised and pleased, and then I felt the old doubts and misgivings – he won't come – it will only be another crashing disappointment. He can find time for the Derbys – but not for me. Of course, if B. stayed on in Paris and Henriette could put me up, I would naturally stay on as long as I could – but I know so well he can never take much holiday, never more than a few days – and he will already have had the whole week at Knowsley.'[83]

The identity of B. has never been definitely confirmed. However, there are a series of interesting letters from Hilaire Belloc[84] to Norah that leave one wondering. It is known that Belloc had a very happy marriage to his wife Elodie, who died in 1910. After her death, Belloc and Norah were often houseguests on the same occasion and for extended periods of time at the Horners' at Mells Manor House and the Howard de Waldens' at Chirk Castle. Belloc is mentioned numerous times throughout Norah's letters as being part of the house party scene as she travelled from place to place.

In 1920 Belloc wrote to Norah:

The Delirious Joy caused by seeing your handwriting again, was dashed by the thought of that great distance at which you lay. I had thought you to have returned with Juliet to the delicious town of London – but you are still by the Adriatic Sea. And then again my misery was relieved by remembering that you found yourself in warmth, in ease, in happiness, with the little mosquitoes singing you hymns of Praise. I also have had my little bit of sunlight in that world. It is now sixteen months since I shot out of Venice in a torpedo boat on my way to Fiume and the Guarrero [sic] – that corner of heaven. Shortly after did I see the Pope, the Vicar of Christ, and respecting his Holy Office, I did not remind him of my former interview with him in '16 when I told him we should win the war and he rebuffed it. They had far

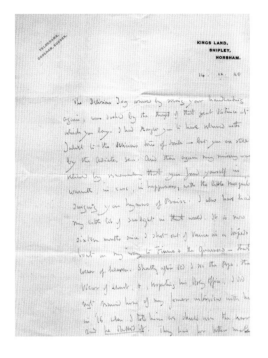

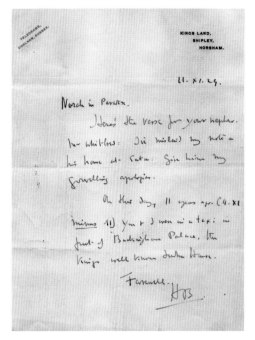

OPPOSITE Hilaire Belloc, a portrait by James Gunn.
ABOVE LEFT One of Belloc's letters to Norah. ABOVE RIGHT Belloc's letter to 'Norah in Paradise'.
BELOW Belloc gave this book of poems to Norah.

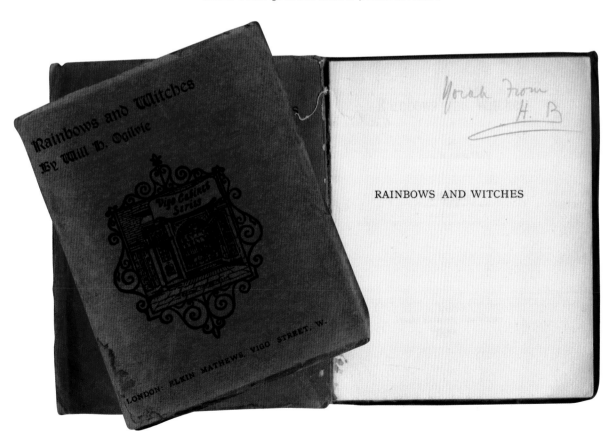

better make me Pope next time they are going to have one of their interesting wars. I should have good judgment as Pope, but the crab would be that I should give scandal by writing you such letters as this, in which I pour out my thinking and beg you to tell me by return and without fail when you reach England. My income stops now all of it on November 11 and I look forward to a black fortune, but am I less gay for that. Oh, no. Farewell till your return. H. Belloc.'[85]

In another letter, nine years later he wrote, 'Norah in Paradise, Here's the verse for your nephew Mr. Whitbread. I've mislaid my note of his home at Eaton. Give him my grovelling apologies. On this day 11 years ago (11 xi minus 11) you and I were in a taxi in front of Buckingham Palace, the King's well known London House. Farewell, H.B.'[86]

Five days later he wrote, 'Yes, yes, Norah and the moment I'm in that way I'll let you know. At this instant I'm off to Sunnys [sic] where I must rest. All my love, H.B.'[87]

B. was not the only man mentioned in her letters. In an undated letter written sometime in 1929, Norah shared her innermost secrets with Philip Sassoon: 'I have been Philandering violently with —————, an old friend and doubly enjoying the warm afternoons on the river, the brilliant scented garden at night and the long discussions about books, people, Horwood and High Life. Osbert Sitwell[88] is coming down this week – as all those who truly love me, come and find me, as they worship me in my works. I find the garden as necessary as its creatrix. Now I must rise for breakfast with the Philanderer out-of-doors under the Jasmine. "So there"!'[89]

On another occasion she wrote to Philip, 'I am enjoying myself wildly and attended the Roman Fete – danced till 3 and received a distinguished proposal, which made me feel quite valuable!!!! I know your cafe au lait Spaniards quite well now – and the bold brown Papa made me tell his fortune last night! So you see, I am quite "The Rage" in the Lounge."[90]

Norah remained discreet about her affairs throughout her written communications with family and friends. She obviously had romantic suitors but never revealed in writing the full names of any of these men. The young suitor from the 'golden afternoon' of years ago, remains a mystery, as does the famous 'B.' who seemed to break her heart repeatedly. Her closest friends knew the identities of these suitors, but no one betrayed her confidence by writing their names out in their correspondence.

Norah's letters often made her sound like a penniless recluse, devoid of friends, but in fact, Sutton served as an oasis for many who enjoyed her company and her gardens. And more importantly, Norah still managed to see and be seen at the best parties and events of London society. Her life was certainly not one of total hardship, as she complained so often to Harry. Norah was able to escape regularly and sometimes for great lengths of time from her troubled life at Sutton into a social world filled with people of privilege, excitement, and intellect.

In a letter addressed to her sister Madeline, Norah described at length a trip in July 1921 in which she again escaped to the solace of Taplow Court. This letter, and those that subsequently followed, clearly reflected a glimpse into the sweeping breadth of her acquaintances, the friendships she prevailed upon, and the unabashed knack she had for finding comfortable (free) lodging whenever and wherever she wanted. Norah wrote, 'at Taplow. Winston Churchill and Clemmy are here, she is a beautiful tennis player and very happy and good natured always and tho' not in the least clever is very capable with her house and her family and he absolutely adores her and she him. Diana and Duff Cooper here too – Diana arrived in a lovely Molyneux[91] model I'd seen in Vogue, of black and white big flowered pattern linen – made with full skirt and thin black chiffon sleeves edged in dull gold – flat hat with orange chin strap. Diana's diving, in an exquisite Maillot with no back was a dream. She looked lovely at dinner in orchid chiffon, with a train and hardly any bodice. I sat between Evan (Charteris) and Winston and had delightful cracks with both. Winston was in a very good humour and painting all Sunday, you know he is really an excellent Artist – some people think him better than John Lavery. I asked him which he'd rather be, P.M. or Velasquez, and he couldn't be sure which, but he declared

he could paint a million times better if he had more time to spare from his Politics.'[92]

Norah was brilliant at casual small talk. The perfect dinner partner, she asked insightful and pertinent questions. At the time she inquired of Churchill as to his opinion of his future, the year was 1921 and he had just been named Colonial Secretary. As to the remark of a comparison to Velasquez, Churchill's artistic talents continue to be heralded to this day, but it was politics to which he devoted his life. He did, of course, reach the political zenith that Norah thought might be in his future, but it was not until 1940, after years in the political wilderness, that Churchill became Prime Minister.

Norah's life that year continued to be filled with excitement: '... dear Katherine d'Erlanger's had a dinner for us and after Nancy [Lindsay] and I and Baba [Metcalf], with 4 young men, went off to Maud's [Cunard] Royal Dance for the Prince of Wales. It was beautifully done and the greatest fun, and Nancy found lots of old partners and friends like Ivo Grenfell, Bim [Lucas], Victor and Edward Cunard, Ronald Storrs, etc. and we stayed till 3 o'clock. The Prince dancing hard with Mrs. Dudley Ward, who looked a vision in orange crepe quite short with her diamond tiara round her tiny waist and doing the Shimmy Shake with the little Prince, too beautiful with her tiny orange satin feet! All the Smarties were there and I was much bucked by Joan telling Adele that she thought Nancy the prettiest girl there.'[93]

Life did not settle down – the next week she attended a dinner party with Chips Channon, sat in a box at the Palace for the ballet, attended a 'tiny, merry chic dinner dance at Philip Sassoon's for the Prince of Wales, and joined the Manners [the Rutlands] for a huge Christmas Ball.' Christmas dinner was spent at the Wharf with the Asquiths – 'up to the Wharf to dine, which was very gay, consisting chiefly of the family – who, when together make up the most brilliant and merry group one can meet anywhere. Puffin,[94] Bonham-Carters, Cis Asquiths, and

Freda Dudley Ward, 'close friend' of the Prince of Wales.

Sir Desmond MacCarthy, Sir Edward Marsh, and Norah Lindsay playing anagrams, 1925. A snapshot by Lady Ottoline Morrell.

4 young men and old Henry, cracking jokes with Puffin and Violet on the subject of Elections!!! He is a wonderful old boy, and seen to great advantage in the bosom of his family, and listening to him and Violet outwitting each other in their dazzling conversation is one of the most enjoyable things I know. We have also had much tennis and a lot of Piano and Piquet by the drawing room fire, so have had a very delicious cosy little Christmas together.'[95]

The emotional and financial maelstrom of Norah's life seemed to ebb in March 1923. Prompted by her two sisters, who were increasingly frustrated by her constant complaining, Norah faced up to the reality of her life, rented Sutton for a period of five months, and continued house hopping in England and on the Continent. Madeline wrote to Anne about 'my darling, unpredictable

Norah – who seemed to me to be having a very, very gay time, when she wasn't having malaria! But she never could manage life unless she had someone by her all the time.'[96]

When she returned to Sutton that summer, she had a renewed energy to work in her gardens, but a sense of hopelessness about her life and friends. She wrote to Madeline, 'Nothing the least exciting has happened here – nor will it ever again. Dear faithful Chips stayed on after you left, and only goes away tomorrow to say goodbye to Paul of Serbia – who goes off to Belgrade at the end of October, marries his Greek Princess out there and is – we feel, quite lost to us forever again! This is making Chips very melancholy, as he has lived with Paul the last six months in London … He has been a great comfort to me, only it must have been a little dull for him – he declares it isn't, as he has my passion for Sutton and its absolute drowsy peace, and after his terrific London season, he has treated his stay here in the nature of a rest cure – and slept a lot, read a lot, and bathed a lot. We have evolved quite a good life, with tennis, which makes us well and thin – and he reads to me whilst I work – and then I practise [the piano] whilst he reads. The Wharfites have been divinely kind. There is a large resident population of the Bonham-Carters and their enchanting children. Puffin, Elizabeth and new Priscilla, and a floating list of visitors including Lucy and Eddy Sackville-West … Ellen Willmott, who was most dear to me and is sending douceurs for my garden. Yesterday we lunched here – and today we lunch again, but there. Peter came down Saturday bringing Eddie Marsh … Chips leaving me is very sad … The garden is really begun to be quite gay again! As the dahlias are coming out and the second bloom of roses appearing at last. But this time of year I always feel a huge and terrifying melancholy at the fact of the summer behind us – and the terrible baffling winter in front – so big and black and expensive – also, it's so sad to think another year gone by.'[97]

In December 1923 money was still very scarce for the Lindsays. Harry, still separated from Norah, was living in a flat in London. To earn money to keep Sutton heated, they agreed to rent their home for the winter months. Norah set off to fulfil her dream of living in Italy for the next four months. By late January 1924, the dream bubble had popped. Her attitude had changed considerably from just a few years earlier when she innocently wrote, 'I would like to spend a winter in Rome and slowly get to understand the intricate web of beauty from the beginning of the world up to now!'[98]

After finally experiencing that winter of her dreams, she wrote with pragmatic candour: 'I think Rome is very depressing, and many people have told me the same. The frightful cold and snow and torrents of rain may have had something to do with it – for a month it's been odious and my house is exceptionally cold, as it's built for summer days and has no fireplaces … Am longing for all this to be over to get back to Sutton. I hate changes and am so dependent on those around me for happiness.'[99]

Before leaving Rome, Norah wrote about the highlight of her winter, an opportunity to attend a gathering on January 18 at the Vatican in honour of Pope Pius XI's second year at the helm of the Roman Catholic Church.

'…I was given tickets to see the ceremony of the anniversary of the Coronation of the Pope with Mr. Leslie and Philip of Hesse, a nice boy I see a lot of. I wore a black crepe de chine dress, black stockings and shoes, black kid gloves, brown fur coat and a piece of black chiffon round my hair. We arrived with an enormous crowd, nuns, monks, upper and lower classes, Cardinals in motors, etc. at the Vatican and proceeded up the magnificent shallow stone Bernini staircase to the Sala Regia. Our tickets really only admitted us to this Hall – where we would see the procession of the Pope being carried through in his sedan throne, followed by the two great white ostrich feather fan-bearers into the Sistine Chapel next door. The big frescoed hall was already crowded – and we were a little disconsolate at the shortness and paucity of our view, when Mr. Leslie bethought him of showing his visiting card to one of the giants of the Swiss Guard. The magic word 'British Embassy' caused us to pass the first Cerberus, the second took for granted we three had proper tickets so without any difficulty we found ourselves suddenly in the Sistine Chapel itself where we found excellent seats amongst the crowd of black gloved, black mantilla'd visitors. Constantly more people were arriving and pushing up nearer and nearer – Monks, Nuns, German women, English tourists – I had an excellent view standing on the stone seat against the back wall of the Chapel and when I was tired I dropt down and sat down, and only saw the lovely Michelangelo ceiling. Getting back on my legs was quite difficult as directly one left one's place, the people surged together and seemed to fill the gap … It lasted about two hours, all the time more and more beautiful uniforms arrived, shown to their places by the Swiss Guards who lined the aisle. The Knights of Malta were rather like our Scots Guards in scarlet uniforms and blue sashes. One pew was filled with priests in enormous white cloth cloaks with high military collars and on one shoulder an intricate red twisted spirallized cross. Another pew was filled by priests in deep fuchsia silk capes and in front of them sat the diplomatic corps. Priests in gorgeous scarlet, brown Capucius-Swiss Guards and Nobles in ruffs and slashed velvet suits preceded the vast Papal Throne borne high in the air and glistening with gold and gems.

The Pope is a fattish sanguine-faced man with specs. He wore heavily embroidered vestments of white and gold. Had the high white tiara covered with emeralds and topped by one huge emerald. One big emerald ring lay on his podgy hand, which he lifted slowly all the time for blessing the people. The two enormous white ostrich feathers were the most pagan detail, moreover the self-same fans have been found in Tut's tomb two weeks ago. These were purely Egyptian on long gold stalks. The procession arrived in front of the Altar to the sound of slow nasal chanting by an invisible choir – the chant was lowered and the Pope took his seat on a high throne on the left and the ceremonies began. The Cardinals in their magnificent cerise silk robes and white tippets looked more splendid than anyone. One of them sat constantly near the Pope when his vast robes were pulled all around him by a sort of 'Maitre de Ceremonies' who then pulled a hand through a small aperture in front and handed the Cardinal his tiny scarlet box-cap! I enjoyed the whole gorgeous medievalism enormously – and had plenty of time when sitting down to examine the great beauty of the frescoes and ceiling – looking their loveliest under a brilliant sun, which made their walls glow like the richest tapestry.[100]

At the end of March 1924, she departed Rome complaining that she had to pay as much for heating the house in Rome as she did at Sutton. Norah wrote, 'Luckily I leave very soon and in a week I go to Lou Sueil, Eze, to stay with the beloved Balsans, Consuelo and Jacques. I have had four months of living alone in a city and am longing to be in a house with human companionship again and to be in the country and to be able to rush out without gloves and sit in the sun and have a room with a real fire.'[101]

In mid-May, during a short lull in her chain of visits before returning to Sutton, Harry, without first consulting with her, let Sutton for an extra two weeks to the tenants who after a long cold winter were luxuriating in the gardens there. Norah, furious at Harry for not thinking of her plight, turned to Frances, Lady Horner for housing to fill the gap until she could move back into Sutton. She and Frances spent eight days in the Horners' garden where she realized that Frances relied on her for all of her garden information and decisions. Frances encouraged Norah to make any changes that she thought the garden needed. Norah wrote out garden plans, dug and replanted and worked to improve an already 'perfect place'. In Frances' 'cosy shut motor they scoured the country and the gardens and shops' for additions to the garden. In the evenings, Sir John read out to them from Jane Austen's *Emma* while they worked until dark in the garden. While there, she realized that her services in the garden were not only worthy of payment but that they kept her mind occupied and happy. She wrote, 'I must plan a busy programme for myself, of intensive work in all directions to use up my time thoroughly and leave no room for personal emptiness.'[102]

The year 1924 began the garden design career of Norah Lindsay.

Norah's Clients

Norah's earliest clients were some of her closest friends. In 1924, at the age of fifty-one, Norah Lindsay began her career at what could be called the top of the 'professional garden design ladder'. She received commissions on the estates of Sir John and Lady Horner at Mells Manor House, William Waldorf and Nancy Astor (Viscount and Viscountess Astor) at Cliveden, Lord Islington and his wife Anne at Rushbrooke Hall, Sir Philip Sassoon at Trent Park and Port Lympne, Lady Howard de Walden at Chirk Castle, and Consuelo and Jacques Balsan at Lou Sueil in Eze, France.

Additionally in 1925, Norah Lindsay decided to capitalize on her well-known letter-writing style and tried her hand at gardening articles, which she submitted for publication to *Country Life*. She was determined to take her garden design career seriously and focused on her skills and knowledge.

A Gardening Style Evolves

Drawn by the sun and warm breezes of the French and Italian Riviera for over twenty years, Norah had been exposed to some of the most prominent gardens in the world. Inspired by the great gardens of the Continent, Norah returned to England after each voyage with new design ideas that she then artfully adapted to the English climate and lifestyle.

Norah realized, 'The thing seeing gardens does, it enlarges one's knowledge to such an extent that one realizes how restricted one's own garden is.'[103] She visited the Baroque landscapes of Le Notre throughout France and was welcomed home by her friends as 'Le Notre Lindsay'.

Like the Italian Renaissance gardeners before her, Norah inserted topiary into her informal designs. She added structure and contrast in her borders using geometric-shaped hedges and trees. After an extended road trip exploring gardens throughout the corners of England with Johnny Johnston and Reginald Cooper, and after spending endless days in their gardens at Hidcote, Cothay Manor, and at Lionel Rothschild's in Exbury, she wrote to her mother, 'You would have loved the amazing gardens I have visited. It has opened my eyes to the possibilities of gardens in other parts of England and was a great education. I feel that I can never again ask anyone to visit mine. I have learned a lot.'[104]

In addition to the travel images etched in her mind's eye, Norah Lindsay re-read the books of Gertrude Jekyll. She had relied on Jekyll's books for inspiration during the early years of the Sutton garden. But now Norah, though still a devotee of Gertrude Jekyll's style of gardening, felt more informed and secure in her own design beliefs. She fine-tuned many of the basic tenets of Jekyll's design theories by adjusting and tweaking them to produce her own version of the perfect herbaceous border.

Norah was also influenced by her gardening friend and sometime houseguest, Ellen Willmott. Willmott was a great plantswoman, but was more passionately interested in horticulture than design. When Willmott first visited Sutton in 1923, the two women spent a day in the garden

sharing ideas, with Willmott leaving behind seeds of her trademark, *Eryngium giganteum*. She encouraged Norah to study the habitat needs of each plant and to plant the 'right plant in the right place' for more successful growth.

The bond between the two women was solidified that day as they walked through the garden discussing their mutual admiration for old roses. Miss Willmott, an expert on the subject, saw Norah's collection of old roses used brilliantly throughout the garden and was impressed by Norah's knowledge of plant names and growth habits. Convinced that she had found a kindred spirit and with the added persuasive coaxing from Norah, Ellen Willmott departed that first day with the promise to dispatch a small shipment of plants from her garden at Warley Place. This was very uncharacteristic as she seldom shared plants with others. Over the years Norah frequently included plants bearing the name of Willmott in her planting schemes. *Iris willmottiana* and *Ceratostigma willmottianum* were commonly found poking through the rose-strewn gardens of Norah Lindsay's border designs.

Between the years 1929 and 1931, Norah wrote articles for *Country Life*, *Vogue's House and Garden Book*, and the *Oxford and Cambridge Magazine*. She also penned a series of nine articles with the intent to sell them to Doubleday & Co. in New York. She had limited success with Doubleday, even though she tried mightily to borrow on her past personal contacts with Mr. and Mrs. Doubleday. While spending a month in Munich, Norah wrote to her son, Peter, 'these last ten days I have been staying behind at home [the Hotel Bayerischer Hof] and finishing five articles, a very great deal of work indeed, as they have had to be written and rewritten and typed and retyped over and over again. Even yesterday, I was working from 9 to 12 when Ossie came to fetch me, and again from 3 to 6 when Bayard[105] called for the second lot of articles. I have made great friends with him and told him exactly how hard up I

The gardens of France and Italy inspired Norah Lindsay to clip her Long Garden topiary into geometric shapes that contrasted with the soft flowing herbaceous plantings, 1931.

am and how tired I am mentally and physically of struggling, and says he will try and get my articles in an American paper.'[106]

She told Bayard of her personal meeting with Mr. and Mrs. Doubleday[107] almost ten years before, when Lady Desborough had brought them to a weekend house party at Sutton and, like so many others, the Doubledays found themselves clothed in the merriment of Norah's home. They had dined in her courtyard, and walked throughout her beautiful gardens along the river Thames, sharing thoughts on colour harmony and garden design. Mrs. Doubleday, an accomplished gardener and author of garden-making books, struck a chord with Norah. As they walked in the River Garden along the Thames, Mrs. Doubleday demonstrated her rare knowledge of birds and the flowers that attracted the birds to Norah's garden. They compared ideas from their own experiences and knew they had much in common as they discussed their love for the garden and its partnership between nature and art. Relaxed in the atmosphere at Sutton and accompanied by Norah at the piano, the group had sung songs and played card and word games long into the night.

Bayard thought this personal connection would be useful and 'suggested my writing a personal letter, which I did, to Mr. Doubleday. I said I was quite willing to write an article for each month of the year if I could get a good offer.'[108] Although Norah's letters indicated that she worked for weeks on the articles that she then submitted through her agent, Bayard, it is unclear why Mr. Doubleday never published them.

From 1927 to 1931 Norah worked at writing a book about her garden design theories. This book, entitled *Garden Idyll*, was never published and the manuscript has not yet been found. Friends and family received updates on the book over the course of the years as she carried the manuscript with her throughout her travels.

From Cap Ferrat in 1928 she wrote to her son Peter, 'I have started my white silk curtains for Sutton and am quilting pale tea colour flowered on them after <u>my favourite theory of ton sur ton</u> [tone on tone]. So I have plenty to do. Also, I am padding along at my garden book, though it is difficult without any flowers to look at and talk about.'[109]

In 1929, aboard a vessel on very rough seas off the coast of Genoa on her way to work at Villa Madama, and fortified by 'Bob Brands infallible pills and a bottle of champagne' she wrote to her mother of the terror she felt when she realized she had lost her lap desk 'with all my life work in it'. When the effects of the pills and the champagne wore off, she found it again and 'all its papers representing the labour of years'. Norah vowed then that it was time to 'get the book typed so as to have a second string to my bow and not again to suffer that awful sense of loss'.[110]

Her family clearly did not follow her writing career. In 1931 a very frustrated Norah wrote to her mother, 'I am disgusted that no one has yet written to me save an unknown man who said he so enjoyed my article on "Roses of Long Ago" in *Country Life* two years ago!!! And that he'd like to put it in his new book on roses. However, I wrote to him to say he couldn't as I was <u>myself</u> putting it in my book.'[111] *Garden Idyll* was to have a chapter dedicated to roses.

In 1928 Norah sent a draft of her book to her trusted confidant Philip Sassoon for his editorial opinion. He responded, 'I loved your Garden Idyll. It is delightfully written – But, in a future edition, please, for <u>my</u> sake, insert a few words on the beauty of a bed of calceolarias against a background of anchusas or something about a bed of Big Onias and Little Elias …'[112]

OPPOSITE The quaint thatched boathouse at the edge of the Sutton River Garden.

ABOVE A letter from Philip Sassoon to Norah Lindsay: 'I loved your Garden Idyll. It is delightfully written.' The manuscript for Norah's book, *Garden Idyll*, has yet to be found.

Design Principles

Norah's amusing letter-writing style spilled over into her garden articles.[113] From these articles Norah's design philosophy emerged.

Norah's first pieces of advice were simple administrative tasks. She advised that serious gardeners 'must send in their orders early to get the best stock from a reputable nursery' and that successful gardeners 'must know the characteristics of their soil and the requirements of the plant'. That 'all gardens must be double dug to a depth of at least two feet and all the soil must be well broken up and mixed liberally with manure – with no exceptions'. That it was imperative to plan your garden with long-flowering plants – with a spring flowerer, next to a summer flowerer, next to an autumn flowerer, for a continuous succession of bloom. The final direction she gave was to 'keep notes – record your successes and failures – then use this information to help you plant again the following year.'[114] On colour in the garden she wrote:

'An elaborate colour scheme should include all the tints of the rainbow, but the colours should be kept in their own group, with delicate shading being preferred to violent contrasts. For example, *ton sur ton* produces a happier result than the placing of blue with orange and scarlet with white.[115]... Colours can be laid on with a lavish hand by planting in bold sweeps. A bold planting scheme affords a harmony in shades where the delicate tones are predominant with swathes of silvery foliage as a foil to the brilliant flower masses.[116]... Nothing is as dull as masses of colour all the same height and shape. What is wanted, given the right space, is a bold treatment of fine foliaged plants to produce a well balanced effect.[117]

Norah Lindsay's double herbaceous borders at Trent Park planted with architectural shapes and a range of colourful contrasts of tone. Norah believed that *ton sur ton* produced a happier result.

On design in the garden she wrote:

> The architecture of the border is as important as the painting of it … There must be a constant variety in design, one group of plants showing off and enhancing the next, and a cunning juxtaposition of contrasts, achieved by planting in patches. For example, the sculpted leaves of funkia [hosta] beside the flimsy fountain of gypsophila or the strong spears of poker and eremuri rising from the low bushes of santolina.'[118] … The patches or plant colonies should be bold and well defined, but of irregular outline, and intimately blended so that there is no set appearance.'[119]

The Italianate style of formalism in layout is preferred, with an informal use of plant substance … Borders should be long and straight with a width proportionate to their length …

OPPOSITE In the Persian Garden at Sutton Courtenay, Norah's borders were long and straight, their geometrical lines softened with delicate planting in pale tones, spilling over in abundance.
BELOW In the Long Garden, Norah used neatly clipped topiary, solid dark yew hedging, and a formal decorative urn to provide an architectural framework for loose-textured shapes of flowers and foliage growing freely. These pictures were taken in 1931.

Attention should be given to the arrangement within the border to the growth form and habit of individual plants so as to secure variety of effect and a series of attractive planting incidents within a greater whole.[120] Different heights are as important as different colours. A rigidly designed border, rising from a few inches in front steadily to a few feet at the back, savours of public institution planting. It is true that the front line must of necessity be the lowest part, but keep the patches of plants in varying positions from the middle to the back and the results are lasting and informal, as if the flowers had chosen their own places.[121]

As summer wears on and plants die back, fill up any vacancies with annuals that maintain or improve the colour scheme and the original design.'[122] 'Above all, let no earth be visible, but crowd up the front with large comfortable mats of permanent things, which can brim over the edge in uneven groups.[123]

LEFT The Persian Garden looking to the house, 1931, the thickly planted borders brimming over with soft shapes enlivened by contrasting textures, such as the spiky, sword-shaped leaves that punctuate the corners of the borders on the left.

BELOW Norah chose to group plants of similar shape and colour in varying heights to add interest and movement to the borders.

ABOVE The Long Garden at Sutton Courtenay in 1930, looking away from the house and showing the framework of Italian-inspired topiary, low hedging, and standard roses that gave structure to the informal herbaceous planting.

OPPOSITE ABOVE Climbing roses decorate a pergola in the garden, 1930.

OPPOSITE BELOW Norah liked to vary the height of her borders, sometimes growing taller specimens, like these lilies, near the front so as to avoid any hint of 'rigidly designed … public institution planting'.

The secret to a successful herbaceous border is to have a profusion of hardy plants well placed in irregular groups and patches, all giving the impression of growing naturally, and producing the effect of a happy and contented companionship.[124] … The charm of a well-planted hardy flower border assumes a delightful informality, yet appears to have a definite orderliness in grouping.'[125]

When not writing, she was sometimes interviewed. Norah was heard on British radio instructing listeners how to grow the best roses and was quoted extensively in magazine articles that were written by others about her clients' gardens.

In addition to writing, Norah was making plans for the gardens at Sutton. The redesign of the gardens took place after Harry had moved out and taken a flat in London. It took over the five years from 1925 to 1930 at a time when Norah was between the ages of fifty-two and fifty-seven.

Norah would wake early, generally around 5 am. While lying in bed she wrote her famous letters for an hour or two, then wrote out long lists of planting plans and plant combinations to be implemented in the garden later that day. As the day progressed she and her gardeners would plant the gardens as she had imagined them hours earlier in the quiet of her softly lighted bedroom. This was a technique that Norah used throughout her career, whether writing from her own room at Sutton, or one of the grand bedrooms that she settled into as she travelled from client to client.

To help with the heavy work, Norah employed one full-time gardener named Walter Carter, and an under-gardener, both of whom lived in the village. She was assisted in keeping the house in order by her new maid, Lily Head, and cook, Mrs. Polden. Lily was a village girl from Somerset who had been recommended to Norah by

Norah's bedroom in 1930. She would lie in bed for hours writing her famous long letters to friends and family. Her window looked out on the Long Garden.

THIS PAGE, CLOCKWISE FROM TOP LEFT Walter Carter, Norah's gardener, at the entrance gate to Sutton Courtenay; Walter Carter with a tilling machine; Walter Carter in the garden; a very proud Walter Carter with his under-gardener.

OPPOSITE ABOVE Lily Head (later Mrs. Walter Carter), parlour-maid and Mrs. Polden, Norah's cook, c.1930.

OPPOSITE BELOW Lily Head at the doorway, Sutton Courtenay, c.1930.

Lady Horner. Within a short time, she became engaged to and was married to the gardener, Carter.

In the gardens, Norah knew her redesigned gardens were exactly as she wanted, so she contacted her friends at *Country Life* and encouraged them to return to do a follow-up article to the earlier 1904 piece. In a two-part series, the Manor of Sutton Courtenay found its way back to the pages of *Country Life*,[126] this time with the renowned architectural historian Christopher Hussey writing an historical summary of the house, and Norah Lindsay an article on the redefined gardens.

Norah allowed the combination of everything she was exposed to from her travels, reading, clients' gardens, and plants from faraway countries to percolate in her mind. Norah's Sutton garden was planned and executed with the same intensity and same approach to life as she lived in her day-to-day existence. Her gardens mirrored her own personality and the attraction that so many felt for her. Norah wrote about the hold the Sutton garden had over all those who encountered its loveliness: 'Some gardens, like some people, have a charm potent to enslave and yet as intangible as dew or vapour … There is an air of spontaneity in the planting, as if the flowers and trees had chosen their own positions, and like the house, been overlooked by the rushing tide of men … You will never want to leave this source of enchantment where peace and beauty beckon and colour and shade and fountains and long green alleys invite and promise a shelter from the unbearable noise of the world without.'[127]

Norah designed her garden for an overall effect of thoughtless abundance and a pleasurable experience. She believed that there should be at least one ideal place to sit in the garden, to rest, to listen and to enjoy the scents of the fragrant lilies, roses and pinks, the sounds from the water in the fountains, the sight of the spired cypress mixed with the rich colours of the herbaceous beds, and the movement of the garden bending to every passing breeze. Her garden was a total experience – a riot to ignite all the senses.

With the limited time she had available to work in her own gardens at Sutton, she explained to her sister, 'Having had to do so many gardens and visit so many nurseries and

attend so many shows I am up on all the best things and shall give you a list. At present what is lovely here at Sutton are the *Lavatera rosea*, shrubby little *Lilac Camp. Molyneux* and huge sky blue thistles with deep pink climbing sweet peas on high stakes, and also enchanting pink *Dierama* which in Ireland they call The Fairy's Fishingrod, owing to its graceful curves. Creamy *Bocconia*. Lemon Mulleins and *Gypsophila* Bristol Fairy make fine patches. Also all the Yuccas are flowering six foot high rods of cream and myrtle and pomegranate and a hedge of blue *Ceratostigma willmottianum* with a cherry *Penstemon barbatus torreyi* next to it and a clump of the most delectable lemon Delphiniums from Afghanistan called *Zazil*. Heaps of silly late but brilliant roses

OPPOSITE The front façade of Sutton Courtenay, softened by planting, in 1930.
ABOVE The Long Garden, 1930, looking back towards the house.

ABOVE A sun-drenched border by the house, looking towards the garden gate between the
Long Garden and the Persian Garden, overflows with roses in 1930. Norah's gardens reflected
her own personality, intense and unrestrained.

OPPOSITE ABOVE The corner around the pool in the Persian Garden, decorated with statuary, an
elegant arched pergola, and faded blue pillars that Norah found in an antiques store in Bath.

OPPOSITE BELOW The long green alleé beckons, 1930.

and two fat tubs of orange *Gazania* and one of the white *Rosa* Mermaid, glorious and in the bog *Astilbe grandis* and *Spirea kneiffii*.'[128]

'Sutton is really too lovely still and so pensive and calm and rather sad in late summer. Absolutely quiet save for the drone of bees and wasps, and the whole place drenched in sunshine and overgrown. The quantities of grapes have broken down the whole pergola, such a blow, as I'm so poor just now, owing to no let, and there are the most gorgeous dahlias and gladioli, *Lilium auratum*, pomegranate and myrtles all in bloom, and the fuchsia tubs as well as the hardy ones all enormous and lovely and pokers good and masses of out of door crinums, figs, mulberries, nectarines, peaches, and pears. I feel rather lonely and long for someone to bear me company, but there's a chance of Victor Cunard[129] rushing over from Paris for the week-end, which I'd love as he adores the garden and would help me to catch up. My gardener is away on a week's holiday and it's all rather rampant, but so lovely. Immense nicotianas in the courtyard.'[130]

'… There are hundreds of Picotees and Dianthus and Pritchard stocks one I think excellent called Mr. G. Pritchard, fat salmon. Hillier has one good one called *Multiflorus salmonea*, in pale salmon. Allwood Nursery has one called Cynthia, pale salmon. Plant these all in one big patch! I go to Bath tomorrow to see some statues for my garden.'[131]

After extensive planting and replanting and with Sutton at its peak Norah wrote to Philip Sassoon, 'If you want to see what a Garden ought to look like – look here, any day, any hour – any old time – it's light till 11 at night and always warm. Do come quickly before the high tide of beauty recedes and leaves a memory only.'[132]

'An overall effect of thoughtless abundance and a pleasurable experience.' An informal contrast of plant forms surrounds the fountain and pool in the Long Garden, in 1930.

'She is an artist and the garden is her paintbox'

THE EARLY CLIENTS

R EADING BETWEEN THE LINES of a letter written from Sutton in 1925, it was obvious that Norah was thriving in her new profession and was gaining enormous amounts of self-confidence in her gardening abilities. Famous people with vast, great gardens wanted her expertise to guide them in the design and planting of their gardens. She wrote to Madeline,

I feel the lush jungley richness of autumn more in this garden than any other place, and a few weeks ago wrote a Gardening Article which you'd like to read as your letter expressed the same feeling as what inspired it. My next article will be headed – "We that are about to die – salute you". And then tell how one day all is lush and well in a last effort – and the next morning nothing but limp black crepe. I am absolutely toiling and moiling at the garden. For this year my knowledge has become a "college" degree. I always knew instinctively, now I have qualified in the higher mathematics – as I have read and studied for my various gardens. Also visited so many nurseries and learnt and learnt and learnt. Result is that I am re-planning Sutton not only nearer to the Heart's desire, but also academically correct – so that everything will grow better and be round pegs in round holes. As long as this work is feasible and the weather accommodating – so long must I stay here and use up my dreaded long black horrid winter. I hope to stick it out till middle of November and perhaps then do a bit of London to see friends and breakup Sutton. And after Christmas – go off to Riviera – as it's January and February that are the worst months to get through here – alone … I've been to Westonbirt for the weekend where a wonderful group of head gardeners were gathered together. Jackson, head of Kew, my friend Johnson, Mr. Balfour, the greatest living authority on Trees, and fat emphatic Mr. James. You can imagine how I revelled in such select company. Moreover, Mr. James played the piano divinely, and Mr. Balfour sang. So we had lovely music as well as lovely flowers. All day we "gardened" first in the

The double herbaceous borders designed by Norah Lindsay at Trent Park, *c.*1930, a beautiful arrangement of contrasting forms and complementary colours. Norah wrote of the Trent Park borders that she had 'trifled over every yard, *every* inch so as to *fill them to overflowing as they are at Sutton.'*

OPPOSITE The scroll that conveyed ownership of Mells Manor to the Horner family in the time of Henry VIII.

ABOVE The central axis of the main garden, looking back towards the house at Mells.

LEFT An overview of the garden at Mells as seen from the church tower.

ABOVE Norah planted magnolias to soften the grey stone walls: (top) a view shortly after the magnolias were planted c.1927, and (below) the current view .

ABOVE The family enjoyed garden views down formally laid out vistas from under the shade of the pergola. Norah wrote about the garden, 'Every garden should be a continuation of the house it surrounds; it should take on the characteristics of the house whether formal or informal.'

LEFT The current view to the sundial.

Arching sprays of roses surrounded the sundial, 1927.

installed borders about 15 feet deep around the 200-square-foot perimeter. In the centre of the Court she experimented with double rows of huge island beds, each planted with her favourite technique, *ton sur ton*. The oval beds furthest back toward the north wall were filled with red and yellow blooms; in the centre beds, blues and mauves; and in the foreground, creams and soft yellows.

Norah wrote to Philip Sassoon of her frustration with the Mells gardener, 'I went to Mells, to Frances's garden and tried to counteract the lethargy of her dear Old Earth Sage of a head gardener who has been there since the days of Noah and is a great fatalist. "Oh, that's the frost", he says when the uncovered fuchsias and syringas are killed in one night. "Oh, that's green fly got them roses", "Oh, that's our soil that doesn't suit pansies", "Oh, that's the dry summer that did that to the stocks", "Oh, that's the rain that blighted the dahlias, Oh, that's the wasps got all the fruit", and so on! He is such a fine old boy that I can't retaliate and say, "Oh, that's the head gardener who ruins the garden." Meanwhile, Frances and I beg away and are goaded every now and then into doing something drastic, such as redigging and putting fresh earth into the big borders and nonetheless, next year, when there is not bloom, he will say in his acceptance voice of utter content and resignation to a Higher Power, "Oh, that Mrs. Lindsay, she did in our borders".'

Norah described Mells: 'Still, Mells has a magic. It has an essential beauty of line and design, and big spaces of green turf and high ancient grey walls shot with gold lichen and crowned in fern and dianthus. In the sitting out gardens, heavy masses of lavender and rosebush, and rosemary, and flowering shrubs of all kinds and tall holly, box mixed with clematis, all as lovely and smiling and bee-beset as one could wish. I always feel at Mells that one moves amongst superior beings where Life is at its <u>grandest</u>. It is like living with Blake's gods and goddesses.'[139]

Sibyl Colefax, a frequent guest, looked out on the peaceful surroundings of the Manor House at Mells and wrote about her feelings for Frances Horner and the gardens that Norah Lindsay designed: 'All the scents of England in the air, verbena, rosemary, roses … the walls and the church … and the shadowing great elms – the walled gardens, the books and above all the woman within … the most healing place in the world …'[140] Sibyl described a week spent with Frances at Mells as 'food for the spirit; the most beautiful of gardens; and wonderful talk.'[141]

A Professional Life

As Norah adapted to her professional life, a life on the road, she told her sister Anne, 'I feel that as one grows older, that there are only two modes of life – one's own home, or travelling about the world. All else is a waste of time and vexation.' Norah was filling her time with travel and work, longed for her home, but found little time for her family. Her brother Nigel, having had his own share of financial problems, moved to British Columbia, Canada, in 1921 to make a new life. There he married and continued a long-distance relationship with Norah. They shared their lives through the family's correspondence. He wrote to Madeline, 'I'm glad Norah is making money. She should go to America where they would cheerfully pay her £500 as a fee. You have no idea how rich they are in the States. A man with £2000 a year considers himself dog poor, brutes!'[142]

In 1926, Norah hadn't seen her son Peter for more than a year. Having inherited the Lindsays' love of adventure, he was now an independent, twenty-five-year-old wanderer travelling the world, stopping off in Ceylon, Calcutta, Kashmir, and Cambodia, all the while sending home vivid letters of his exploits. He had clearly inherited his his mother's gift of description.

Nancy, in 1926, still unmarried at thirty, was living in a flat in London, but dutifully cared for Sutton whenever Norah was away. In addition to her interest in gardening, she had taken up the practice of botanical drawing and was slowly building up a portfolio and selling her artwork to Norah's friends and clients at £5 per picture. Although they saw each other from time to time, which is all that could be expected of two people with busy working lives, Norah complained about trying to stay in touch with Nancy, 'Not one single line from Nancy after sending her all my turquoise rings and £5. It's like posting into the sea.'[143]

Norah's separation from Harry continued. She never stopped thinking of what life could have been like if she and Harry had stayed together. With her defences at a low point after attending the wedding of Joscelyne, Madeline's daughter, on April 27, 1927, Norah wrote with profound melancholy, '… you seem to be so blessed in your home. Your three perfect adoring children – your husband who never wants anyone but you – your garden you can fill with any flowers you want to buy – your glorious houses, motors, furs, <u>tiaras</u>! – oh you seem so lucky. Do you know I was married 27th April – it seems another Norah when I think of it.'[144] Sadly this would have been the thirty-second wedding anniversary for Harry and the fifty-four-year-old Norah. Harry, now sixty-one, was living in London in a small flat. He continued with his quiet antique and interior career at Sindlay's.

Hidcote Manor

It is unclear exactly when Norah's friendship with the American-born Lawrence 'Johnny' Johnston began. The first reference to Johnny appeared in Norah's letters in the early 1920s when she talked of a visit to his garden at Hidcote. After that point, she included him so frequently in the correspondence that it is assumed that if she had had a close relationship with him before about 1920, he would have appeared in earlier letters.

In June 1926 she wrote a letter from Hidcote describing her stay, '… But here all is <u>beauty</u>, peace and spoiling. Delicious dinner last night out in one of the glasshouses full of lilies and scents and everything quiet and restful and no bother at all.'[145] By the spring of 1927, the friendship had become so close that Norah and both of her children were spending weeks at a time at Hidcote enjoying Johnny's hospitality.

When Johnny's mother died, Norah reflected on the amiable companionship she shared with him: 'He is such a cosy companionable creature and has my three passions in Excelsis – gardening, travelling, and reading out. He has had to rush home as his poor old Mother died suddenly – a great release as she was Ga Ga. But he's had all the barbarism and work of an English funeral down at Hidcote and thank God the weather was so fine it made it all easy. He told me he'd ordered a Pall of violet silk entirely covered with violets with a cross of palm fronds in the middle and you wouldn't see any coffin and that it was lovely. He is a good little man – that's why I like him.'[146]

They shared a friendship and love, not only for his gardens, but for all gardens. Norah accompanied Johnny on frequent garden excursions throughout Great Britain and the Continent. Norah consulted, coaxed, and strongly influenced Johnny, but he was never a money-exchanging client. Johnny provided Norah with financial support by generously letting her use his houses whenever she wanted and his car whenever she needed. 'Johnny has lent me his shut Daimler for the expedition to go off to Bodnant to see the Aberconways' wonderful place in Wales to bring back sheaves for Sutton.'[147] He was also a patron who paid for the trips they took together to Venice and the Riviera.

Norah, often accompanied by her daughter Nancy, enjoyed a life of simple pleasures at Hidcote. 'We have had an extremely enjoyable and cosy uneventful week here, leading the most comfortable existence with dear Johnny. Every morning he goes off to plough at 8:00 am, and as most mornings have been gloriously fine and warm no doubt it's

Hidcote Manor Garden, Gloucestershire.

a very healthy occupation. Nancy and I go for a long ramble over the little hills and copses of this enchanting Cotswold country. We lunch at one and sometimes go for an expedition afterwards, or merely another walk. Sometimes I go and practise on Heather Muir's piano, as I dreadfully miss that when I stay here. Johnny is contemplating building a big room for a new dining room, and then he would put a piano in the hall which would be a lovely big room to sit in. I wish he would, as I am miserable if long away from a piano. But before that, he will build an indoor tennis court which I do see would make the winter here very agreeable as we could play indoors all the time. We've had excellent bridge with various neighbours, chiefly the Muirs who are first class players …'[148]

Serre de la Madone

As at Hidcote, Norah did not design the gardens at Serre de la Madone, on the Riviera, but rather counselled Johnny Johnston as he planted. After Johnston acquired Serre in 1924, Norah described it in detail:

Every single day I wake to golden flooding sunshine and flawless hard blue stone sky, which I'm told is always the case here till Christmas. Reggie and Johnny and I generally go up to his garden about 11:00, after he has had tennis with the pro, and meet the architect or builders or someone who is working on the house. The house is tiny, but going to be in time, quite lovely. It stands up behind his garden terraces so that there is quite a climb to get to it. Good exercise for one, but in rainy weather rather tedious, but he means to make a big road when he returns, for driving up, and a lovely one it will be, through olives and orange trees, the views getting more and more gorgeous and remarkable as you mount. The outside is cream and inside too, save the little hall which is amber. He has three or four very pretty doors and a lovely front door and lovely old stone Provençal ornament for over the door. Which is up a small flight of steps – I've made Reggie draw a rough

sketch and plan to show you. The dining room is one side of the hall with a window looking right over the valley into the big mountains beyond with the tiny town of Gorbio perched on the nearest spur. A really immense panorama which will make the room enormous. An old table, amusing chairs and old puce curtains fill this room, small as the whole villa is small, the three bedrooms have each a bathroom. Mine leads out of my room and has pink tiles of flowers. It is so lovely up there as the lemon trees are all in bloom and smell quite delicious, and just behind the villa is the wild hill covered in pine, olive, arbutus, rosemary, myrtles with the loveliest walks all along the top where you look down upon Italy and Bordigherra. The walks here are quite famous as almost every day you can take a new one, nice and sandy, or with big rounded boulders pushing through the path, and the sweet scents are intoxicating as one goes along in the hot sunshine with leaping locusts and bright golden butterflies flitting about and the sandy floor red with fallen arbutus berries, delicious to eat if my inside was well. But what I do eat and adore every day for breakfast are the ripe golden red Khaki [*Diospyros khaki* – persimmon] from Johnny's garden. His trees are covered and look like trees in a fairy tale. After the morning spent planning up by the Serre, or wandering through his absolute flowery jungle of the fuchsias, high shrubs covered in purple, scarlet, and lilac blooms, tanks full of heliotrope, water hyacinths, vast cactus, and prickly pear, rose hedges in every shade and countless rare, unknown sweet scented trees, and huge flat white camellia bushes, etc. etc. etc. we drive back to the flat, lunch and then go on for some expedition and return when dark. I then go to bed till 7:30 pm, when we have our simple dinner, afterwards we three play bridge or talk or sometimes go round to a local movie. Yesterday we took lunch and went for a delicious expedition past Biot into the interior. Spread lunch out in a hot olive grove where we lay basking with the empty pastoral country all round. Peasants were cutting grapes and carrying them in the big washing baskets

ABOVE Lawrence Johnston's home, Serre de la Madone, Menton, France, c.1930.

RIGHT ABOVE The dining room at Serre de la Madone with a view over the mountains to the tiny town of Gorbio, c.1930.

RIGHT BELOW Norah's bedroom at Serre de la Madone with her personal items on the dressing table on the right, c.1930.

below us, far away like busy ants. Great thick rich woods rose on ridges and gave way to valleys and more ridges and finally came the background of far high grey filmy mountains. After lunch we climbed up the ruined stone path of St. Julien to the romantic plateau above with its vast ilex trees, broken stone parapets holding seats at intervals and its tiny pink washed church. I also long to buy it and live there and create a wonderful iris garden.[149]

Like three musketeers, Norah, Johnny, and Reggie Cooper rolled around the countryside exploring and shopping. Life at Serre was relaxing, filled with creativity, and the simple pleasures of food, gardening, and exercise. But

Norah was not always on holiday at Serre. On some occasions she threw herself into the real, physical work of gardening alongside Johnny. She described a few days work in the heat on the rugged hillside,

Came down bright and early as usual and consecrated the day planting in the garden. Johnny had an enormous conglomeration of pots waiting to go in. So I spent most of the day with him finding places for about thirty buddleias, new mimosas, etc. It's quite dry, with sandy, grassy terraces behind the house, which are already planted with minute seedling shrubs you do not notice unless you plop a plant on the top of it. All the cocos [macaws] were joyously

swinging about in their perches, the vast big one clambering everywhere and finally settling in the mandarin tree on the terrace. You hear them imitating the various calls – "Norah" – etc. Too amusing. It was a lovely day and difficult to tear oneself away and come indoors. Johnny worked hard planting, carrying up pots – as everything is up hill and then lugging huge cans of – water too!

The next day Norah continued her letter,

We were having a lot of people to see the garden in the afternoon … the party included Ginger and Norah Warre, Col. and Mrs. Des Voeny, and Sir Ernest Wills, a nice oldish man who has bought Littlecote. All very keen gardeners. We very slowly proceeded along all the little narrow paths, through the enclosure of huge tree ferns like a tropic jungle, which has a sort of pergola roof hung with *Clematis meyeriana*, just out in a froth of pale cream. Then through the lower plant house, where an enormous orange *Begonia venusta* in vast wreathes of flower was the attraction. Then to the tangly jangly terraces where violets and white broom and almond blossoms are just coming out

and the two terraces of enormous succulents, one on the top of the other. Vast high erections of prickly fig cicads, dracenas, yuccas and phormiums, etc. and lots of rare tiny asphodels and ranunculus nestling at their base. Then to the half-roofed-in terrace with rare shrubs ... We slowly wound upwards past the heather bank with the hellebores and cyclamen to the sitting out terrace by the house, where the five macaws were spread about on their perches ... After tea I took them all down the hill and packed them into the smallest road taxi I've ever seen. I returned to the house and Johnny said "Norah, you are quite invaluable" – poor darling, he gets tired and no wonder, going to

ABOVE LEFT TO RIGHT The old stone Provençal ornament over the entrance doorway at Serre de la Madone; the flowery jungle at Serre de la Madone filled with citrus, tanks of water hyacinths, and walkways lined with prickly pear and roses; views through the front gate to the distant mountains; the terrace steps bordered with ivy, violets, and sweet-scented almond blossoms.
All photographs taken c.1930.

see one's friends off to "the garden gate" means a terrific climb back up again.[150]

Chirk Castle

Meanwhile, Norah's garden-designing life took on a very fast pace. One of her dearest friends was Margherita, Lady Howard de Walden, who, like Frances Horner, had listened to and counselled Norah on the many miseries of her life: those caused by Harry; her lack of money; her relationship problems with her daughter, Nancy; and her ever present maladies.

Norah was known to spend weeks at a time at Chirk Castle in Wales with the Howard de Waldens. Although the Myddelton family had owned the property since 1595, in 1911 the castle was leased to Thomas, 8th Lord Howard de Walden, and his wife Margherita. At Chirk, Norah felt protected and loved by the large and active Howard de Walden family. She escaped to its strong, broad walls when she felt at her most vulnerable over the loss of Harry, or when the thought of making ends meet seemed impossible. She huddled in its solid warmth with her

children when the walls of icy Sutton were more than they could bear. And best of all, she enjoyed the constant flow of guests who filtered through the halls of Chirk. Lady Howard de Walden, who had a sweet soprano voice, was known for her brilliant house parties and musical evenings. She was often accompanied by Norah at the piano, as they entertained for guests such as Rudyard Kipling, G. B. Shaw and Hilaire Belloc.[151]

Buoyed by the first few wage payments from Mells, Norah mentioned to Lady Howard de Walden that in her new capacity as a professional landscape gardener, she had suggestions to make to change the scale and form of the

BELOW An engraving of Chirk Castle, near Wrexham, in Wales, the home of the Howard de Waldens.
OPPOSITE ABOVE Chirk Castle surrounded by topiary. Norah softened the walls at Chirk with her signature plantings (left); a current view of Norah's Shrub Garden at Chirk Castle, including *Magnolia wilsonii*, pteris, and azaleas (right).
OPPOSITE BELOW Many of Norah's clients' gardens would eventually boast small stands of these shaped topiary specimens that Norah called Welsh hats.

topiary surrounding the castle, and ideas of how and what to install in a vast new shrub and herbaceous border that could ultimately supplant the hideously overgrown border already in place. The terrace had been planted in about 1870 with yews shaped like Welsh hats, all surrounded by a high yew hedge. Lady Howard de Walden agreed to pay Norah for her services and she began at once to instruct the eighteen gardeners with the clipping of the topiary and the planting of the beds.

Years later Margaret, Lady Myddelton, recalled, 'Mrs. Lindsay made her enormous herbaceous border backed by double *Cupressus macrocarpa* hedges. It reached from the steps of the long lawn to the path to the rock garden and was the same width all the way. The necessary staking must have been a tremendous labour … it reminded one of a timber yard when the stakes were put in the spring!'[152]

Norah's gardens occupied approximately five acres on the easterly side of the Castle. The soil was well drained and slightly acidic, but the challenges came from planting on the windy hillside, 700 feet above sea level, where the average rainfall was approximately 45 inches per year. The rains could trample the borders and cause unsightly messes of spires and stalks flopping about or lying flat on the ground.

Norah had designed and tended the gardens at Chirk for more than a decade when she wrote, 'Yesterday started gloomy and wet and ended an exquisitely fine day here which made all the difference to my work, as I was out till 6:30 pm. The head gardener is charming and likes all I've done and loves my visits, and last year I planned redoing the whole border which is now absolutely beautiful, also I had started a very good shrub plantation and am pleased to find all the various hydrangeas species from Hilliers, *sargentiana, arborescens, grandiflora, villosa* and *quercifolia* all in magnificent flower. Also *Hortensia* and *Tricuspidaria*, most gratifying, also masses of lovely fuschias etc. etc. I always love the family, each has individuality, beauty and grand health. Margot is still delicate, but looking very pretty and they are all so happy and kind to me, there is the most enormous gladioli here I've ever seen! It's big as an orange Regale – bigger!'[153]

Lou Sueil

Apparently the challenges of varying soil and climate did not foil Norah's expertise in the garden. From the wind-chilled slopes of Chirk, Norah moved on to Lou Sueil, a Riviera garden built on a sun-drenched, rocky knoll opposite the old town of Eze high above the Mediterranean coastline.[154] This was the winter home of her good friends, Colonel Jacques and Consuelo Balsan.

Norah's mother had long been friendly with Alva Vanderbilt Belmont, Consuelo's mother, and their two daughters had shared a decades-long friendship. Consuelo Vanderbilt's unhappy first marriage to the Duke of Marlborough ended in divorce after a period of fourteen years of separation and two children. In 1921, her second marriage to Jacques Balsan resulted in profound happiness.

Soon after their marriage they purchased the 150-acre estate known as Lou Sueil, the Provençal expression for 'hearth'. It was there, under the guidance of the architect Duchêne, that they built a warm and comfortable home, made of stone, complete with a cloistered garden. The Balsans lived at Lou Sueil during the winter months, and for the next seventeen years gaily entertained their many society friends.

As the Balsans were building the gardens, Norah was hired to oversee the design and installation of the herbaceous borders. From modernized guest rooms in one of the old peasant houses on the edge of a cliff surrounded by pine woods and olive trees, Norah wrote her planting plans and settled into the life at Lou Sueil. The other guest houses and the main house were usually brimming with visiting friends.

Consuelo wrote: '… Norah Lindsay, whose Irish beauty recalled Sir Joshua Reynolds's children, those puckish faces with elfin eyes … She was an accomplished pianist, a tireless reader and possessed the Irish gift for an amusing tale. She often helped us plan our flower borders and laughed with us over the French gardener's dismay at the riotous disorder of an English herbaceous garden. One day in trying to explain why the phloxes had not kept true to colour, waving despairing hands, he cried, "But Madame, I cannot prevent the butterflies from playing with the flowers!" – a lovely description of nature's propagating act.'[155]

Norah worked in the Lou Sueil gardens for a period of about ten years. An article published in 1928 in *Country Life* describes a portion of the garden that Norah and the Balsans developed together:

'… so well cultivated is it and so rapidly have the plants grown that it looks as if it had been in existence many years. Owing to the rocky nature of the ground, this garden has had to be clothed even more than is usual on the Riviera, as its bare bones were too rugged and sun-scorched to allow for mere patches of colour. The varying contours in the natural lie of the ground have sufficient grace to allow for an adequate clothing. This has been done so skilfully, with such a pleasant mixture

to as the Main Formal Garden) with long double flower borders, the Water Garden, the heather garden, the herbaceous border along the forecourt's brick walls, the Rose Garden, the shrub border along the wall below the Great Terrace, and the shrub and herbaceous border along the Tennis Court.

The agreement surrounding the retainer entitled Nancy Astor to call upon Norah at any time, which she did. Numerous letters to her family and other friends reference, 'Nancy wants me at Cliveden for a bit'[172] and off she would run. Many of those on the staff at Cliveden frequently felt Lady Astor's impatient wrath. Frank Copcutt, Nancy Astor's house flower decorator, once said, 'The difference between Lord Astor and her ladyship was that if he wanted anything done in the gardens he asked if it was possible to do it, whereas her ladyship demanded that it be done.'[173]

Lady Astor reprimanded Norah on numerous occasions over the lifetime of their professional relationship for spending too much money on the Cliveden gardens. In the spring of 1927 Norah posted a letter to Nancy Astor in response to a complaint made by the Astors for what they thought were overcharges and 'neglect of their interests' on an invoice from Norah. It is clear that Norah was furious, but also very worried about losing her job at Cliveden. She plied her letter with a hint of fury, disdain, and a stab at promoting jealousy and sympathy in order to rectify the matter. Throughout the letter she wove in facts that demonstrated to the Astors that she was working with others who trusted her, others who did not complain about prices, and others who were spending large quantities of money for her services and were willing to pay top prices for rare and unusual specimens.

Using the principles she employed in the redesign of her garden at Sutton and the ideology that was appearing in the magazine articles that she was publishing, the Cliveden gardens emerged. They were a 'subtle blending of a strictly Italianate style of formalism in garden planning with an informal use of plant substance, a marriage between an architectural conception of gardening and a greater freedom in the use and disposition of plant material.'[174] The width of the Forecourt herbaceous garden was in faultless balance to the extensive span of the borders; all lined with an edging of paving stones artfully concealed by the drooping heads of pinks, saxifrage, and dwarf phlox planted along the garden's edge. This technique was a compromise, designed by Norah as an expression of beauty and informality, and insisted upon by Camm, the head gardener, for the ease of mowing the great lawns.

After an extended stay in Venice during the winter of 1929, Norah arrived home to a frantic phone call from Lady Astor. She wrote to her sister, 'Nancy Astor telephoned to get me to Cliveden just after I had arrived on my doorstep, so I had to go over there and go round with the new gardener and explain that we hated a narrow earth edging to every bed and border and preferred the flowers to lop over on to the path, nor did we like the 100 years old magnolias in a straight

OPPOSITE ABOVE Norah surrounded the Water Garden at Cliveden with shrubs and trees for autumn colour and a springtime burst of German iris and lilies. She edged the sloping banks with blankets of primroses.

OPPOSITE BELOW The Water Garden as it appears today.

line with the balustrade!! He was rather amusing when he said there were three kinds of gardening: good gardening, bad gardening, and employer's gardening. He is really quite clever and nice but has to learn the ways of the place.'[175]

In July 1930, when Edward Hudson, founder of *Country Life*, suggested that they would like to photograph the gardens at Cliveden, Nancy Astor insisted that Norah be present. One can imagine the pride that Norah felt escorting Hudson throughout the grounds of Cliveden.

Yet Nancy Astor was very hard to please. Complaints about the status of the garden and a constant, frugal monitoring of the finances prompted yet another carefully worded letter to Norah warning her to take care with their funds. In addition to Lady Astor's personality, Norah now

had to contend with Glasheen, the new head gardener. Norah and Glasheen never developed a comfortable working relationship. Norah thought Glasheen a total incompetent, Glasheen thought Norah usurped his responsibilities. Nancy and Norah's quibbling continued for years about money, the state of the gardens, and most vehemently about the competency of the head gardener.

From St. Georges-Motel in late September 1931, Norah wrote to Lady Astor, 'Dearest Nancy: I have just cut this out of *Country Life* (Sept. 26th) to send you as they had an article on planting borders, and though they never put in where the borders came from, which I call 'Sauce' – or <u>who</u> did <u>them</u>, which is still more regrettable, they have picked it out of all their thousands of borders as the best example of a well-done border. I, of course, recognized my own work at my beloved Cliveden in a flash, and as it was done

OPPOSITE The wall below the Great Terrace with shrubs
planted by Norah Lindsay.

ABOVE The Forecourt Garden at Cliveden in 1931. Norah
encouraged everyone she knew to 'buy the September 26th
issue of *Country Life*' to see this photograph of what the
editors called, 'the best example of a well-done border'.

RIGHT The Forecourt Garden as it appears today.

two years ago, I thought it would comfort you to feel they used it as <u>their best border example</u> and indeed when I look at all its sunny glory I feel my heart turn over with its loveliness and the enjoyment I had doing it.'[176]

Again they argued and compromised. 'I only returned from working at Blickling Monday after five days of glorious bracing Norfolk air, when I got an S.O.S. from Nancy Astor to go to Cliveden … when I arrived at

gorgeous Cliveden … it was in full summer plumage and as grand, bowery and beautiful as a Fragonard screen. No one was to be seen. Empty splendour! As they were all at Ascot. I stole into the house and approved the flowers! One huge vase of lemon *Eremurus bungei* and sky blue belladonna delph was glorious, also another of salmon foxgloves and deep blue Spanish iris. Then I got hold of the gardener and we had a glorious walk round. Really I was proud of all my old plans – come now absolutely to perfection. Everything had grown and flourished apace. And I was very satisfied. Nancy has called me in to supervise – at £50 a year which is always a help and I can just prevent the gardener from dotting everything about, as all head gardeners dote on dots, and he had ruined the terrace by six pink daisies and four blue dots, etc. … We were about thirty for dinner and after that a very good game of bridge … The next morning I took Eric Dudley and Sim Feversham all round the glorious borders, to such effect that Eric has asked me to Himley, which fits in with Kelmarsh. I hope he gives me work. With difficulty I dragged myself away from the loving crowd and returned to my own garden.'[177]

With the new compromise of £50 per year, Norah 'finished up' her garden work at Cliveden, limited her yearly trips, and aggressively pursued other garden work. She and Nancy Astor did not have a complete falling out, but their time together was definitely curtailed. Norah did not actively return to Cliveden for any major work or for any extended periods of time for the next five years.

Trent Park

Of all Norah's clients, the one she was probably closest to was Sir Philip Sassoon. He was her confidant, travel companion, best friend, referral source, and all-round provider of money, stability, advice, gossip, intellectual discussion, and political, social, and artistic contacts. They carried on a lengthy correspondence for many years filled with gossipy, private jokes about their friends, silly pet names for each other, their changing views on different

OPPOSITE Sir Philip Sassoon, who became Norah's greatest friend. She often confided in him and once wrote to him, 'Work is a great appetizer and gives one a zest for life which becomes greatly shortened just when you wish it to stretch out like elastic.'
ABOVE Springtime at Trent Park, 1931.

religions, and sometimes rather bawdy discussions of their health. These letters also included their worries about the political stability in the world and, of course, detailed discussions about Philip's gardens at Trent Park and Port Lympne. Their love for each other was seen in the closing line of every letter, never a mere Yours Sincerely, but rather Much True Love, 100 Loves, or Lovingest.

Philip Sassoon was descended from an affluent Jewish family whose fortune, generations earlier, had been made in India in the opium trade. When his father died in 1912,

twenty-three-year-old Philip, the youngest Member of Parliament, was living in lavish style in a townhouse in the centre of London at 25 Park Lane. His mother, Aline Rothschild, had died a few years earlier, and when Philip, the millionaire bachelor, inherited the family's country house estate in Hertfordshire, he decided to renovate the house to accommodate his entertaining tastes.

Norah's letters refer to their first meeting at a party at Taplow Court in 1921. There (where the mix of house-guests included Winston Churchill, Sydney Herbert, and

Evan Charteris) she and Philip Sassoon struck up a lasting friendship.[178] Very shortly after that first encounter at the Desboroughs' home, she attended a small, chic dinner dance at Philip's for the Prince of Wales. She was a first-time houseguest at Trent Park on Christmas Eve, 1921.

Trent Park is located on the outskirts of London, thirteen miles from the centre. Sassoon used the estate for entertaining during the months of May to July. From 1924 to 1926 the house underwent vast interior and exterior reconstruction. At the same time, Norah Lindsay was overseeing a small army of gardeners as they constructed 'the glory of the magnificent grounds with long flower borders and pergolas of Italian marble clothed with vines, wisteria and clematis.'[179]

Shortly after receiving a letter from Philip Sassoon congratulating her on the progress being made in the gardens, she wrote, 'It was sweet of you writing me that <u>comforting</u> line about your borders, as I am so nervous and diffident underneath my brazen shell and really dislike being a

BELOW Pages from the Trent Park Guest Book: 1934 (left); 1935 (right).

OPPOSITE ABOVE View down Norah's herbaceous borders to the Trent Park pergola, 1931.

OPPOSITE BELOW The pergola, Trent Park, 1933.

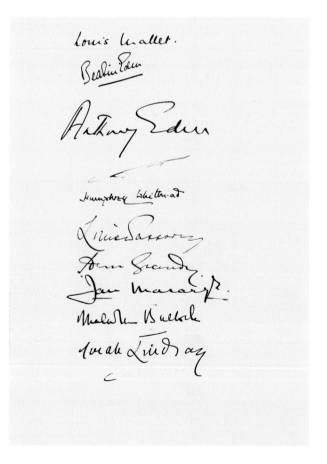

professional and at the mercy of criticism more than <u>I can say</u>. If only I work hard and make money from a lot of gardens or a book, I could stop and would stop tomorrow, but as things are at present, I foresee working much more intensely and being more and more the slave of ignorant owners till at last I shall be vetting the church yards!!!! … I do think myself your Trent garden lovely and my whole heart is in it and ever since I left I have written four times to Wilson [the head gardener] on various lovely plants and suggestions about raising for next year. It's a pity you cannot see my garden now – it is a lesson in beauty and the lilies – regalis, ostrowskias, madonnas <u>all wonderful</u> – now it is at it's height and so lovely I could put my arms round it … I am so gratified to hear you're liking your borders!! But I find them very good and I am the severest critic. It would be strange if they were not good as I have trifled over every yard, <u>every</u> inch so as to <u>fill them to overflowing</u> as they are at Sutton. And planned and planned till I was dizzy to make <u>them dizzy</u> with colour. When we put the poppies right they will be perfection – no less. Also, I'd have you know Wilson is the most arduous taskmaster. Not only does he ask me two million questions, the answers to which are hastily inscribed in a notebook, but as well, he wishes imploring me to tell him "<u>which colours go together</u>". I wrote him an exhaustive list at which he writes back "Would I please tell him which colours <u>didn't</u> go together". Is he by chance laughing at me in his trowel?'[180]

In 1929 Norah was commissioned by *Country Life* to write an article for publication about her work at Trent Park. Norah took this opportunity to express the principles of design that she employed in the garden and to uncover the secret of her borders. This article, perhaps one of the finest written by her, and certainly the most revealing, illustrated her design philosophy.

She described how Trent's 'wide borders, lie in pairs, on a gentle slope, with broad grass paths surrounding them on every side so that the untrammelled eye can rove easily up this glade of brilliance, noting the incandescent orange and scarlet of the distant beds, the rich purples and blues of the middle ones, and the soft assuaging creams, and pastel shades of the two at the end.'

ABOVE Norah frequently used large patches of blue meconopsis in her border designs, as seen here at Trent Park, *c*.1930.
OPPOSITE ABOVE Norah planted many water gardens during her career, such as this one at Trent Park, 1931.
OPPOSITE BELOW The terrace at Trent Park, 1933.

OVERLEAF

LEFT The Red Border at Trent Park with its fiery accents, planted for the height of the season in July.
RIGHT ABOVE The Pool Garden at Trent Park in the 1930s with its soothing colour palette of soft blues, whites and yellows.
RIGHT BELOW The view from the pool house to the main house, Trent Park, 1933.

Norah successfully employed one of her design 'tricks' in Sassoon's Trent garden: 'I find the paler blues of delphinium make a better effect than the darker. They look glorious with groups of rich rose and pink herbaceous peonies, while sky blue, pale pink, and lilac lupins rise in great sheaves behind long stretches of rose-coloured valerian.'[181]

She excelled at 'playing the game of the gardener's ego', often pitting Philip Sassoon against Nancy Astor. Norah enticed work out of each by sending tempting letters describing the great plans and plantings she installed on the other's property. She realized that petty jealousies and estate-owner egos created a certain tension that helped sell more shrubs and plants. Norah wrote to Philip '…went to Hilliers today where we chose a huge specimen for Nancy's garden'. Shortly thereafter she received instruction from Philip to load up on the same for him, only this time buy more and buy them larger. It became commonplace for Norah to write to Nancy of the exquisite plants that she found for Philip, thereby perpetuating the circle of covetous buying.

Port Lympne

Port Lympne, overlooking Romney Marsh in Kent near Hythe, was designed as Sassoon's country retreat on the land once dominated by Roman legions, an ancient river called Limene, and an extinct town called Porta Lemania. Its name derives from this Roman station.

In the early decades of the 1900s, Sassoon employed the noted architect Sir Herbert Baker to build a rather modest house on the hill with views to the sea beyond. A few years after its completion, and fuelled by his exotic taste, Sassoon chose to make changes to the house. Baker, busy in Delhi, was dismissed, as the impatient Sassoon was ready to complete his dream. The architect Philip Tilden was retained to realize the neo-classical concepts in Philip's

creative mind. Sassoon instructed Tilden to add Moorish rooms and extraordinary pools and fountains; John Singer Sargent was consulted to direct the finished texture of the walls; Rex Whistler was commissioned to grace the rooms with fanciful cartouches and embellishments; and Norah Lindsay was hired to design the grand herbaceous borders and plantings along the face of the building.

Norah's task was to design gardens that were at their most beautiful during the months of August and September when Sassoon planned to be in residence. Norah worked closely with Philip on the gardens for more than fifteen years. She admired and had a good working relationship with his head gardener, Wallis, who oversaw a staff of up to twenty gardeners.

Norah's double herbaceous borders, the Long Borders, were 135 feet long and ran from the top to the bottom of the garden on a windy slope overlooking the sea. She chose plants that could withstand the elements and wrote to Madeline about her cold days in the garden: 'I've been working at Lympne where it's all blowy and most awfully cold as we are so high above the Romney Marshes, we get a lot of wind here.'[182] The borders were divided by a large swathe of perfect green lawn to set off the subtle rolling colours of the plantings.

Norah softened the face of the stone walls on the Front Entrance, Loggia, East, West, and South Terraces with herbaceous plantings, and her favourite magnolia trees. She found large yews at Hilliers to back the stone figures in the central forecourt in front of the house, and advised Philip on the correct choice of colour in the Chess Board Garden. She advised, 'I hope your cutters and carvers are already at work on the Vernal chessmen who will adorn your Tudor Squares at Lympne. Make them stand on gay rugs of low dazzling colours – the best aniline dyes – as in azure blue, crest gold and ash of ruby.'[183] Adjacent to the Chess Board Garden she advised on the plantings in the Striped Garden.

OPPOSITE ABOVE Port Lympne, rear façade.

OPPOSITE BELOW Port Lympne, as it is today.

ABOVE Norah's double borders at Port Lympne with Romney Marsh in the near distance.
RIGHT ABOVE Norah's long borders at Port Lympne looking back to the house. From a postcard.
RIGHT BELOW The Port Lympne long borders looking back to the house, current view.

ABOVE Norah softened the
horizontal lines of the terraces at
Port Lympne with herbaceous
plantings.
LEFT The Terraced Borders, Port
Lympne, current view.

ABOVE The upper terrace of the
Terraced Borders, filled with
dahlias.
RIGHT The dahlia terrace, Port
Lympne, current view.

'A continual va-et-vient – what a life it is'

GARDENS LARGE AND SMALL

Rhodes House, 1928

I N ADDITION TO PRIVATE CLIENTS, Norah was also commissioned to make public gardens. From 1928 through 1929 Norah spent about fifteen days planting the beds and gardens designed by architect Sir Herbert Baker at Rhodes House, Oxford University. It is certain that Norah was recommended for the job by Philip Kerr, as they had a personal relationship. Norah wrote to Philip Sassoon, 'Tomorrow I work <u>all</u> day in Oxford at Rhodes House.'[184]

On his death in 1902, Cecil Rhodes, the British/South African diamond magnate, created the Rhodes Scholarships. Rhodes chose Oxford University as the site from which these scholars would study 'to broaden their views, improve the lot of humanity, and work towards maintaining peace between nations'. The Rhodes Trust, which administered the scholarships, was based in Oxford at Rhodes House. The views from within the building were designed to direct the eye toward the intricate garden rooms surrounding the building. The focal point from the dining room was the view to the Warden's Garden.

Norah planted the 15-foot-deep borders along the 150-foot north wall in the Warden's Garden. She filled the beds with lavender and roses. In her book, *Oxford's College Gardens*, Eleanour Sinclair Rohde described the garden. 'From the terrace one now looks into the garden of Rhodes House, which was formerly part of the Warden of Wadham's old extensive kitchen garden. When the garden of Rhodes House was being made the most attractive feature – the north terrace walk – was most unfortunately destroyed. This was part of the original fortifications and bounded the Warden of Wadham's kitchen garden. The garden of Rhodes House is overflowing with lavender – more lavender I should think than in any other garden in Oxford. The Warden of Wadham's garden has been greatly changed. The present beautiful rose garden was formerly a clump of ilex and holly and the lovely herbaceous border merely poor shrubs. Against the house the shrubs and the small rockery have been cleared away, so that now one can see the whole of the façade. The most attractive view now is from the dining room – on one side the beautiful old wall and

The parterre garden at Blickling Hall, newly restored according to Norah Lindsay's plant lists.

phloxes who in turn blend with the blue and pink hydrangeas. The magnolias in the moat are entrancing. So are myrtles and lots of fuschias and veronicas and that ever beloved Dutch honeysuckle with its incomparable sweetness … Oh, it is so lovely and so peaceful and so romantic and in sunshine the rosy brick seems to radiate light and sweetness.'[198]

An interesting side note – of which Norah's clients were unaware – is that Norah customarily exchanged and moved plants from Sutton or from one client to another. This exchange was predominantly between Cliveden, Trent, Port Lympne and Blickling. 'I was getting plants at Cliveden for Blickling as Glasheen has such an enormous surplus from the vast unrivalled collection I put in.'[199] It is safe to assume that Nancy Astor had no idea that this exchange was practised, nor would she have approved of it. She would have been outraged if she knew any of the plants she had paid for were being shipped off for someone else's benefit.

ABOVE The eastern end of the Parterre garden, showing one of the stone sphinxes and one of the herms at Blickling Hall.

OPPOSITE A current re-creation of Norah's colour-filled parterres at Blickling Hall.

Kelmarsh Hall and Ditchley Park

Norah enjoyed the hospitality of Ronnie and Nancy Tree at their houses at Kelmarsh Hall[200] and Ditchley Park. From about 1928 to 1933, Norah was hired to advise as she worked alongside the Trees, both keen gardeners, in the planting of the double herbaceous borders, Fan Rose Garden, Long Border, and Lavender Garden at Kelmarsh Hall. She helped plant thousands of bulbs and recommended the best shrubs for use in the Wilderness area and Oak Walk. When the Trees later employed landscape architect Sir Geoffrey Jellicoe to design and plant the landscape, Norah never mentioned Jellicoe in her letters nor did she ever mention anyone else giving advice to or being employed by the Trees. She seemed to be quite content in the amount of work they gave her, and never felt jealousy or regret that someone else was designing around her. As was the case with many of her larger clients, the Trees paid Norah a yearly retainer of £100 for which she was 'on constant call'. In November 1930, while Norah was enjoying a stay with Johnny Johnston in

Menton, she complained, 'I am peeved at having to go to Kelmarsh, but Nancy Tree's wire was so imperative and as they pay me by the year, I have to go when sent for so insistently. Also, my last visit was in August, so it's time I went.'[201] However, after a particularly relaxing stay at Kelmarsh, Norah wrote to Philip Sassoon, 'It was delicious staying with the Trees. Their house a gorgeous affair with vast fires and sofas, and lots of unusually nice people – Nora Phipps, and the two Jenkinsons and Phyllis and Juby just round the corner and Bruce Ogilvy for dinner and bridge – The Yorkes to lunch Sunday with the Wyndhams. So that there was a continual va-et-vient and lots of music, imitations, letter games and mere lounging. I cornered Bobby Jenkinson on gardens and find he knows every rare shrub and possesses most of them – what a life it is!'[202]

The Trees shared the same taste for fine things. Ronnie, a connoisseur of all things Regency, purchased furniture and paintings, while Nancy, who became renowned as the interior designer Nancy Lancaster, decorated their houses with her distinctive and influential interpretation of what became known as English Country House style.

LEFT Kelmarsh Hall, the home of Nancy and Ronald Tree, 1932.
ABOVE Kelmarsh Hall, rear façade, current view.

OPPOSITE ABOVE Kelmarsh Hall in 1932. Norah worked side by side with the Trees, planting in the herbaceous borders.

ABOVE LEFT The herbaceous border as it is today. ABOVE RIGHT Kelmarsh Hall across the garden, current view.

OPPOSITE BELOW A view to the Topiary Loggias in the Kelmarsh Hall garden in 1932.

ABOVE LEFT A current view of the Topiary Loggias. ABOVE RIGHT Box-edged beds at Kelmarsh Hall today.

Ronnie Tree described his first memories of Ditchley Park, Enstone, Oxfordshire, the home he purchased in 1933: 'Everything we saw that afternoon gave us the impression of a Sleeping Beauty waiting to be called back to life. We had the temerity to believe that we could undertake this gigantic task. No baths, no heating, no lighting. But we did not care. We would put them in. A fortnight later the house, its contents, and its three thousand acres, were mine.'[203] Ditchley Park became the centre of the Trees' world and became known for their grand entertaining, beautiful gardens, and important house-guests. During World War II, the Trees' home was renowned as the weekend retreat for Winston Churchill who, 'when the moon was high and the German bombers could easily spot his home Chequers', would escape to the safety of the darker corners of Ditchley.

Ditchley Park, 1941.

There was no garden when the Trees purchased Ditchley. They employed Sir Geoffrey Jellicoe to plan a garden, inspired by the Italian masterpiece, Villa Gamberaia, near Florence. Jellicoe added formal gardens, stone terraces, a pleached lime alleé, and a stone-tiered fountain large enough to hold swimmers. The *pièce de résistance* was a 300-yard-long stone terrace running the length of the house and overlooking the lake and temple. Ronnie Tree indicated in his memoirs that a Herb Garden was installed by Jellicoe, but Norah's letters point out that she did much of the planting in that garden.

Norah worked in the gardens of Ditchley Park from 1933 until 1946. Her letters detail her many trips to Ditchley, and the hours working alongside Nancy and, more often, Ronnie, whom she adored.

A series of letters written by Norah to her sister Madeline between 1938 to 1940 document the work performed by Norah at Ditchley. She wrote, 'Now I must bundle off to Ditchley as there is a lot of planting to settle.'[204] Norah packed up a few enticing things for the Trees, including upright hellebores and blue primroses which Nancy Tree liked so much, and set off for Ditchley. When she arrived she found the beloved Trees and their sons, Jeremy and Michael, just sitting down to tea. They all rushed out to meet her. 'Jeremy is the fat, adorable boy still at private [prep] school. Michael the tall, elegant one at Eton. Both have enormous charm and are on the sweetest terms with their parents. As both boys and Ronnie and Nancy hug each other constantly with the deepest fervour and say "How I adore you" quite openly and simply. They never have any sort of disagreement. After tea Ronnie and the pro and Jeremy went off to play tennis, and Nancy and I wandered everywhere making tremendous plans for the next year – when we mean to plant a magnolia walk, a room of white cherries and another of camellias in the thick and sheltered woods here. We had Peter Beatty, Ronnie's half-brother at dinner – he owns Reigate Priory and is very fond too of gardens. He praised my handiwork in the gardens here.'[205]

At Ditchley, as at most of the gardens designed by Norah Lindsay, a significant planting of magnolias was included in the plan. A portion of a letter that she wrote to Philip Sassoon expressed her feelings. After a day 'hobnobbing with dear Mr. Hillier [owner of Hillier Nurseries]' she expressed what would be her most perfect and accurate epithet (albeit somewhat heartlessly): 'I wish he [Hillier] would suddenly die and leave me all his magnolias and *Phyllanthus* and *balearica* Box. They just intoxicate me … I believe the only perfect garden is sward and huge evergreens, ilex and magnolia I've done at Sutton and Cliveden. Vast dark masses sitting on Turf – When I die, Magnolia will be written on my heart.'[206]

Norah's letters described her work in the Ditchley gardens, 'I planned a whole new Herb Garden which I think will be lovely. Also the big scheme made of Wallflowers here is a great success, but there is no rain and all the forget-me-nots I planted are shrivelling up.'[207] Contrary to this letter, it has been written that Russell Page also sent a plan to Nancy Tree, in April 1938, instructing what should be planted in the Herb Garden.[208]

Norah left Ditchley, where as she said, 'they shower love and sweetness on me', and drove with Peter Beatty back to Sutton to see her gardens. 'He said he had never seen such a delicious place. Peter Beatty wants me to give him a spot of advice for his garden at Reigate Priory, so I go there for two nights on Thursday.'[209]

ABOVE Current views of Greenaway, where Norah designed a garden for Viscount and Viscountess Weymouth:
(top left) the front gate; (top right) the 'prim little Jane Austenish house'; (below) the remnants of Norah's garden as it looks
today. This topiary might have been clipped long ago in her favoured Welsh hat design.
OPPOSITE The house and stables at Dalham Hall were constructed in about 1705. The large square house is made of red brick
surrounded by vast spreading lawns and parklands rolling off into the distance across the Suffolk downs.
Cecil Rhodes owned the property for a number of years until his death in 1902. The property then passed
on to other members of the Rhodes family, and finally Norah's clients purchased it in 1925.

Greenaway

Norah's clients included many small country houses. 'I don't ever remember such a hot golden day or the garden looking more scrumptious. Imagine banks of the hardy blue agapanthus with white and the dull pink echinacea with six-foot high *Thalictrum dipterocarpum* behind it? And masses of pink sidalcea with grey artemisia. Quite lovely. Alas, at 9 am this morning I leave for my next job, staying at the young Weymouths at Longleat, and am very much looking forward to seeing that famous house, though I am operating at one not far off that Lord Bath has given them where I believe there is no garden at all, merely a hideous piece of ground.'[210]

When the 5th Marquess of Bath presented his son, Henry Frederick Thynne, Viscount Weymouth, and his pregnant wife, Daphne, with a small house, Greenaway, near Longleat, the ancestral home, Norah Lindsay was invited to design the gardens. The house was a 'prim little Jane Austenish house in Warminster, built of pink brick with grey corner-stones.'[211] Writing from Reggie Cooper's house, Cothay, in Somerset, Norah described the garden to Philip Sassoon: 'Johnny fetched me from Longleat last

Monday where I had been turning a perfectly hideous flat plantain ridden field into a garden for the exquisite young Weymouths to live and love in! It was a hard task – but I have made a lovely Plan – with beech walks and yew arbours (très Cranford) and as the garden at Longleat is merely groundsel and seed pods it will easily shine as a great example of my Cunning. I adored the woods at Longleat and the queer little rabbits that always sat at the door of their houses watching the motors pass. Quite a fairy tale world. Daphne is on the verge of her second baby and as Diana is coming tomorrow we talked obstetrics a lot, mingled with Max [Beaverbrook] and his strange life.'[212]

Dalham Hall

Dalham Hall, Dalham, near Newmarket, was originally constructed in medieval times on a chalky hill overlooking the downs of Suffolk.

During the winter of 1925 the horse-racing-mad Sir Laurence Philipps purchased the property as a stud farm to be nearer to the centre of the racing world at Newmarket. Ethel, Lady Philipps, familiar with Norah's

reputation, hired her to design the herbaceous borders along the Front Terrace wall, the Sunk Walk, Rose Garden, Yew Walk and along the walls of the old Kitchen Garden. Norah was hesitant about working at Dalham as over the years she repeatedly expressed her dismay at living among strangers while she worked, but she took the job and worked there for a period of two years from 1929 to 1930.

She wrote to Philip Sassoon, 'I lunched with Gerald [Berners] … and then flew off … to Newmarket and Lady Philipps. The usual longing to buy golden yews and sundials and to remake the house nearer to the heart's desire – still, it's a job! But the evenings are so queer with total strangers! I'm getting a horrible "sweet smile" on my face like a lady-in-waiting. Anyhow, I say to myself – I am only here for three days then back at Sutton and shall spend all my time lying in bed and playing the piano.'[213]

Woodcote Manor

Norah never overcame her fear and loathing of spending time with strangers. In the following years she was faced with this problem on more than one occasion. She was summoned to Woodcote Manor, Bramdean, near Winchester, the home of Captain and Mrs. F. H. Tudor-Owen. She complained to Philip Sassoon, 'I was fetched in Winchester after three hours <u>waiting</u> – acute standing on my legs by a Mrs. Tudor-Owen and was motored to her quite nice house and quite nasty garden where in pouring rain I was expected to suggest a <u>perfect</u> new plan that would entirely <u>remake</u> it more like mine and yours. Oh dear – Philip darling – how I hate these <u>visits to strangers</u> and evenings with them by the fire. – I so understand why goveys [governesses] <u>prefer</u> dining alone after the day's work is over!'[214]

She also wrote to her mother of this fear as she travelled about the countryside: 'Do write to me at Port Lympne where I go on Friday morning to stay with Philip till Monday. And then to Port Ledge, Fairy Cross, Bideford, Devon, with Lady Joanie Grigg – to do her garden, 27th to 30th – then to Chirk on the 30th and on to Maureen

Stanley's at Witherslack – all jobs! It's so queer to travel about violently and stay with mere acquaintances for two nights and then tear off somewhere else … But then life is very queer. As to me, who hates society, adores leisure and privacy, this work seems like a madness. Still it's worse if the madness was withdrawn and I was left to live on £9 a week! Well it's no use making speculations as there is no answer anywhere to one's questions, but I do thank God for my friends, they have come to my succour when I was in absolute distress, and I think I am getting back my nerve again and hardening up against this hellish thing called life or fate!!'[215]

After another quick stop at Sutton, this time for three days, enough to enjoy its lovely splendour, she began her 'intensive work of rushing everywhere as it was the time for replanning and settling where to put in bulbs.'[216] She told Madeline that the garden at Sutton was 'still lovely with wonderful dahlias, all with the most dazzling dyes, and one wall of huge white clematis like china plates, though the fluffy *Clematis grata* is too, too lovely. All the various fuchsias are at their best…The best autumn things now are *Senecio brachystachys* – a low bright yellow edging for a border, *Physostegia* 'Vivid' – very pretty, low pinky mauve perennial, group it under *Aster acris*, the two go well together, and with them put big patches of the low blue aconite, backed by the tall *Aconite fischeri*, and near them the deep dark pink *Echinacea purpurea* 'The King'. There darling, I've told you all my trade secrets as you are so good to me.'[217]

Garden Club of America

Norah's gardening skills received international fame on several occasions. A trip to England by the members of the Garden Club of America was organized in June 1929 under the auspices of The English-Speaking Union in the hopes of strengthening the link between English and American gardeners. Organized by well-connected and wealthy driving forces in both countries, ninety women from the United States and another one hundred British

ABOVE Norah's view of Woodcote Manor upon her arrival. Woodcote was a stately Elizabethan house that had once belonged to the surgeon, and talented artist known for his etchings, Francis Seymour Haden, dubbed the 'Apothecary of Hants' by his brother-in-law, Rex Whistler.

BELOW LEFT The entrance, Woodcote Manor. Current view.

BELOW RIGHT The remnants of Norah Lindsay's favourite topiary Welsh hat design which she clipped for the Tudor-Owens.

women joined together to visit the finest gardens in England. The week began with a pilgrimage to Kew, the Royal Botanic Gardens, Hampton Court and the Royal Horticultural Society. For the remainder of the week, motorbuses conveyed the party on day-trips throughout Oxford, Buckinghamshire, the Cotswolds, and Kent. Norah wrote, 'Darling Mad, … I am so tired of racing off though never miss one single chance of a job as to protect my house, no "let" has yet appeared!! Isn't it awful – I seem to be so little here too as Monday I was at Cliveden gardening and in the afternoon receiving 200 garden clubbers from America. It was a glorious day, and I never got home till 8 pm … My soles were blistered, but Tuesday the 200 garden clubbers all came here and I sucked in their crazy appreciation and praise and loved them all. It was so lucky they came the finest day we had … Chips and George Gage suddenly arrived Friday, "sick of London". They brought a vast hamper and bathed and adored the garden saying "they expected any moment to meet a Unicorn!" Christopher Hussey arrived Saturday morning an hour after they left, to see about doing photos for *Country Life*, and then departed.'[218]

As the buses pulled into Cliveden, Nancy Astor presided over tea in the French Dining Room, while Norah guided the groups on tours of the gardens. The next day, when the buses arrived at Sutton Courtenay, Norah was in her glory. Mary Helen Wingate Lloyd, one of the American organizers and the author of several articles written about the trip for the Garden Club of America's publication, the *Bulletin*, singled out Norah's brilliance: '… it would be hard to find a more exciting planting than Mrs. Harry Lindsay had in her old garden at Sutton Courtney [sic], very tall poppies of a cool pure scarlet floating high above gray artemisia, and *Santolina incana* with dark old yews as a background. Not one poppy, but <u>dozens</u> in each box-edged section.'[219] The tours that week also included stops at Hidcote Manor and Port Lympne, two gardens that left further impressions of Norah Lindsay's brilliance in the minds of the American gardeners.

Norah's gardens were also visible when the National Gardens Scheme was instituted in 1927 to raise money for

ABOVE Three views of the Manor House of Sutton Courtenay. when the gardens were open to the public.

OPPOSITE The allure of Sutton Courtenay and its enchanting courtyard.

charity. Gardening in Britain was unquestionably a national pastime. When the National Gardens Scheme arranged for the great gardeners of Britain to open their gardens for a few days each year to the viewing public, a tradition was born. Norah and many of her clients opened their gardens to all those interested in a glimpse into gardening on a grander scale. From the beginning, the list of gardens showcased included Southill Park, Trent Park, Port Lympne, the Manor House of Sutton Courtenay, and Cliveden. The guide to these gardens, which in later years came to be known as the Yellow Book, was first published in 1932. Its pages expanded from the success of the public's interest in the scheme and the dozens of generous landowners willing to share their gardens. In its first year, it was illustrated with photographs of Norah's borders at Port Lympne and Trent Park. In the following years, the book was filled with Norah's clients and

gardens, offering the public an opportunity to view and mimic her swaying borders. Regulars on the list included Norah's clients' gardens at Mells Manor House, Chirk Castle, Blickling Hall, Trent Park, Port Lympne, Hidcote Manor, Rotherfield Park, Dalham Hall, Mottisfont, and Ditchley. By 1936, the Manor House of Sutton Courtenay was opening its gates three times a year, in May, June, and July, and the crowds were swarming inside to enjoy Norah's seasonal procession of bloom.[220]

On another occasion Norah welcomed the Rhodes Scholars from Oxford: 'They are all nice middle aged earnest wives from all over the Empire whose husbands have been at different times Rhodes Scholars. You can imagine their raptures over the house and garden … The next morning, they all returned with their husbands or brothers or sons, as they were so extremely happy here they begged to return and bring their belongings. But at 12:15 pm I had to fly to the sanctuary of my bathroom and change as Mr. Curtis and Mr. Kerr arrived to take me to Cliveden where the whole Rhodes Scholars in three huge chars-a-banc again turned up!! I had a very pleasant afternoon showing the garden to Mr. Hudson and Violet Leconfield.'[221]

Years later, in 1938 when a group called The 50 French Gardeners toured Hidcote, Mark Fenwick's Abbotswood, and the Trees' Ditchley, it was Sutton Courtenay that was the highlight of their trip. Norah was pleased to report, 'it was a dazzling morning and hot and the garden had never ever looked so beautiful. The vote was at the end of all – that my garden was the loveliest.'[222]

The women of the Garden Club of America were impressed by Norah Lindsay's brilliant planting schemes. This photograph of Sutton Courtenay was taken by a member of the club, Mrs. Lloyd, who considered it to be one of her favourite gardens.

'If you had money, she was the one to spend it'

ARISTOCRATS, PRINCES, AND PRINCESSES

FROM 1928 UNTIL 1939, Norah's letters tell of the meteoric climb of her career as she dashed from the garden of one famous personality to another, with stops in between at Sutton where she managed to find the time to redesign her own gardens. The return address lines of her letters and their noted destinations were a veritable Who's Who of the titled and the crowned society of Britain and the Continent.

From the Palazzo Contarini in Venice she wrote to Nancy Astor: 'Dearest Nancy, I have to go on the 15th September to Hungary to carry out a fixed plan to do the garden of Princess Stephanie of Belgium so I cannot cut that short, for the promise was to stay a <u>whole</u> week, though I don't care a bit to go amongst strangers, never having the faintest spark of adventure in me and only liking to huddle with the people I love.'[223]

Princess Stephanie of Belgium

The trip to Princess Stephanie's was indeed an adventure. An air of intrigue still hung over the Princess as her first husband, Crown Prince Rudolph of Austria, had been involved in a famous scandalous suicide with his young mistress at the royal hunting lodge in Mayerling. The Princess

and her second husband, Ambassador for Hungary in Paris, Count Elmer Lonyay, lived in a castle in Oroszvar in the Moson Megyei region of Hungary. Princess Stephanie was a kind employer, highly complimentary about Norah's ideas. Norah and the Princess got on very well, and chatted easily in French about plans for the garden. Norah was left on her own much of the time and remained at the estate until the end of September as she planned and directed the planting of the herbaceous gardens.

ABOVE Norah Lindsay in 1936. OPPOSITE The Duke of Windsor working in his garden in France.

life, tho' it's amusing to gleam the latest gossip from her. Much love to you, Ever your loving, A.'[234]

Norah's letters indicated that she spent about one day a week working at the Fort during the remaining months of 1930 and 1931. She considered working for the Prince a great honour, but described it as tiring, hard work. 'Thank you darling for letting me sleep Wednesday and Thursday after always a very tiring day at The Fort as H.R.H. is iron made and as alert as a robin and rushes about from 10 o'clock until 2 o'clock and from 3 o'clock to 5 o'clock without pausing to take a breath.'[235]

'Yesterday I was at the Prince's which progresses very slowly, but I think what we've done is good. The enormous structural alterations have taken all the money, as I've moved the front road and the back had to be banked and surrounded too!'[236] And she bragged to Madeline, 'You would have been amused to see the Prince's new stream-line motor he sent to Reading to meet me. It is the most extraordinary shape, and when I came out of the station I felt most important as there was such a crowd collected. It was marvellously roomy and comfy and lots of glass so that I engaged watching the surprised faces of everyone en route. The Prince himself was well and charming and Prince George was there and a golfer and an equerry. Of course, it poured so that the Prince lent me a large mac which went all over my fur coat … Prince George is such a clever, sensitive, attractive young man with a great sense of humour, and love of the arts. He made me play some Chopin to them before I went off to work after lunch.'[237]

Norah was very proud to have the Prince as a client even though she grumbled to others of the hard work that she was putting in at The Fort. She made herself available whenever she was needed and revelled in a trip to a Royal Horticultural Show in the company of the Prince. 'I am just going off to the Fort by early train in this cold, not at all pleasant, but the sweet Prince answered my phone himself and said "Tuesday would be O.K. if I'd come early as his family were arriving to lunch"'[238]

And a few weeks later: 'I had a lovely time at the Iris Show yesterday with the darling Prince, and then back to York House with him which he showed me all over.'[239]

'The day I gardened at the Fort was so cold I caught a bad chill and was in bed three days with a sort of flu. I had been warding it off for two or three days beforehand on purpose to carry out my engagement at the Prince's, but to no purpose tho' to be sure I did carry out the day's planting and successfully, as the Prince was there, gave me lunch, and seeing I was seedy, sent me up in his motor! But he most particularly wanted me to see the coloured photos of his garden, which I'm glad I did – as they are quite lovely and were in a photographers in Conduit Street the next day. That delayed my getting home to bed and by the time I got back was in full fling of an awful cold and flu, and lay in bed wretchedly.'[240]

After working at The Fort for about four years, Norah had become more relaxed in the company of her famous client though never quite blasé about the perks of working for such a charming fellow. The strain and pressure of working for the Prince had dissipated as the gardens took shape and her confidence grew. But during all the years she worked for him, Norah never forgot that it was a great privilege to work for the Prince of Wales.

'At 9:45 am the Prince's motor called for me and I spun down the road I know so well that I always read the papers now instead of look out the windows. It was drizzling – cold, windy, but I worked all the morning with him and then we had a tiny lunch, he only tea, whilst I was eating cold tongue, cheese and fruit, he went off to change as he was to open a Fete at Maidstone. We got into his motor and drove to his private landing place in Windsor Park, – about ten minutes away. There, the smart red and blue and silver machine was waiting, with Piers Legh, his equerry, Capt. Fielden, his pilot, and a mechanic. I never saw weather look so uninviting. Slanting rain, grey mists, and swishing melancholy wind. He hopped in, followed by Legh, and off they went. First of all running a good way along the ground, then rising, turning round and returning in the air over our heads. Ladbroke, the nice fat chauffeur who I know so well, stood by me and we watched the plane flying into the teeth of the wind and rain, and he told me how marvellous it was that one could keep contact all the time with the wireless so as to know exactly where one was … then I bowled off to London …'[241]

Knowing that Anne found her work with the Prince irresistible, Norah sent off a long descriptive letter recounting one of her more remarkable days at The Fort: 'I had a busy unexpected morning yesterday. Tuesday evening, I was in bed when I heard the telephone ring and Gertrude [the maid] came up to say that the Prince of Wales was on the telephone, which she switched from below to my room. He is always so polite and does all telephoning himself. "Good evening, Norah, could you come possibly tomorrow to The Fort as the garden is looking quite lovely and my Mother is coming over and I want you so much to meet her, and Winnie Portland and Sim Feversham want to see you." Naturally, I was delighted and said I would. He was at Windsor for Ascot. So off I went (tho' I really wanted a quiet few days here) and his motor met me at 9:30 am at Reading and I wore a red and white foulard skirt on to which Gertrude had tacked a cream shirt of two years old which I'd never worn as it was too satiny, but it made quite a nice dress, and a coat Henriette Davis had sent me, which I'd dyed the same red. A long plain coat, with the seams alas, a trifle white if you came very close. Red shoes from the Lido days, slightly sandalled and my gents boater with black ribbon. Smart I hoped, yet not too smart.

'I arrived about ten minutes before the Queen and found G. Trotter and the footmen in their white linen coats and medals all standing waiting at the door. I had a slight preliminary rush to look at things and was more satisfied than usual, as none of my gardens are quite what I hope for!! It takes three years to be perfect, but I hadn't gone down to the Iris Walk. A telephone message came to say "They'd left Windsor" and we waited in the Hall. Soon four motors drew up, and out came the Queen, who the Prince introduced me to at once. Prince George, the Lascelles, and Winnie, Blanchie, Sim Feversham and Lady Airlie, and May Roxborough. "We've all come" someone said. And I headed the procession with the Queen.[242] She wore a creamy dust cloak and toque to match and had a white veil and looked very pink and smart.

'We went first all round the house where fremontia and mauve shrubby linum looked too lovely. Then down to the Iris Walk below the battlements which really was a sight of beauty. Masses of Iris's, blue poppies, and pink rock roses all sowing in happy profusion whilst up the battlemented walls were some perfectly glorious roses, climbing Mme. Edouard Herrriot, Souvenir de Claudius Denoyel, etc. Enchanting sight for me. The Queen was properly delighted, though she's no gusher. "Very pretty", "Charming", "What's the name of that?" etc., etc., and said she thought it lovely. But what filled me with pride was my own gardening friends taking notes already. Winnie was like a girl in a pale blue tussore suit and blue crinoline hat, really lovely she looked. Sim was very amusing and said "Windsor" was much too important for him!!

'Altogether it was a great success and they then all whisked away for Ascot, and I went over it all again and saw terrible secret sadnesses – rabbits having eaten lots of things, brooms died back – etc., etc. I hope no one saw it but me, still on the whole it's doing better. I came back by car. It was sweet of G. Trotter to arrange it. I was glad to get back home and rather tired and slept for an hour … then I practised a bit and in the cool of the evening cut off all

FORT BELVEDERE, SUNNINGDALE.

The battlement walls at Fort Belvedere softened with poppies, rock roses and linum.

the dead heads of the tulips down the valerian wall and then a lot of watering of Dahlias. It was almost like a backdrop scene for beauty. Quiet light with a tender lemon glow over everything. A high brilliant moon and tall white Eremurus, and the groves of brilliant poppies were lovely. But though I'd have liked to stay out all night, I was so tired that finally I went to bed … after a most perfect day.'[243]

The Prince appreciated Norah's talent, learned from it, and years later wrote about her. After the abdication, when he and the Duchess moved to France, *Life* magazine sought to photograph his spectacular gardens outside Paris. In the article, in which he described his love of gardening and of the influence that Norah Lindsay had on his gardening style, he wrote:

I think my deep enjoyment in gardening must have been latent; at least I did not inherit it. My grandfather, I remember, liked gardens in a very grandiose sort of way. His interest in them was sporadic … My father's interest was even less; he liked shooting best, and after that collecting stamps. And while my mother liked flowers and used to take me as a child to admire the famous herbaceous borders at Hampton Court, near London, she liked them best in vases, in their cut-flower state. This was perhaps fortunate, for kings and queens rarely have the opportunity to indulge in practical gardening. Of course all the royal estates had fine gardens, and I remember those at Sandringham and Windsor as vast impersonal places where we children were not encouraged to play. They made a fine show in summertime, but people did not really live with them. This kind of long-distance gardening always seemed a bore to me. By 1930, after 18 years of travelling all over the world, I had seen more gardens – more elaborate gardens – than most men can see in a lifetime. Some were beautiful; some were impersonal. They all confirmed my earlier impressions. A garden is a mood, as Rousseau said, and my mood was one of intimacy, not splendor. It was not until that year when my father lent me Fort Belvedere, bordering Windsor Great Park, that I had a chance to try out some of my own ideas. There, at 'The Fort' … I became a 'dirt gardener' with a vengeance. The Fort was surrounded by a hundred-acre wilderness when I arrived, and I enthusiastically set about my work, hacking up laurels, which I hate, installing herbaceous borders and exhausting my weekend guests. It was at The Fort that I first became fascinated with the problems of landscaping, and in the space of six years I patiently, and to a great extent with my own hands, transformed this wilderness into a tidy and organized landscape of shrubs and flowers until it conformed to the noble countryside that stretched through birch and giant cedar down to the vistas of Virginia Water. It was from The Fort that I handled the negotiations leading to my abdication in 1936, and there and then my first gardening activities came to an abrupt end.

As the article continued, he described his French garden at The Mill and in particular the Norah-Lindsay-inspired herbaceous borders. With the help of Norah's plant palette taken from the gardens at The Fort he created his new masterpiece:

'…the two main herbaceous borders stretch from my big room, which we call The Barn, clear across to the wall along the river. The flowers that fill them are the old favorites, like delphiniums, lupines, phlox, chrysanthemums, fall asters and anchusa. To cover the bare walls we planted fast-growing vines like Virginia creeper and honeysuckle. We put in hybrid floribunda roses like Vogue and Fashion, which dot the beds with scarlet, crimson, salmon and rose right up till the October frosts … The unusual use of roses in the herbaceous border, was taught me by Mrs. Norah Lindsey [sic], a charming English lady who used to help me in my first gardening efforts at The Fort. She specialized in herbaceous plantings, and if you had money she was the one to spend it. I think now that her use of roses alone was worth the tuition fee.[244]

Norah would have thought that article worth all the tiring days she put in at The Fort.

ABOVE Rotherfield Park, Hampshire, the home of Sir Jervoise and Lady Scott.

BELOW Norah planted the shrubs along the windows to soften the walls of the house.

OPPOSITE ABOVE An invoice from Mrs. Lindsay for work performed at Rotherfield Park.

OPPOSITE BELOW Norah Lindsay did not usually draw outline plans. Instead she wrote several pages of instructions for each of her estate owners and their gardeners. These instructions included suggestions for plant removal or transplanting, soil enhancement, locations for new plantings, and extensive plant lists.

brown velvet and gold belt and had been to some party – so she'd dressed for the Roxburgh wedding and hadn't gone – which she seemed to think fearfully funny! She wore a pillbox on her forehead and a lovely black fox cape. Then came Paul and Olga of Yugo Slavia. They are such old friends of mine and we flew affectionately together and Paul settled himself by me on the sofa. Olga looked beautiful in a dark grey suit, long coat trimmed with grey astrakhan and usual grey alpine hat and lovely pearls. Then came Poppy with a seductive red parrot cap and velvet dress, and Prince George and Ivor Churchill and Teeny and Juliet and Diana. The latter in good looks, a black velvet tammy and a most elegant coat of cloth with two pinky fur long stripes going all round her neck and down the two fronts – very chic. Then came Grace Vanderbilt and she was deadly smart having come from the Roxburgh wedding. She was all in pink velvet and shoes to match and her bosom was one huge fluffy inappropriate crysanthemum from her chin to her waist!! You know she was called The Kingfisher in old days as she worshipped royalty, and she was exuding happiness as she had had a long talk with the Queen. Then came Mrs. Simpson – a slim, neat figure in black astrakhan and a neat pillbox of the same on her forehead. Very friendly she was and reminded me of 'when the dog bit my ankle and I said a nasty little thing' and I said 'I always hated being bitten', but couldn't remember anything of the kind.

Had a nice talk with Prince George who asked me to lunch next Tuesday. And then a long talk with Paul who wants to take me off with him to do his garden near Bled. It's a lovely stroke of luck and he said 'Darling Norah, we said there's only one person who can make

gardens and that is you'. So in about three weeks I shall join him in Paris and go back with him and Olga. Isn't it thrilling?! I believe his Schloss is not far from the Austrian frontier (I must get a map and examine where it is). Alice Hofmannsthal (who was there looking lovely in black velvet and a tiny feather toque of bright blue green) declares it is the most lovely enchanting place with great beauty and all kinds of picturesque peasants with their legs wound round and round and hats with shawls over them. She adores her life out there and has a lovely chateau – or Schloss. I went up to see Honor and was staggered by her beauty, as it's most becoming to her to have a baby! She had a bright green nightgown and bright green set of sheets and pillows with an edging of broderie anglaise all in vivid apple green. And she showed me a lovely diamond and ruby clip Chips had given her for the son and heir. Of course, her room was a bower of flowers for the occasion as people from the tea party below were coming up at intervals to see her and the baby. I must say I never saw such a proud father as Chips is. He simply must show the baby to everyone and hangs over him with an expression of absolute adoration. Well it was very exciting and I returned by a late icy train full of new thoughts and plans. 'Must get my passport seen to, and snow boots, and a thick jersey or two.' When I told Mrs. Denton, my cook she said, 'Well, you must be proud, and if you are not proud yourself, I am very proud for you.'[250]

When the entourage arrived in Yugoslavia they travelled directly to Brdo, an old sixteenth-century Austrian castle recently purchased by Prince Paul. The central portion of the sturdy square castle contained an open courtyard accented with enormous turrets at each corner. Prince Paul was sparing no expense to make the house beautiful. The landscape architect Cecil Pinsent had been called in to design the fountains and steps and Norah was to design the herbaceous borders filled with flowers and shrubs. The royal party remained at the castle for four days. That gave Norah enough time to explore the grounds, and make notes before returning to England to plan the gardens.

OPPOSITE ABOVE Brdo Castle, Slovenia, front façade, formerly the home of Prince Paul and Princess Olga of Yugoslavia. OPPOSITE BELOW Brdo Castle, rear façade. Norah's herbaceous plantings filled the parterre gardens to the rear of the castle. Today they are planted in grass.

'Out all day and dining early in tea gowns'

GRAND GARDENS IN ENGLAND AND FRIENDS ON THE CONTINENT

Norah's social life continued to flourish around her garden clients. She attended dinner parties, concerts, and on one particular evening , wrote to Frances Horner about comments made by the artist, Paul Maze. 'He said, "There was a lovely lady there in a black velvet coat and red gloves and shoes, who was holding a sort of court"! He meant me.' And to her sister she wrote: '"My red gloves seemed to be very popular as even Paul Maze said I must sit to him for a picture – which I did, but as I said I had only time in between my gardens, I doubt it being more than an *esquisse* [first sketch]. It was very nice to put on the motley and see some friends again in between my days away working. Ava gave me a dinner of twenty! At which Lady Dumfries, one of the most beautiful young things I'd ever seen, Gerry Wellesley, Evan and Dorothy Charteris, Philip Sassoon, Gerald Berners and Bogey were some of my friends there, and afterwards I went on with Terrence Philips who would drag me forth to Alice Wimborne's ... I went up to Jean's for a night and had one most delightful evening with Emerald at the Old Vic where Beecham made his debut as conductor under the new regime of National Opera. Maud had two boxes for Pauline Raber and I, Gerald Berners, Tom Mitford, Maud, Mabelle Cory, Siegfried Raber. It was highly enjoyable ... I then went to Johnny's on Friday, who for once had quite a party, as he had Mark Fenwick and old Charles James, and Captain Kingdon-Ward who is delightful to meet like all explorers.'[251]

Norah had thrown open the doors at Sutton on a cold day in February 1933 and all who entered were once again warmed by her unquenched flame of spirit. Her neighbour, Margot Asquith had organized an auction placing some of her belongings for sale.

We had such an extraordinary incursion of people here on Sunday to see Margot's things that I have only just recovered from the joyful surprise of unexpectedly receiving to lunch Ethel Sands, Nan Hudson, Reggie Cooper, Lee Ashton, George Churchill who owns the lovely pictures in Glos, Johnny Baird who telephoned he was at Rhodes House, and wanted dreadfully to come

At Serre la Madone, Johnny would start his day each morning with a swim in the pool.

186

mossy pool – though last night he declared he felt cold! He is a sort of Rumpelstiltskin isn't he, and can't be altered in any way. Muriel has just returned from Venice where she said life went on just the same. They say all the Italians out of Italy are keeping out and not going back.[259]

Three days later Norah wrote:

We have quite suddenly abandoned Venice and all our elaborate plans for this 'general mobilization' news is too definite to disregard and we might well have an incident in which we might get embroiled and it would serve us right. When we arrived back at Serre Johnny suddenly said he thought that Gourdon, May Norris' place, was being sold and that it would not fetch

LEFT Norah and Johnny spent hours in front of this fire with the dachshunds curled up on the sofas.
BELOW A view of the countryside beyond the gardens of Serre de la Madone, where Norah and Johnny walked the hills amidst the wild shrubs and masses of heather.

Norah met Maud and Gilbert Russell at Mottisfont Abbey, Romsey, Hampshire in the final days of 1935 where, inspired by a small window over the front door, she designed a small parterre garden. 'Arrived at the Gilbert Russell's. Mottisfont is magnificent and romantic too. It is all stone, rushing rivers, vast old yew trees, cedars and lawns and a charming atmosphere of the past. Inside are long corridors, late Georgian white panelled rooms, beautiful mantelpieces and great comfort. We gardened in pelting rain two days running – and in mud up to one's knees. I nearly caught cold but didn't. It's a small job and not much to do yet, but might swell out later …'[269] Norah worked at Mottisfont at the same time that Rex Whistler was painting the interiors. During a break in the day at the completion of the Parterre Garden installation, Whistler and Norah shared a walk through the garden and admired her plantings.

Norah's letters rambled on with a list of client names and projects to be completed. '… I arrive in London to work all day at Audrey's [Audrey Field] garden in Regent's Park – then work at Mrs. Maugham's [Syrie, Mrs. Somerset Maugham] garden all day Friday … then spend the day gardening at Aylesbury … then off to Scotland and on to Johnny's at Menton.'[270]

Serre de la Madone was exactly what Norah needed to lift her spirits in January 1936. With a perfect piano, endless letters, and her bit of needlework to finish on her quilt, she was quite content to do nothing. She was also pleased to report that many improvements had taken place and Johnny had done all the things in the garden that she had suggested the year before. Johnny wanted to build a smaller house on the property at the top of the hill, but at present had 'erected a tent to sleep in during the summer heat. He had to be satisfied with a tent, as he was so overdrawn he had abandoned all his schemes, is going to have to rent Hidcote, and is just going to stay quietly and receive his friends and stop buying.'[271] Her only complaint was '… if only he

wasn't so addicted to ivy, I would think this place quite perfect. I've always minded ivy in England, and trebly do I mind it out here taking up a lot of precious room where a gorgeous southern creeper or even a rose or honeysuckle would look better … The four doggies are sweeter than ever and the cocos wander about and one came in my room because he heard my voice, and was most affable … All the hotels at Cannes are shut up. The war scare and the idiotic high prices have kept everyone away…life is ultra quiet.'[272]

Johnny had a small circle of friends on the Riviera whom he frequently visited. Norah often accompanied him on his visits around the countryside and had formed close friendships with some of their favourites in this circle: Robert Norton, Charles de Noailles, May Norris, and Edith Wharton. One of their favourite jaunts together was to Sainte Claire le Château, Hyères, the home of the novelist Edith Wharton, where they could always count on great conversation, wonderful books, beautiful gardens, and a mix of interesting people.

On one such trip on their way to spend a few days with Mrs. Wharton, Norah and Johnny stopped off for tea with Evan and Dorothy Charteris. Norah was overcome with the news about the death of King George V and wrote to Madeline, 'We had a long talk about the King and the sorrow over his illness. Now I hear he has died in the night. It's so terrible to lose such a steady well-loved King and just at this juncture it's very precarious the Prince with his impulses and unsteadiness coming to the Throne. Poor Prince – his gay little private life at the Fort, his garden, all over, all finished, no private happiness any longer, just a dedication of his time and thoughts to his great task. However, he has such splendid sides and such great sympathy with the under dog

ABOVE The view overlooking the stone wall at Edith Wharton's home, Sainte Claire le Château, in Hyères, France.
RIGHT Edith Wharton with her Pekinese dogs.

ABOVE Robert and Elsie Tritton on
the Western Terrace stairway at
Godmersham Park.
RIGHT The Western Terrace
stairway as it is today.

East of the house through an iron gate in the stone wall was the swimming pool court, the site of Norah's first project. She planted her favourite flowers with her foremost principle in mind, *ton sur ton*. At each corner of the pool, at a distance of 12 feet off the sides, she laid mown grass rectangles 15-feet wide by 38-feet long to soothe the eye and to help cool the air from the heat of the pool's stone paving. On an axis with the centre of the pool, as the eye gazed off to the far end of the pool, were a set of steps leading up to a statue of Neptune sitting alone on a pedestal 10 feet high. The whole effect was reminiscent of her work at Trent Park in the area of Sassoon's orangery and swimming pool.

Directly east of the swimming pool court was the kitchen garden, rose garden, and tennis court. Norah planted the kitchen garden with cutting flowers for the house, and herbs and vegetables. Before passing through another small iron gate into the honeysuckle-vined walls of the tennis court, Norah installed a large formal rose garden buzzing with bees.

To the west of the house, Norah assumed her next project. Here the lawn rose steeply, with a broad flight of steps which she lined with roses and small flowering trees, leading to another terrace facing the west end of the house. Norah softened the stone walls of this lower terrace with garden beds six feet deep containing her favourite magnolias, roses, and climbing vines. Wall fountains gurgled with soft cooling sounds as water trickled down gently to dampen the ferns and other shade-loving plants at the base of the walls. The whole effect was one of lush, uncontrolled abundance. It was a sensual paradise.

Norah designed these cool, shaded Western Terraces as the antithesis of the hot, simmering Swimming Pool Courtyard. Each garden, while equally beautiful, offered a different atmosphere and attitude. The bright, reflecting sunshine bouncing off the stone pavement around the swimming pool offered a feeling of joy and conviviality. It was a place to gather with friends, enjoy the sights of the gardens, share a meal, or occupy oneself with physical activity in the pool or on the tennis court; whereas, the cool ambience in the sheltered Western Terraces of the Stag

Courtyard emitted a more contemplative aura. It was a place perhaps to go to be alone, to wander slowly around, or to sit on a bench amidst the coolness of the vines to read or reflect.

The Sutton Garden in 1936

Norah returned to Sutton and described the garden to Madeline: 'On Sunday Sibell Glyn brought Lord Listowel and a Baron Rosen to see my garden – which now that the sun and rain has come is a mass of glorious iris, tree peonies, poppies, and lupins and marvellous cream-coloured foot-high huge lemon meconopsis, mixed with the blue Baileyii and forget-me-nots and pink columbines. An exquisite grouping eliciting such praise. Another delicious bit - rare cottage pink peonies and sky blue polemonium and lapis *Aquilegia* 'Hensol Harebell'. Another perfect bit is yellow tree peonies, blue ceanothus and Rose Fortune's Yellow. Quite glorious. The Iris border has never been so good, some of them are formed with vast enormous heads like sham flowers … I thoroughly enjoyed my own garden and set out the dahlias and weeded and tied up and sighed for more gardeners, though I do pay four now as the month of May always wants more labour. Still I reflect, I would not get the jobs or the reputation I have but for the crowds who visit Sutton and see exactly how I lay it out and run it. Today I lunch with Alice Hofmannsthal and give her advice on her garden.'[283]

RIGHT Norah's hospitality at Sutton Courtenay:
(top) Norah (second from left) entertaining friends
and animals;
(middle) Norah (fourth from left) never tired of sharing her
table with her many friends;
(bottom) Norah's friends relaxing near the front door at
Sutton Courtenay.

'These extraordinary events'

THE KING AND MRS. SIMPSON

AUGUST WAS THE MONTH each year that Philip Sassoon wanted Port Lympne to be at its finest. Norah set out in early August to check on the gardens to be sure they were ready for the impending onslaught of houseguests. This year she packed into a car with Chips Channon and his wife Honor and started the long drive on the road crammed with traffic to Lympne. 'Of course, they gossiped madly all the way. The usual topics the King and his speech, the King and his yacht trip…The King…The King…The King!'[284]

> We found Philip, Teeny and the Aberconways walking up the long drive as we arrived. The Duffys [Duff and Diana Cooper], Helen Fitzgerald, the Simpsons, and the Brownlows were there. Diana and Duffy start Tuesday for their holiday motoring, planning to stay with Daisy Fellowes at Cap Martin and then on to join the royal yacht wherever and whenever they are told. Diana is marvellously calm as she hasn't yet had any orders or plans told her, but she says H.M. has a party at The Fort this weekend, so she'll probably hear any moment. She is quite delighted at the change from the stale Riviera to the thrill of the Dalmatian coast. But says Duffy can't stay away long because of his duties and work. I sat by Duffy last night who was exceptionally gay and entertaining. He can be more delightful than anyone and I'm told he is not so violently anti-German as the gossips insist. After dinner I played bridge with him.[285]

As expected the gossip quietly turned to the King, and the whispered comments (because after all, the Simpsons were there) talked of nothing but the imminent yacht trip along the Dalmatian coast.

Some time later, after she had received the letter from Norah recounting the weekend chatter, Madeline wrote across the back of the letter then filed away her thoughts on the matter: 'Duff ought to have refused to go with H.M. as Mrs. Simpson was included in the party – and because he was in the government he should have refused to go on this trip. H.M. was so badly served by his friends who never told him the truth. So that he really did believe he could marry her and make her Queen and was shocked when he found he couldn't – If his friends had really told him the truth and showed him that they did not like her – or think his behaviour wise – then he might have realized what he was doing – but they never attempted to make him understand how utterly

The Duke and Duchess of Windsor (photographed by Dorothy Wilding).

Ditchley Park by Alexandre Serebriakoff (1907–1995). Madeline wrote of this room's 'gorgeous cornices and perfect golden trophies on the walls … covered with Genoese dark red cut velvet … on a golden ground'.

Normanby and a new client, Bushie Peakes, at Lownd Hall. But no mention was made of Harry. On June 3, 1939, Norah was hit again with an intense shock when she learned that her dear friend Philip Sassoon had died that day at his house on Park Lane.

Life at Sutton during the War

On September 1, 1939, Hitler invaded Poland and on September 3, Britain and France declared war on Germany. The months that followed Britain's declaration of war were referred to as the 'phoney war' because Britain saw no military action. Nevertheless, a fearful chill seized every citizen.

Norah wrote to Madeline:

One line in the lull of early morning to say it's sad to go through all the horror and misery of another war away from each other … Nancy is marvellous. She has turned into the upper housemaid as well as the gardener. We have only old Evans left, so we have this time to literally dig and weed and double dig for vegetables – all day. We have painted over several windows with black paint and pasted black paper – all very boring meticulous work on ladders – but now we have six rooms and all the basement to do. Even in Abingdon there are no candles, no meat, no stuff for windows save expensive green velvet, no blankets, no radio, hardly any black paper left and no more paint to darken windows!! Nancy has to do the pumping before we get a drop of water in the house. You see the water system is so primitive here you have to pump two solid hours a day to get a bath, that's why the officers haven't quartered children with us. It ought long ago to have been seen to by Harry and as he raised such a huge mortgage, he might have improved living conditions here with one quarter or 10th of it …

Norah with Sir Philip Sassoon, in 1925. The snapshot was taken by Lady Ottoline Morrell.

224

This morning as I woke … we had our first air raid warning. We rushed about getting gas masks, but the blessed sirens soon blew … I can tell you it gave me a horrible fright, waiting, and this house is cardboard and would flop if anyone leant against it. Still darling, I don't know if my work will still go on or clients will pay me! I have a feeling it's going to be a very long war – isn't it awful darling, all the horrors and sufferings beginning again of those four years … We have … moved the piano downstairs to use only the downstairs rooms and shut up the drawing room and banqueting hall … Life seems so futile – all this lovely weather and I look at the garden and wonder how it will survive. We both cut wood every day a little, but it's hot and tiring and goes very slowly. Anyway it uses up our sad bodies and tires our brains – but manual work here has to be done.

There is awful discontent in the village over the refugees [sic] as some are filthy, very rude and want to go back to London, and won't help in any way. One woman was so rude they reported her to the evacuation officer who had her removed. Our attics are full of 'Denton' and 'Alston' relations from London.[315] I feel Hitler will take Poland and then the real attack will start in France and Germany. How ghastly and stupid it all is, and Hitler ought to be hung, drawn and quartered for insisting on war and having all these innocent men killed … I was in church when our clergyman starting his sermon said, 'Well, the catastrophe has happened' – and I knew war had been declared. Luckily I was sitting down, as I felt I was fainting, only eight people in church – as they had all heard on the wireless. I bought a wireless yesterday – I had to. I wish to God you were nearer … I feel absolutely corpselike, from want of sleep. I envy you a huge busy house, as I think size is important – small houses are silly when one wants to huddle hard together…[316]

For now, we live in the old dining room and thus have one fire only and eat at the long table in the middle. But luckily have two bedrooms blackened-out so could have two guests. Gerry Wellesley thinks that inflation must come and that anyone who has a piece of land – like this – must stick to it, as only land will have any value after the war, and he says we'll have no chance of selling this place now and we'd better stick to it just living in one room and living on our potatoes and apples. Oddly enough, Bob Tritton writes this morning in the same view, saying all that will remain will be land – of any value. But we will have somehow to find Peter's mortgage for next January! Well, whilst we were lunching, a man was also going all over the house in case it might do for a school!!! After lunch Gerry tactfully went out in the torrential rain for a walk, so I had Peter to myself. He was in good spirits and talked chiefly about my health and how important it was I should leave this icy house and stay with friends and I assured him he mustn't worry about me as I was making a very good plan with my various friends – Chirk, Welbeck, Violet Woodhouse, Anne Islington, Joanie Gregg, Francis, and fitting in my last two small jobs – Trittons and Menzies. Luckily, each place I can stay as long as I like – at least three or four weeks each.[317]

In October Norah and Nancy packed all the china, books and knick-knacks in huge chests in the cellar and 'shut up' Sutton. Unable to afford to keep Sutton heated during the winter months and with little money for necessities, Norah and Nancy set off for Hidcote. Johnny had come back to Hidcote for a brief time and had invited Norah to join him before his return to Menton in November. Norah stayed with Johnny until the end of October, when she moved on to Chirk.

On Christmas Day she wrote to Madeline, 'They say Hitler's Nazis will either shoot him or he will shoot them all first as he's beginning to realize they distrust him … Everyone is very upset and angry over Kennedy's speech.[318] Ronnie Tree tells me he is really a very ordinary Irish man who has made masses of money and only thinks of holding on to his money, and wants to be President in four years. Ronnie bet me (1d that's all I would take) that America would come in. Perhaps at the very end she might like last time and then say they had saved England. I believe what are wanted are ships and more and more ships which if only America would come in would be the greatest help to us and we could then send big guns to Romania and Yugoslavia. Last time, America sent us a ship a day.'[319]

Norah continued to send Madeline updates from her politically connected friends, while Madeline was learning to live with aspects of the war in her own front yard. The Whitbreads'z estate was being used as a camp, with thousands of soldiers congregating for manoeuvres and sleeping in tents on the Southill Park property in preparation for shipment to the front.

Up until now, life was not all that changed for those lucky few living on the large, wealthy estates in England.

Norah moved in with the Trees at Ditchley and while there continued the usual complaints about the dearth of servants and taking one's coffee without sugar or foregoing the morning buttered toast – two guaranteed complaints from Norah each morning – their lifestyle had not deteriorated. Before a game of tennis, a typical lunch at the Trees was a delicious mix of *pâté de foie gras au aspic* with salad, creamed chicken and asparagus, followed by ice with strawberries.[320]

Norah continued to lose clients as the war intensified and she wrote,

I am rather sad, as I have lost one of my precious gardens as Mr. Menzies is shutting up and going to work in his firm in Edinburgh. The loss of £100 a year is terrifying. I could not even afford dear loving Daisy [her maid] but that a friend [Jean Hamilton] paid me her wages as she said she could not bear I should have no one with me – no husband – no house – or child. Indeed, I often get the dumps longing for my own blood, but also realize I must be content for the moment to be here, as any time this may be taken and then I'll be able to come to you. I am absolutely hungry darling to see you – longing for the

LEFT Hidcote Manor was always a comfortable retreat for Norah.
OPPOSITE ABOVE Southill Park, another retreat for Norah, the home of Madeline and Howard Whitbread, seen from across the lake.
OPPOSITE BELOW Southill Park, front façade, as it is today.

Friday, February 5th, Lady Colefax's luncheon party; but she had bronchitis and stayed in bed. Norah Lindsay acted hostess in her place. She was wearing a flat, black hat like a pancake on the side of her head, pulled down over one eye. It was adorned with cherry-coloured buttons. Her white frilled blouse had more cherry buttons. She is kittenish, stupid-clever, and an amusing talker. On her left was Osbert Peake, now a Minister of some sort, a boring, stuffy man. Jamesey was on my right and in the circumstances we had nothing, but nothing to say to one another. On my left was Laurie Johnston, who had just seen my father at Hidcote. A man called Palewski, who is General de Gaulle's *chef du cabinet*, and rather spotty, talked about North Africa. He has just returned from Casablanca where he attended the Churchill–Roosevelt meeting. He said Roosevelt was in high spirits; he had to be carried in a chair from the aeroplane for he cannot walk at all and can barely stand unaided. After luncheon, which was delicious, Laurie Johnston took me aside to ask if the National Trust would take over Hidcote garden without endowment after the war, when he intended to live in the South of France for good. He is a dull little man, and just as I remembered him when I was a child. Mother-ridden. Mrs. Winthrop, swathed in grey satin from neck to ankle, would never let him out of her sight.[342]

Norah returned to Southill Park on June 1, 1943, and told Madeleine of her affairs. 'It appears that David Astor suggested, rather tentatively, buying Sutton, but thinks the price – £14,000 – too much. Norah has written to him explaining that if he doesn't pay £14,000, then there "will be hardly enough for me to buy a cottage"!! She is impossible, isn't she!! She never sees but her own point of view. But he won't buy or consider Sutton unless Nancy goes away from the gardener's cottage, and Norah says "Peter gave Nancy the gardener's cottage." – but I imagine that if another cottage were found she would have to move. Anyway, lovely as Sutton is, I have always thought it was an impossible possession for Peter or Norah. David Astor wrote that one of the reasons he could not give

£14,000 is because he would have to do a lot of repairs and modernization and Norah wrote to him and told him "there was nothing he need do to the house, I had made it quite comfortable, and now that there are fifty children there, it has to be kept clean and tidy!!"' Madeline continued, 'Nothing will ever make Norah see things as they are, only as she wishes them to be. Norah wrote, "And in some ways it would be well having David there, for I could live there a lot, and he could pay me to keep the garden going"!!! – But there is no doubt that her outlook is a very poor one financially. Although she received £500 from Jean Hamilton and £200 from Robert Norton when they died, she has lost £75 that Portland gave her each year.'[343]

Wartime Friends

Norah returned to Southill Park for Christmas and immediately took to bed with flu. While lying in bed she and Madeline read out *The Eagle and the Dove*, Vita Sackville-West's book about St. Theresa. They enjoyed the book so much that, prompted by Norah who was too weak from flu to write, Madeline wrote to Vita. Vita replied, 'My dear Madeline, How very nice of you to write! And of course I was delighted to hear that you had read and liked my book [on St. Theresa]. I must say, I do find it a fascinating and mysterious subject, and one that so few people (apart from Catholics) know anything about. I thought the only way I could make it palatable to the general reader was by making it "human" too. Most books on saints and mysticism, written by devout believers who accept blindly all the teachings of the Church, are almost repellent because their authors have nothing but their sincerity to recommend them. I thought it was high time that somebody with some literary training tried their hand at it! I am so sorry to hear that Norah's Peter has been ill. I didn't know. If she is still with you, please give her my love, and tell her that Mrs. Drummond[344] is much the same and as indomitable as ever. With love and thanks dear Madeline, Vita.'[345]

'Her beauty gladdened our eyes

THE FINAL CHAPTER

NORAH'S ERRATIC BEHAVIOUR and vagabond life caught the attention of those closest to her in 1944. This was the year when her friends and relatives realized that her future needed securing. Norah was now spending almost six months a year at Southill, intermixed with lodging with one friend or another for weeks at a time.

In early June, Madeline and Violet (Letty) Benson of Compton Bassett began a discussion for the best option to secure Norah's future. Madeline suggested finding an inexpensive flat in London. Letty responded, 'I do not know of any ideal flat for Norah, but I am certain that what you are thinking of for her is the right thing. What about Dolphin Square – it is near the Tate – or has that been requisitioned? There they have a restaurant and many other amenities attached. Michael Asquith lived there when he first married and they loved it. Poor Norah, I agree with you about Peter – it is difficult for him to be a dutiful and careful son with all the distractions in his life right now. Do let me know how your plan proceeds. Perhaps I might help – I'd like to if I could. How would it be to get 20 or 30 friends to guarantee £5 a year each? It is so little really, and if one signs a banker's order one forgets about it quite cosily. I do it for one other very poor friend.'[346]

Norah had no idea that Letty and Madeline were so worried about her future, and with typical *joie de vivre* went off to see the Astors and the Trees. When she was due to return home, Madeline kindly said, 'Norah comes back, so the flow of wit will once more sweeten the routine of our days.' The gossip that Norah returned with stunned Madeline: 'Norah home, and the gossip of Astor–Tree milieu, and Tree's wife who thinks her husband "the most marvellous man", but needs other men too!!! All very difficult for Tree!'[347] The Trees' marriage was clearly breaking up.

At the end of August Letty Benson was still working on raising money for the 'Norah Fund' or at the very least, finding homes for her temporary visits. Letty contacted Anne Poynder, now a widow watching her own money closely, who wrote to Madeline, 'I am so sorry about Norah. I leave here tomorrow and go to Scotland, and that is so far away, that I am sure Norah could never manage it. Also, I have so few servants and know she wants waiting on and can't do for herself. I have learned to do most things for myself. I wonder where she will go. She has so many friends – perhaps to Welbeck. I heard you had decided on a flat in Sussex Square. I think that's a good idea. I would have liked that, but I am too poor nowadays.'[348]

When Peter finally met Madeline at Southill Park, Madeline wrote, 'Peter here, and full of plans

Portrait of Norah Lindsay painted by Harrington Mann.

for Norah. He seems to think that she could not be expected to live on less than £1,000 a year! I give her £100 a year, and I think I could give her £200 – but not more. There is a faint hope that Sutton may be sold to David Astor which would net her £200 or maybe £300 a year – and Letty's collection from all the Friends has brought in £150 – so that makes £750 a year total. And Peter's <u>future</u> plan was – really future – that she should have a tiny house in the South of France. All her friends who had houses there want to return there so she would have a colony of friends round her. I don't think this is a very good plan – but I am only too glad to let Peter settle and plan … I still don't think Peter's plan of £750 a year will work – but I think she will still make something with gardens after the war. Poor Norah – she has always lived with people who have huge incomes and she can't learn to live poor. Not, for instance, to buy <u>quantities</u> of newspapers whenever she goes on the smallest journey – not to send cables and long telegrams – but there it is, she is too old to learn now!'[349]

The 'Norah Fund' was firmly in place by December. Madeline wrote, 'The collection for Norah is now complete and she has been told and thank goodness is pleased, though plaintive at having to rely on <u>friends</u> and not relations.'[350]

Norah replied to Madeline after she was told of the plans to increase her income:

Norah's bedroom (middle floor, second window from the left) looked out on the rhododendron alleé at Southill Park.

All yesterday I carried your letter about and every now and then read it again. It is such a huge relief to feel I am not quite so indigent and down in the ditch and that I needn't worry so cruelly about the future, which always seems so dire and menacing when one has no home and no money to get one. … Then came my lunch with Letty, and when she told me all about her scheme I was so taken aback at her utter kindness in thinking of helping me – only an aunt by marriage, and her industry and zeal in writing all those letters when she has five sons to worry about – three in battle – that I nearly laid my head on the table and boo hoo'd, which would have surprised everyone in the room. What gave me a real gust of joy was her realizing all I'd been through in misery, as not having been there for a year she must have guessed it instinctively! Sympathy, real sympathy, in other people's troubles and listening and giving time to listen is a sane and heavenly gift. So when Letty suddenly started telling me I'd given so many people so much happiness in my life, I was spellbound, but didn't know why she should tell me this. Then she explained why – and I was really very uncomfy, but so emotional I could only nod, as somehow I minded her asking people for money for me … it's a huge help and a comfort to me and you can imagine how grateful I am.[351]

January 1945 was ushered in with good news. Peter announced that he had reached an agreement to sell the Manor House and all its furniture to David Astor, though the transaction was not signed nor did money exchange hands. Norah was somehow under the delusion that the deal provided her with the benefit of living at Sutton whenever she wanted and that she could redo the garden again. Norah planned to use Southill as her 'headquarters till the war was over' – then move back to Sutton. Peter was still talking of buying her a cottage in the South of France and letting her stay with friends in England for a portion of each year, and Madeline and Letty continued in their search for a small, inexpensive flat for Norah in London. Madeline wrote, 'I smile, without surprise, at

Peter's idea of how she should live. I expect actually he is right. I don't mean that it is right that she should live extravagantly, but I don't see her for long living wisely – cheaply. It is impossible to think Norah can use buses, and her love of beauty must be satisfied, etc. Perhaps I am wrong.'[352]

In mid-January Norah wrote to Madeline, 'I think Sutton is all right but mums the word till it's really settled. But I got a sweet letter from David and it's wonderful if it comes true that I have still one friend who loves it (and me) and wants it. He so loved it when he was at Oxford and absolutely lived in my house – at last there is a Sign. But mums the word. My chief happiness is not the money, but that I shall see Sutton again.'[353]

Norah gardened at the Trittons' in the early spring, travelling to London occasionally to enjoy friends. When Ronnie Tree called her to Ditchley in mid-March, she went without hesitation.

I spent all Saturday gardening with Ronnie, settling where to plant lilacs and roses, etc. and at night we gossiped madly, alas he told me of many marriages just splitting up owing to the war. Lord Stanley of Alderley has 'walked out' on the lovely Sylvia. The young Rothschilds are parting as she has been 'gay'. He has bought her a house near Ditchley. Then he said he'd heard Sim Feversham's marriage wasn't too secure as she had fallen in love with someone, and Wissie's [Astor] wasn't going too well. Only don't repeat any of this darling, it's only to you I say it and probably they will all settle down in the end. On the other hand, Barbi [Wallace] is marrying that fine American writer, Herbert Agar, who wrote *A Time For Greatness*, which is a splendid book. They have been madly in love and I am thankful she's going to find happiness. A tall, dark giant with a lovely low voice – evidently he adores her and she him and they have the same tastes and will have a very happy life – he writing and she gardening. I hear Nancy Tree is much better, but still nervy and melancholy, but ever so much better than last year. Ronnie has bought her a lovely house in Queen Anne's

Gate next to her old one which ought to please her. Ronnie was so loving – I am so fond of him, and so sorry. He is so, so good and patient.[354]

August 1945 brought good news and bad news. Mid-month, Norah rejoiced when World War II ended with a victory to the Allied forces. But at the end of August, when Peter Lindsay and Janie announced that their marriage was over, Norah suffered from the news more than anyone else involved! Although, it is interesting that Madeline fumed, 'we've never had a divorce in our family before,' obviously viewing Norah and Harry's unsuccessful marriage and separation for life as being much more acceptable than a divorce (a common view at this time in Britain).

Norah stayed at Ditchley until it was time to move into her new flat, in Wilton Place, on October 1. She wrote, 'Well, it was heavenly being here again amongst the fleshpots. Huge room, private bathroom, bath salts – everything. Darling Ronnie. Charming party. David Beattie, who I've always liked though known very little, and a very pretty Mrs. Bragg he's going to marry … They all go over to Blenheim to shoot today and Blenheim comes over to shoot with us Monday. I go off to Myrtle Hood's small garden all day … A small job – still a job. Evidently Nancy Tree not returning here – as her bedroom is being used (don't repeat this). Ronnie wants to go off to America and round world for six months in October, but says it's awfully difficult to get a place.[355] … We also had Anthony Eden, quite charming, gay and talkative – and George Carlisle – an old friend – mellow, travelled, ironic and very nice to talk to. Ronnie and I have been gardening. We are going to go see 'Lady Windermere's Fan' tonight. I wish I didn't have to go to Diss[356] in this weather, it will be so cold there, but it means money and my flat is so ruinous I must work hard to pay for it.'[357] (At the age of seventy-two, Norah could still be a bit of a martyr about her lot in life.)

'I was very sad leaving Ronnie, who I love and has put me up for three weeks', wrote Norah on the day she officially moved into her new flat.[358] She put some of her own creative efforts into the flat, fixing it with her books and vases of flowers, until she at last was able to say she was happy and cosy in *her* new home. She let it to a friend for the month of November as she went off to do a few small garden jobs and saved her money with the intent to fix the flat to her liking in the spring.

Norah's declining health became worse while she gardened at Godmersham in April so she returned to Southill where she knew she would have extra care. Norah's health had been a problem for several years. She continually complained to anyone who would listen about a

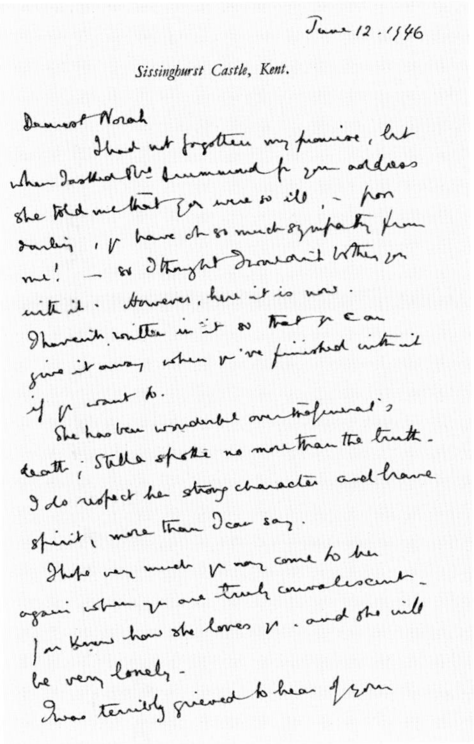

June 12. 1946

Sissinghurst Castle, Kent.

Dearest Norah

[handwritten letter from Vita Sackville-West to Norah]

[continuation of handwritten letter]

Your loving Vita.

OPPOSITE Norah's life-long friend, Vita Sackville-West. A photograph from Norah's personal scrapbook.

LEFT AND ABOVE A letter from Vita to Norah.

constant pain in her stomach and she developed frequent bouts of flu-like symptoms. She was examined by doctors on numerous occasions, and was generally sent off with medication and told to rest. Norah was convinced for years that she was dying of some cancer that was working its way through her body. Her friends, and especially those who had so often housed her in the most recent years, were accustomed to her taking to her bedroom for days on end, with trays of food shuttled to her while she recuperated. Norah demanded a great deal of care and attention and eventually Madeline's daughter-in law, Helen, encouraged her to check into a nursing home in early May as no one could adequately care for her. Norah checked out after only one night's stay because the cost was all too dear and moved back into Southill. Letters of encouragement flowed into Southill when news spread of Norah's ill health. Vita Sackville-West wrote to Madeline, 'I wonder how Norah is? I was deeply sorry to hear how ill she had been. Mrs. Drummond [Norah's former housekeeper] wants to know her present address if you could very kindly put it on a postcard. Yours affectionately, Vita.'[359]

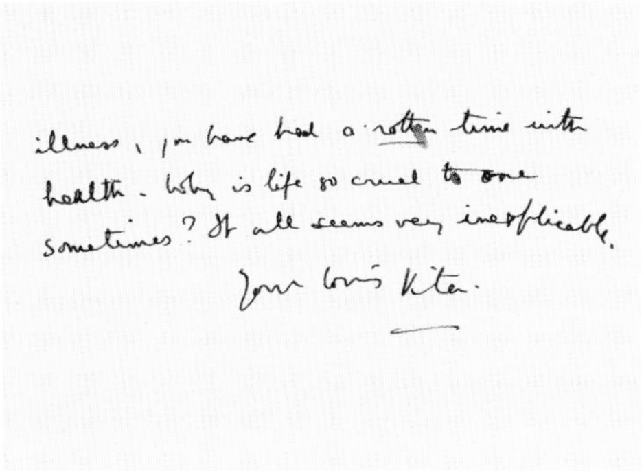

Norah's clients were starting to put the war behind them, and she was called to the Bensons' to plant, to Baba Metcalfe's, Peter Beatty's, the Allendales' and back to the Trittons'. Gerry Wellesley wanted her to go to Stratfield Saye House before the cold set in to help him in the garden. She went anywhere she was asked, as she was 'so fearful of losing the tiniest job I never turn down anything.'[360] However, Norah's health continued to deteriorate during the winter months of 1946 and 1947. She moved out of the flat at Wilton Place into a more spacious and comfortable apartment at Flat 410, Carrington House, Hertford Street.

In March, Norah moved back into Ditchley for a six-week stay, from which she now complained, 'It's twice as cold here as in my new snug flat. However, there are lots of compensations.' Norah settled in with the other house-guests, including 'Dr. Macleod, a young very clever psychiatrist who is treating Nancy Tree, a very calm competent agreeable young man, who looks like an Oxford Student – and Bobbie Shaw is here.'[361]

Norah used Ditchley as a home base, recovered from her recent ailments and went off to Peter Beatty's at Astrop Park, King's Sutton, where she worked 'on the tulip borders, planted thousands of white narcissi in the lawns and directed the pruning of the roses, all the while earning a few wages, before falling quite ill again and taking to bed. I am totally unable to stand, though have got so much better here that I can now walk, but cannot stand. Fear some deadly weakness of tummy. I hope I'll be able to go off and work at Mrs. Baron's and Mrs. Tritton's.'[362]

When Easter rolled around, Ditchley was filled with guests, 'including Lord and Lady Moore – she is a glorious pianist and gave us brilliant recitals every night, Pat Wilson, Kitty Gurney and Elizabeth Winn, Peter Beatty, and the lovely and exciting film star, Paulette Goddard and her charming husband, Burgess Meredith. She is very lovely, with enormous dazzling eyes and flawless teeth, very slim and gay and sweet and untough, and she and her husband, who looks rather like a writer, adore each other. He is a delightful man and has been a lot in England in the war and an old friend of Ronnie's. They were very easy and simple and we all liked them very much. They left early this morning to go and begin their work on their separate films. She is doing Mrs. Cheveley in Oscar Wilde's 'Ideal Husband'. She wore an unending succession of strange clothes – sox to her knees of red wool and very amusing shoes covered in nails for out of doors. And lovely modern jewellery. Daisy was thrilled, as Mrs. Meredith took Daisy to see her when dressing for dinner and she gave Daisy her autograph.'[363]

She wrote to Madeline, 'You know, the Trees are now divorced, but for six weeks it's not announced so bury it!'[364] 'I was interested Ronnie quite simply referred to his divorce saying he was advised to say nothing to the reporters as nine times out of ten if you ask them for silence one of them blabs … Ronnie and I are going out this morning to make plans for a better spring garden in the orangery next year. The gardener has been very bad at weeding and Ronnie had to give him a talking to. It's no good my planting if he doesn't pick out the ground elder. Now I must get up and have my bath, which is not as nice as it used to be as tiny black tadpoles have somehow got into the cold water cistern and the cold tap has to be covered with a piece of muslin!'[365]

In early June, Norah wrote to Madeline, 'Ronnie is just married [to Marietta Peabody] and I suppose goes to Barbados for his honeymoon, where he means to settle about the building of his house which he means to go to in February. I hear from the Beattys that Nancy Tree is behaving very badly over Ronnie's wedding.'[366]

Norah's health declined during the coming months. She worked at the Trittons' and Beattys', but spent as much time in bed as in the gardens at each of these houses. She was now making weekly visits to doctors, receiving injections for her kidneys and liver, and had her entire family worried about her well-being.

In mid-October, she returned to Ditchley for the last time, and reported, 'I really am feeling better, not so feeble. The new Mrs. Tree is quite lovely, very young and gentle and fair and no wonder Ronnie loves her, she is really loveable. A big party coming tonight – Ismays, Bill Ciston and his wife; David Niven is bringing Vivien Leigh and Laurence Olivier to lunch on Sunday.'[367]

But Norah's health had not improved. After the exciting festivities with the film stars at the Trees', Norah was driven back to London. Madeline went to Norah's flat each day to check on her; Daisy, her faithful maid, took loving care of her; and Peter came back from France at intervals to check in on her. Madeline recognized, after recently watching her own husband die, that Norah was very ill. She wrote in her diary, 'I have done the job of seeing my beloved's through the last bit of life and the agonizing familiarity of it all hurts terribly.'[368] Word spread quickly of Norah's condition and dozens of letters flowed into Madeline's flat with best wishes and encouragement.

Norah was admitted to hospital in February 1948, but the doctors determined that she had such a serious infection and high fever that they were unable to operate on her. She remained in the hospital, heavily medicated, barely conscious, and unaware of her surroundings for weeks, with Madeline sitting at her bedside.

The letters continued to arrive. Victor Cunard wrote from Barbados, 'I am more distressed than I can say. I simply cannot believe that she is not going to get well. She has meant more in my life than any friend I have got, and I cannot think what life would be like without all the fun and beauty she brings to it. I know how deeply you must be suffering, and I wish I were in England to give you all the sympathy I feel. Yours ever, Victor Cunard.'[369]

At the end of March, Norah showed small signs of improvement and was released from hospital. Madeline and Daisy continued to care for her on a daily basis, but Norah was still so weak and in such pain that she could only lie in bed all day. She was unable to write her famous letters or read any of the latest books, and was so heavily medicated that for the next few weeks she was often in and out of consciousness.

A Vivid Portrait

Norah Lindsay died of cancer of the kidney on June 20, 1948.[370] Her brother, Nigel, wrote to Madeline, 'Poor darling Norah, a real release for her. I do wish I could have seen her again. I last remember her though as gay and full of those brilliant spirits and wit she possessed.'[371] Norah Lindsay left an estate of £2,442 to be divided equally between her two children, Peter and Nancy.[372]

Madeline, the devoted sister, the dependable caretaker, and the keeper of the family correspondence now had the final task of approving the changes to the announcement that she and Gerry Wellesley, the Duke of Wellington, had composed in preparation for Norah's passing during her last dying weeks. Gerry Wellesley wrote from Stratfield Saye House, 'Dear Madeline, I have received the typescript. I certainly agree that there should be a paragraph about

Sutton and all that it meant. The addition of this and the abbreviation of the rest has certainly been an improvement. When the sad moment at last comes, would you like me to send it to "the Times". If so, I would explain that it has the approval of the family and that as it is the result of collaboration it should be published "A correspondent writes", not "W. writes". Yours affectionately, Gerry.' This loving tribute, submitted to *The Times* in the form of an obituary, described Norah's personality and life as only those closest to her could express.

Mrs. Harry Lindsay

A correspondent writes: –

Norah Lindsay has gone, and we who knew and loved her realize that we shall never see anyone like her again. In years she was no longer young, but she was quite ageless; and as she did not cling to any particular standards of behaviour and was utterly uncensorious, young people loved her, not as a revered elder, but as a gay fellow-conspirator. In her talk she had a curious power of detachment from any period, and no one was ever less set in her ideas.

Norah Lindsay was lavishly endowed by nature. Her beauty gladdened our eyes. Her music enchanted our hearts. She had an acute and critical appreciation of literature, especially poetry. Her brilliant letters were received with delight by her friends – and – she was an unrivalled talker. Her conversation sparkled with unexpected analogy and lightning repartee.

The happiest years of her life were spent at Sutton Courtenay, her home. There, as one entered the gate, care sloughed off one's shoulder. In that loveliest of all gardens, her friends gathered: Oxford boys, Cabinet Ministers, gay girls, wits and poets, beautiful women, and with Norah radiating gaiety, life touched a higher level of vitality and happiness than in any other place.

Above all, she was a gardener. Laying out and planting were her career. When her wit and charm are forgotten, her gardens in England, France, Belgium and Italy will remain as a permanent memorial to one whose mastery in that art amounted to genius.

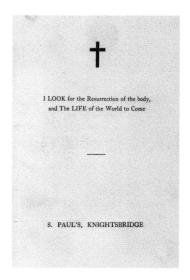

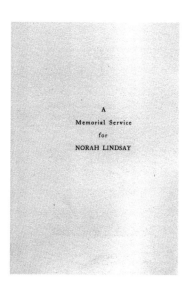

ABOVE The programme for Norah Lindsay's memorial service.
BELOW Norah is buried in the churchyard of the Parish Church of All Saints, Sutton Courtenay.

A lifetime's collection of family, friends, and clients lined the pews of St. Paul's, Knightsbridge, London, to bid Norah adieu at a memorial service organized by Madeline. In addition to her family, the mourners milling about so sombre and silent included: Sir Henry 'Chips' Channon, Reginald Cooper, Gerald Wellesley, Duke of Wellington, Mr. and Mrs. Sacheverell Sitwell, Lord Morven Cavendish-Bentinck, Lady Violet Benson, Gerald Villiers, Victor Cunard, Michael Tree, the Honourable David Astor, Vicountess Nancy Astor, Nina, Countess Granville, Viscountess Allendale, Viscountess Esher, Lady Glyn, Lady Alexandra Metcalfe, Mr. and Mrs. Robert Tritton, Lady Keppel, Mrs. Leo d'Erlanger, and Sir Edward Marsh. Norah Lindsay was buried that same day in the churchyard behind the Parish Church of All Saints, Sutton Courtenay, directly across the road from her beloved Manor House.

Deeply saddened, Chips Channon wrote in his journal: 'June 20. Norah Lindsay has died. She was one of the most brilliant, fanciful and altogether amazing of women. Her wit was extravagant, her conversation an ecstasy, her garden the finest in England, her appearance exotic to a degree. She had Renaissance hair, tight lips, treacherous eyes, but she was a fine friend, a lover of poetry and a worshipper and begetter of beauty. Everything that she touched sprang to life, and Sutton Courtenay, where she lived for so long, and where I spent the happiest days of my youth, was a terrestrial paradise. Long ago she influenced me more than anyone.'[373] Chips also included a conversation that he had with Emerald Cunard: 'I suggested that women were the world's greatest letter writers, and Emerald agreed. She cited Norah Lindsay, Lady Desborough, Mme de Sévigné and herself!'[374]

In his memoirs, Philip Sassoon's architect at Port Lympne, Philip Tilden, wrote about Norah's enchanting qualities, disarming demeanour, and natural flair for garden art. 'Norah Lindsay was one of the most instinctive gardeners of this generation. I wish that she had written more about it in the manner that old William Robinson did. Miss Jekyll had held the day in garden literature, and there was no one of quite the same calibre to follow her. I think that Norah Lindsay could have done that, and if she had written one-tenth as amusingly as she talked, she would have become a best-seller… Her monument must be in very truth the gardens that she has made, and would that they could retain their first pristine touch of genius that put scents and colours in their places… Norah Lindsay dealt with the sheer effect of it all.'[375]

A note clipped into the back of Madeline's diaries was marked 'Extract December 1937 Yorkshire Post'. The society correspondent who wrote this article knew nothing of Norah's long hours standing in the pelting rain with mud up to her knees, or of the years spent on cold dirty trains traipsing from one garden to another. Instead the author only knew of the vibrant outer shell that Norah so convincingly presented to others. References to Norah's work, as in 'gardener' or 'employer', were placed in quotation marks as if these words were euphemisms for gratuitous consultations or divine flowers that she bestowed upon the gardens with the flick of a magic wand. The references to 'three years supervising gardens' and to endless holidaying in warm climates, further hides the real life and hardships that also filled Norah's world. But the

correspondent stated one undisputed truth in his article; indeed, Norah Lindsay was a woman of the century:

> In the last Social Diary I wrote of Mrs. Norah Lindsay being a week-end guest of Lord and Lady Allendale at Bretton Park. Mrs. Lindsay, a cousin of Lord Mayo, is one of the best-loved members of that indefinable community of art, letters and refinement that knows no national frontiers. She is exquisite, even exotic, yet a very real person. Her visit to Lord and Lady Allendale was as a friend and as their chief 'gardener'. For three years she has been planning, planting and supervising the gardens of great houses not only in this country but in as distant places as Bled, the summer home of Prince Paul of Yugoslavia. In Yorkshire Lord and Lady Feversham are also her friends and 'employers'. Her own gardens at Sutton Courtenay in Berkshire are among the most delightful in the world. Every summer Mrs. Lindsay visits friends in Venice and every winter she goes to a villa in the foothills of the Riviera, feeding her love of sunshine and beauty. But her greatest joy is in the flat fields of the Thames valley, where grassy orchards, rare plants, and mossy statues surround the Elizabethan manor house which is her resting place. 'Employers' value her as a guest not only for her gardener's hands, but for her conversation and wit; for the turn of phrase in her letters, for being a musician and able to make all listeners understand the composer's thoughts. Perhaps her Irish ancestry gave her the temperament which makes her appreciated by the discerning of every land as a woman of the century.

Sir Edward Marsh sent Madeline an extract of his thoughts on Norah. Eddie's goal was to make Madeline smile. He told Madeline he had written these words years ago and had included them in a book he had previously written:

> Mrs. Harry Lindsay – born Norah Bourke – if she had been an 18th century Frenchwoman, she would be celebrated in all the memoirs for her gifts and graces, her wit, her beauty, her hospitality, her zest and sunny

ABOVE LEFT Handwritten letter, Norah Lindsay to her sister, Madeline Whitbread.
ABOVE RIGHT Handwritten envelopes, Norah Lindsay to Lady Desborough.

temper, her buoyant courage, her music, her fascinating scrap books, and her exquisite art of gardening. She lived on the river at Sutton Courtenay, and in those old summers used to have parties called Allegresses, when the Manor House and all its dependencies became one great doss house for guests from London and undergraduates from Oxford – and all saw 'golden days fruitful of golden deeds, with joy and woe [love] triumphing'.[376] One of her best letters described her first country house visit after a rather hectic winter in Italy – 'It's extraordinary to be here again among all these women with real hair, real busts, and real husbands – so different from those boy-dowagers in Rome and Venice.' I have always treasured the reason she gave for

not riding, 'I hate sitting up on the back of a great big horse that keeps throwing meringues in my face.' She once took it into her head to write some extra verses to the poem of Blake's which contains the couplet

'A robin redbreast in a cage

Puts all heaven in a rage.'

But unfortunately the only one I can remember is –

'He who vexes a canary

Puts the Pope in Quandary.'

After a visit to a film in which Miss Anna May Wong had played an oriental vamp who alienated the hero's affections from his perfectly good European wife, she was asked what it was like, and answered, 'It was about a man who didn't know White from Wong.'

The letters carefully filed away in Madeline Whitbread's letterboxes were no longer long, rambling, deliciously descriptive letters written by Norah. They were no longer Norah's 'self portraits' of life, which were greedily read and enjoyed by Madeline, then passed on and reread by her mother, her sister, or her children. Instead they were treasured thoughts from those who knew Norah best, and those who loved her most. Some of the letters Madeline received include:

June 26, Darling, So the sad parting of the ways has come. Everyone will say and feel that your poor Norah has been stretched on the rack of this rough world long, long enough and that without you she could scarcely have endured. But you are left with the aching sadness, that void that aches on. Bless you, Madeline, you have indeed been a sister of mercy and loving kindness. Ever loving, Anne Islington.

Trent Park, July 11, Dear Mrs. Whitbread, How kind of you to have sent me that life-like and charming description of Norah. It brought her back so vividly to me after reading it, it really is difficult to realize she is dead. I am so very glad to have it. One thinks of her in the garden and one thinks of her indoors. She filled both places like no one else. Many grateful thanks, Yours sincerely, Hannah Gubbay.

1, Cambridge Square. I cannot think of anyone past or present that one enjoyed being with as much. Even those who did not see her often have such delicious memory pictures of her. Quite unique and for you losing such a pearl among women is dreadful. You loved her so and she loved you. All my love, Evy Marshall Field.

La Moubra, Montana, Valais, Switzerland, July 12, Dearest Madeline, How nice of you to lend me the typed copy of what you and G.W. wrote about Norah! I shall treasure it amongst a few other 'appreciations' of the wonderful people one has known who have truly enriched one's life. Norah will indeed be remembered by the beautiful gardens she made. I wish it were possible to associate her in some way with this National Trust scheme by keeping up a few of the most notable English gardens (I believe Hidcote is almost first on the list). But I suppose that even if all her friends subscribed to a 'Norah Lindsay Fund' it would not be enough to make an appreciable difference – one knows only too well what a big annual outlay is needed on a lovely garden. Yours affectionately, Sibyl Colefax.

'Marlborough House, S.W.1, July 15, Dearest Madeline, However long we had been expecting it and however thankful we might be that the end of suffering and so much misery has come – when the blow falls it always comes as a catastrophe and leaves such a dreadful sense of 'missing', which one knows will always remain. Indeed, one could not wish it otherwise – so much of the past and of one's whole self is bound up in the loss. I do most truly grieve with you and send you all my love and sympathy. Your Norah was a very gifted and remarkable person and will be deeply missed by a very wide range of friends. Queen Mary wished me to tell you informally how sorry she had been to hear of your loss. How ghastly these disasters must be for those who feel that a candle has been blown out for good. Yours very affectionately, Cynthia Asquith.

Pamela Lytton, a friend from childhood wrote,

July 5, Dearest Madeline, I go back a long way, for my most vivid and abiding memory of her is when as a little girl I was invited to see her in her 'Presentation Dress'! She is clearly before my eyes, in her long white dress and train and her tulle and feathers – and her lovely radiant face! Standing in a corner of the Great Cumberland Place drawing room, admired by so many and worshipped by me! Surely she had run her course and has gone to a world of lovelier gardens and perfect contentment.

July 30, Knebworth House, Knebworth, Dearest Madeline, I am so glad you sent me a copy of the beautiful service you arranged for Norah. I like especially 'Go forth upon thy journey from this world, O Christian soul!' ... and the words of the anthem and the quotations from Ecclesiastes, Psalm 16 and Romans. I am sure the music was very perfect. How wonderful for you that Norah was 'exquisite to look at' – how

deeply comforting that must have been. I do understand. Some day I hope her letters will be collected and published in some form. You must do that. It would be an absorbing task of love and memories. Much love and thoughts of sympathy from, Pamela Lytton.

I can't begin praising Norah or summing up her great qualities. We both think no sentence could be more lovely than "in the heyday of her great beauty ... shedding gaiety about her and filling our hearts with music and our gardens with flowers." Affectionately, Monica Gage.

And finally, from Norah's devoted and longtime maid and companion,

Manor Cottage, Sutton Courtenay, October 15, 1948. Dear Madam, I am so sorry for such silence, but I have thought of you and dear Miss Cooper so often. I just couldn't write, as I have been so disappointed about all I have tried to do. I was so happy about going to America and did lots towards going – and then when I got home Mother cried and begged me not to go, saying she was 74 and was all I had left in England. So I just gave it up feeling quite wretched. And now I work in Oxford in a shop as a saleswoman. I leave home at 8:30 am – arrive home at a quarter past six. And knit in the evenings or do some needlework. Every Thursday is my half-day and I go down to dear Mrs. Lindsay's grave and put on some flowers. I put roses on it out of Mother's garden last Saturday. Oh, I still miss her so, so much and know how you miss her daily. You and I were with her so very much. I had a most lovely letter from Prince Paul yesterday and he was so miserable about it all. Now goodnight Madam and keep well. I remain, Yours sincerely, Daisy.

LEFT Doris (Daisy) Alston.
RIGHT Norah Lindsay, 1910.

NOTES

1 Norah Lindsay to Madeline Whitbread. MBW Letters, Southill Park Archives. [Henceforward **NL/MW**] 1925.

2 NL/MW November 9, 1926.

3 Hertfordshire Archives and Local Studies. Ref: D/Erv C1600/1–32 Desborough 1910–1947.

4 *Ibid.*

5 The names Aunt Nornie and Aunt Nornor were used interchangeably by the family.

6 Author's interview with Penelope Dare, March 4, 2002.

7 *Miss Madeline*, privately published memoir, Madeline Bourke Whitbread, Southill Park Archives. [Henceforward ***Miss Madeline***]

8 *Ibid.* p. 12.

9 *Ibid.* p. 14.

10 *Ibid.* p. 15.

11 *Ibid.* p. 25.

12 Lancelot 'Capability' Brown (1716–1783) British landscape gardener.

13 Cooper, Lady Diana, *The Rainbow Comes and Goes*, p. 76.

14 Balcarres, Fifeshire, The Seat of the Earl of Crawford. *Country Life.* August 9, 1902. Vol. 12, p. 176.

15 Charles served as Lieutenant–Colonel of the Grenadier Guards and Colonel Commanding of the St. Georges Rifles. From 1865 to 1874, Charles was a Member of Parliament serving Abingdon. See Biographical Notes.

16 *Lord Wantage, V.C., K.C.B. A Memoir by His Wife*, p. 349.

17 Anne Bourke Burroughes Journal, 1892. Courtesy Penelope Dare Family Collection. [Henceforward **ABBJ**]

18 ABBJ 1892.

19 Mrs. Adela Maddison was an accomplished musician. See Biographical Notes.

20 ABBJ 1892.

21 ABBJ 1893.

22 The Army Reserve of Officers List dated July 1899, p. 1514 indicates that Lt. H. E. A. Lindsay transferred from active duty to the reserve list of the Army on March 20, 1895. He returned to the Gordon Highlanders active duty list during World War I. The Gordon Highlanders Museum Archives.

23 *Lord Wantage, V.C., K.C.B., A Memoir by His Wife*, pp. 301–302.

24 Lord Wantage purchased the Manor property on August 20, 1886 for £6,586 at an auction at the Queen's Hotel, Abingdon. The sum total of the value of the estate and the money given to Norah was a vast amount at that time.

25 Hampton & Sons auctioneers circular.

26 *Miss Madeline*, p. 50.

27 *Miss Madeline*, p. 50.

28 Maurice Baring (1874–1945) Author, poet, and journalist.

29 *Miss Madeline*, p. 50.

30 *Chips: The Diaries of Sir Henry Channon.* Robert Rhodes James, ed., p. 68.

31 Cooper, Lady Diana, *op. cit.* pp. 66–67.

32 NL/MW June 1925.

33 Norah and Harry referred to the property as Sutton.

34 The derivation of Peter's name was in honour of his Lindsay ancestors: David being the name of 7 of the first 12 Earls of Crawford. Ludovic was the name of the 16th Earl of Crawford.

35 Sutton Courtenay was part of the county of Berkshire until 1974 when boundary changes included it in Oxfordshire.

36 Madeline Bourke Whitbread Journal, entry dated March 19, 1897. [Henceforward **MMWJ**]

37 ABBJ April 26, 1898.

38 ABBJ April 28, 1898.

39 Marcus Stone (1840–1921) Influential genre painter known for graceful, pretty, restful portraits.

40 ABBJ July 19, 1898.

41 These were the years when there emerged a – relatively new – subdivision in the publishing industry, namely magazines relating to women's interests. The influence from this rapidly growing field was enormous. Articles, many of them by women, were published in *House and Garde*n, *The House Beautiful*, *The Century Magazine*, and *Country Life*, and *Country Life in America*.

42 Norah Lindsay to Philip Sassoon. Sassoon Correspondence, Houghton Hall Archives. [Henceforward **NL/PS**] Letter XXI, Box 21. Undated, *c.* 1926.

43 NL/MW 1919.

44 Madeline Whitbread to Jocelyn Whitbread. MBW Letters, September 1925. Southill Park Archives.

45 NL/MW September 1941.

46 MBWJ January 30, 1905.

47 MBWJ 1912–1918.

48 MBWJ 1912–1918.

49 MBWJ Undated.

50 Their marriage in 1908 was one of companionship and convenience for Emmie. When she married Clarendon she assumed that she would be financially taken care of for the rest of her life, but she did not inherit wealth from Clarendon when he died in 1914.

51 Letter from Edward VII to Lady Clarendon. 1909. Southill Park Archives.

52 MBWJ July 1915.

53 NL/MW 1918.

54 NL/MW April 1918.

55 NL/MW 1918.

56 Lady Gwendoline Churchill. See Biographical Notes.

57 Herbert Henry Asquith, 1st Earl of Oxford and Asquith, and Prime Minister. The Asquiths had a home, The Wharf, in Sutton Courtenay adjacent to Norah's home. The two families were kind and hospitable to each other sharing meals and tennis matches. See Biographical Notes.

58 NL/MW April 1918.

59 Norah Lindsay to Emma Bourke. MBW Letters, Southill Park Archives. [Henceforward **NL/EB**] Spring 1918.

60 NL/EB May 1918.

61 NL/MW May 30, 1918.

62 NL/MW May 30, 1918.

63 NL/MW December 1919.

64 NL/MW Summer 1918.

65 Hassall, Christopher, *A Biography of Edward Marsh*, p. 125.

66 NL/MW September 1918. Southill Park Archives.

67 Norah Lindsay to Anne Burroughes. MBW Letters, Southill Park Archives. [Henceforward **NL/AB**] September 1918.

68 NL/MW 1918 and 1919.

69 NL/MW Winter 1918.

70 NL/MW Winter 1918.

71 NL/MW May 1920.

72 Norah Lindsay to Madeline Whitbread and Anne Burroughes. MBW Letters, 1919–1921. Southill Park Archives

73 NL/MW 1919.

74 NL/PS Letter V, undated, Box 21.

75 *Ibid.*

76 NL/MW August 1919.

77 NL/EB, September 1919.

78 Haddon Hall – High Peak. www.highpeak.co.uk

79 Cooper, Lady Diana, *op. cit.* p. 58.

79 Norah Lindsay to Jean Hamilton, Hamilton letters 20/2/35, August 1, 1920. College Archives & Liddell Hart Centre for Military Archives, King's College London, University of London.

80 NL/MW June 1920.

81 Norah Lindsay to Jean Hamilton, Hamilton letters 20/2/35, August 1, 1920. College Archives & Liddell Hart Centre for Military Archives, King's College London, University of London.

82 Knowsley Hall, the home of the 17th Earl of Derby (1865–1948). He was a successful owner and breeder of racehorses.

83 NL/MW March 17, 1925.

84 Hilaire Belloc (1870–1953) British writer and poet. See Biographical Notes.

85 Hilaire Belloc to Norah Lindsay. MBW Letters. Southill Park Archives. [Henceforward **HB/NL**] September 14, 1920. In 1916 the Pope had doubted Belloc's assertion that the Allies would win the War.

86 HB/NL November 11, 1929. Belloc and Norah were in a taxi outside Buckingham Palace at 11 o'clock, Armistice Day, 1919.

87 HB/NL November 16, 1929.

88 Sir Osbert Sitwell (1892-1969) Poet, essayist and novelist. See Biographical Notes.

89 NL/PS Letter XIII, Box 21.

90 NL/PS Letter XXVI, Box 21.

91 Edward Molyneux (1891–1974) Irish couturier who worked in Paris between the wars. See Biographical Notes Appendix.

92 NL/MW, July 1921.

93 NL/EB 1921.

94 Anthony Asquith. See Biographical Notes Appendix.

95 NL/EB 1921.

96 Madeline Whitbread to Anne Burroughes. MBW Letters, 1924. Southill Park Archives.

97 NL/MW August 28, 1923.

98 NL/MW 1920.

99 NL/MW January 1924.

100 NL/MW February 1924.

101 NL/MW March 1924.

102 NL/MW May 1924.

103 NL/AB, May 1927.

104 NL/EB June 1927.

105 The identity of Ossie and Bayard have not been determined.

106 Norah Lindsay to Peter Lindsay. MBW Letters, Southill Park Archives. [Henceforward **NL/PL**] September 1928.

107 Frank Doubleday Founder of publishers Doubleday & McClure. See Biographical Notes.

108 NL/PL September 1928.

109 NL/PL January 1928.

110 NL/EB October 16, 1929.

111 NL/EB August 1931.

112 NL/PS Philip and Norah exchanged letters which often used their own sort of secretive language with references to religion – Onias and Elias, the Jewish pontiffs – and to legendary or historical figures, Norah as Serena B. or Philip as Guy Fawkes.

113 Norah Lindsay's articles and interviews appeared in the following: 'Planning the Spring Garden.' *Vogue House & Garden Book.* March 1929, pp. 21, 48. 'The Garden in July.' *Country Life.* Vol. 66. July 20, 1929, pp. 78–80; 'Cliveden – II, Bucks. The Seat of Lord Astor.' *Country Life.*Vol. 70. July 18, 1931, pp. 68–74; 'Roses of Long Ago.' *Country Life.* 1929; The Manor House Sutton Courtenay, Berks. – I: The Gardens by Norah Lindsay. May 16, 1931.

114 Lindsay, Norah, 'Planning the Spring Garden.' *Vogue House & Garden Book.* March 1929, pp. 21, 48.

115 Lindsay, Norah. The Garden in July. *Country Life.* Vol. 66. July 20, 1929, p. 79.

116 Taylor, G. C., Cliveden – II. Bucks. The Seat of Lord Astor. *Country Life.* Vol. 70. July 18, 1931, p. 70.

117 The Garden in July, *op. cit.* p. 78.

118 *Ibid.*

119 Taylor, G. C., Cliveden *op. cit.*

120 *Ibid.*

121 'Planning the Spring Garden', *op. cit.* p. 48.

122 Planning the Herbaceous Border.' *op. cit.* p. lxi.

123 'Cliveden – II. Bucks. The Seat of Lord Astor,' pp. 68–70.

124 The Garden in July, *op. cit.* p. 78.

125 Taylor, G. C., Cliveden – II. Bucks. The Seat of Lord Astor. *Country Life.* Vol. 70. July 18, 1931, p. 70.

126 *Country Life*, May 16, 1931.

127 Lindsay, Norah, 'The Manor House – I. Sutton Courtenay, Berks. The Residence of Mrs. Harry Lindsay.' *Country Life*. Vol. 69.May 16, 1931, pp. 610–616.

128 NL/MW August 1930.

129 Victor Cunard (1898–1960) Diplomat. See Biographical Notes.

130 NL/MW September 3, 1930.

131 NL/MW September 22, 1930.

132 NL/PS Letter Vii, Box 21.

133 Hillier's Nursery in Hampshire. Norah often consulted directly with the owner, Edwin Lawrence Hillier (1865–1944) when making her plant selections.

134 NL/MW November 1925.

135 Horner, Lady Frances, *Time Remembered*, p. 196.

136 Norwich, John Julius, *The Architecture of Southern England*, p. 559.

137 Asquith, Cynthia, *Remember and Be Glad*, p. 195.

138 Asquith, Cynthia, *op. cit.*

139 NL/PS Letter xix, Box 21, undated.

140 McLeod, Kirsty, *A Passion for Friendship: Sibyl Colefax and Her Circle*, p. 139.

141 *Ibid*.

142 Nigel Bourke to Madeline Whitbread. MBW Letters, January 16, 1926. Southill Park Archives.

143 NL/MW January 1930.

144 NL/MW April 29, 1927.

145 NL/MW June 1926.

146 NL/MW December 17, 1926.

147 NL/MW May 3, 1927.

148 NL/MW December 1931.

149 NL/PL, November 1930.

150 NL/MW February 1933.

151 *Chirk Castle*. The National Trust. 1998. p. 56.

152 Lady Margaret Myddelton to David Locke, Head Gardener, Chirk Castle.

153 NL/MW August 1936.

154 'A Riviera Garden, Lou Sueil.' *Country Life*. Vol. 64, December 22, 1928, pp. 900–903.

155 Balsan, Consuelo Vanderbilt, *The Glitter & the Gold*. p. 221.

156 'A Riviera Garden, Lou Sueil.' *Op.cit*

157 NL/MW January 10, 1930.

158 Alfred Potocki (1886–1958) Polish count. See Biographical Notes.

159 Jacques Balsan suggested that 'Charlie Chaplin poisons everything, and what lunacy to give him the Legion of Honour'. Philip Sassoon defended his friend by saying that 'I like him very much and he is a great friend of mine.' See Biographical Notes.

160 NL/MW April 1, 1931.

161 NL/MW March 1929.

162 NL/MW March 27, 1929.

163 NL/AB March 31, 1929.

164 NL/MW August 1930.

165 NL/MW September 7, 1935.

166 A novel by Elizabeth von Arnim, published in 1922. The story revolves around a month in the lives of four women in an old Italian castle. Later made into a film in 1992.

167 NL/PL September 7, 1935.

168 NL/MW September 8, 1935.

169 *Cliveden*. The National Trust. 1994.

170 Tyack, Geoffrey, *Cliveden and the Astor Household*, pp. 5–7.

171 Astor, Michael, *Tribal Feeling*, p. 132.

172 NL/MW December 1926.

173 Harrison, Rosina, *Rose: My Life in Service*, p. 147.

174 Cliveden – II. Bucks. The Seat of Lord Astor. *Country Life*. Vol 70. July 18, 1931, p. 68.

175 NL/MW April 12, 1929.

176 Norah Lindsay to Nancy Astor. September 1931. Papers of Nancy Astor, Viscountess Astor. Reading University.

177 NL/MW June 1933.

178 NL/EB, July 1921.

179 Horsley, E.M., ed. *Lady Cynthia Asquith, Diaries 1915–1918*, p. 60

180 NL/PS Letter XXI, Box 21.

181 'The Garden in July', 1929, p. 78.

182 NL/MW July 31, 1936.

183 NL/PS Letter XXVII. Box 21.

184 NL/PS Letter IIII, Box 21, 1928.

185 Rohde, Eleanour Sinclair, *Oxford's College Gardens*, pp. 132–133.

186 Letter from Mr. Wylie, Secretary to the Rhodes Trustees to Mr. Kerr, Secretary of the Rhodes Trust, dated May 22, 1929. Rhodes House, Oxford University Archives.

187 Letter from Philip Kerr, Lord Lothian, Secretary of the Rhodes Trust, to the Rt. Hon. H. A. L. Fisher, Warden, Rhodes House, Oxford, dated June 19, 1930. Rhodes House, Oxford University Archives.

188 Garden notes made by Sir Herbert Baker, dated May 8, 1933. Rhodes House, Oxford University Archives.

189 NL/MW August 1932.

190 NL/MW May 25, 1928.

191 *The Coming of Christ* by John Masefield. See Biographical Notes.

192 NL/PL, May 29, 1928.

193 NL/MW June 8, 1932.

194 Norah Lindsay's letters and the Blickling Archives confirm that she began working on plans and plantings for Blickling Hall in November 1932.

195 NL/MW July 11, 1933.

196 Compiled from ledger accounts. Blickling Hall Archives.

197 NL/EB, June 1934.

198 NL/MW August 9, 1936.

199 NL/MW November 1932.

200 The Trees leased Kelmarsh Hall from 1927 to 1937 from Col. C. G. Lancaster, who became Nancy Tree's third husband. See Biographical Notes.

201 NL/MW November 28, 1930.

202 NL/PS Letter XI, Box 21.

203 Tree, Ronald, *When the Moon Was High. Memoirs of Peace and War 1897–1942*, p. 40.

204 NL/MW April 15, 1938.

205 NL/MW April 16, 1938.

206 NL/PS Letter VIII, Box 21.

207 NL/MW April 19, 1938.

208 Becker, Robert, *Nancy Lancaster: Her Life, Her World, Her Art*, p. 228.

209 NL/MW April 19, 1938.

210 NL/EB, July 1929.

211 Fielding, Daphne, *Mercury Presides*, p. 138.

212 Daphne's second child, Timothy was born October 13, 1929. He died eleven months later. The press baron, Max Aitken, Lord Beaverbrook [see Biographical Notes Appendix] was Timothy's godfather. The Weymouths lived at Greenaway until 1933, when they moved to Sturford Mead on the Longleat estate.

213 NL/PS Letter XXIII Box 21.

214 NL/PS Letter XIX, 1927, Box 21. Houghton Hall Archives.

215 NL/EB, August 1929.

216 NL/MW September 1932.

217 NL/MW September 1932.

218 NL/MW June 13, 1929.

219 Garden Club of America *Bulletin*, November 1929. 'Plant Material, The Papaveraceae.' p. 86.

220 Compiled from the National Gardens Scheme Archives at the Lindley Library, Royal Horticultural Society.

221 NL/EB July 1929.

222 NL/MW July 17, 1938.

223 Norah Lindsay to Nancy Astor. Astor Collection. 1928. Envelope #73. Reading University.

224 NL/PS Letter XXVIII Box 21.

225 NL/MW August 1929.

226 The background information for Villa Madama courtesy of the Villa Madama website www.esteri.it/eng/2_9_2.asp

227 NL/PL October 1929.

228 Belvedere, literally 'beautiful view'; a building positioned to offer a fine view of the surrounding area.

229 *A King's Story, The Memoirs of The Duke of Windsor*, p. 238.

230 Cooper, Lady Diana, *The Light of Common Day*, p. 161.

231 *A King's Story, The Memoirs of The Duke of Windsor*, p. 239.

232 Prince George, later Duke of Kent (1902–1942) Edward VIII's younger brother. Married Princess Marina of Greece in 1934.

233 From a notation made by Lily Carter, parlour-maid, in her autograph book, dated June 15, 1930. Courtesy Carter Family Archives.

234 Anne Burroughes to Madeline Whitbread. MBW Letters, August 20, 1930. Southill Park Archives.

235 NL/MW September 1930.

236 NL/MW May 1931.

237 NL/MW November 1931.

238 NL/MW April 1932.

239 NL/MW May 1932.

240 NL/MW 1932.

241 NL/EB June 1934.

242 Queen Mary (1867–1953) Mother of the Prince of Wales.

243 NL/AB June 16, 1932.

244 'My Garden' by H.R.H. The Duke of Windsor. *Life* Magazine, July 16, 1956, p. 62–74.

245 NL/MW November 1931.

246 Norah's lawyers advised Norah to invest the £5000 that she had received from Uncle Bob as a wedding gift in the stock market. These investments were estimated to yield £200 in dividends per year. When Harry learned this, he reduced his yearly support to £100. He considered the dividends as coming from him, since the capital was a gift from his relative.

247 NL/MW November 1931.

248 NL/MW October 1932.

249 NL/MW September 1930.

250 Norah Lindsay to Joscelyn Whitbread. MBW Letters, November 1935. Southill Park Archives.

251 NL/MW December 1932.

252 Norah Lindsay to Anne Burroughes and Madeline Whitbread. MBW Letters, February 1933. Southill Park Archives.

253 NL/MW May 1933.

254 Virginia Parsons, later second wife of the 6th Marquess of Bath. See Biographical Notes.

255 NL/MW June 1933.

256 Madeline Whitbread Journal. 1935. Southill Park Archives.

257 NL/MW September 10, 1935.

258 NL/MW September 11, 1935.

259 NL/MW September 11, 1935.

260 NL/MW September 14, 1935.

261 NL/MW September 16, 1935.

262 NL/MW September 24, 1935.

263 NL/MW November 7, 1935.

264 NL/MW December 1935.

265 NL/MW December 1935.

266 NL/MW December 1935.

267 NL/MW December 25, 1935.

268 NL/MW December 25, 1935.

269 NL/MW January 1, 1936.

270 NL/MW January 8, 1936.

271 NL/MW January 17, 1936.

272 NL/MW January 17, 1936.

273 NL/MW January 21, 1936.

274 NL/PL January 22, 1936.

275 NL/PL January 22, 1936.

276 On March 2, 1936 Hitler issued final orders for troops to re-occupy their former garrison posts in Rhineland towns. Further he instructed that if the French forces took action, the troops would be instructed to withdraw. Five days later on March 7, 1936, Hitler denounced the Rhineland provisions of the Treaty of Versailles and the Locarno Treaty.

German troops marched in to re-occupy the Rhineland. German representatives informed foreign ministers and ambassadors of the German re-occupation of the Rhineland, and outlined a peace plan including twenty-five-year non-aggression pacts for all countries bordering on Germany.

277 Norah Lindsay to George Burroughes. MBW Letters, March 1936. Southill Park Archives.

278 Pierre-Etienne Flandin (1889–1958) Prime Minister of France 1934–1935.

279 Norah Lindsay to George Burroughes. MBW Letters, March 1936. Southill Park Archives. Baldwin appointed Sir Thomas Inskip Minister for the Coordination of Defence.

280 Scant information on Sir Louis and Lady Baron and the gardens at Holmbury Hall has been located to date.

281 Nicolson, Nigel, *The World of Jane Austen*, pp. 61–69.

282 NL/MW May 30, 1936.

283 NL/MW June 4, 1936.

284 NL/MW August 2, 1936.

285 NL/MW August 2, 1936.

286 Madeline also wrote, 'This was the yachting trip when Edward took Mrs. S. with him and made such a bad impression on all the ports where they put in. It was supposed to be incognito – but of course was photographed everywhere.' Madeline Whitbread, handwritten notes on the back of a letter dated August 2, 1936 from Norah Lindsay. MBW Letters, August 2, 1936. Southill Park Archives.

287 NL/MW August 3, 1936.

288 Boris III of Bulgaria (1884–1943).

289 Norah Lindsay to Madeline Whitbead and Peter Lindsay. MBW Letters, Letter dated August 31–September 9, 1936. Southill Park Archives.

290 NL/MW October 1936.

291 House of Jansen. Interior Design firm founded by Jean-Henri Jansen in Paris in 1880.

292 NL/MW November 1936.

293 NL/MW November 1936.

294 NL/MW November 1936.

295 NL/MW November 19, 1936.

296 NL/MW November 19, 1936.

297 NL/MW November 1936.

298 NL/MW December 1936.

299 NL/MW January 6, 1937.

300 NL/MW January 1937.

301 *Marie Claire* was formally launched in 1947.

302 NL/MW February 1937.

303 NL/MW February 1937.

304 NL/MW February 1937.

305 NL/MW February 1937.

306 NL/MW August 12, 1937.

307 NL/MW September 1, 1937.

308 NL/MW September 12, 1937.

309 NL/MW September 2, 1937.

310 NL/MW September 1937.

311 Harry Lindsay to Madeline Whitbread. MBW Letters, September 1937. Southill Park Archives.

312 Henry Edith Arthur Lindsay, Certificate of Death. Kensington Registration District.

313 Norah did not attend the service, nor did she mention Harry's death in any letters written to Peter, Nancy, or Madeline. Two assumptions can be made from this. Either she never wrote about her feelings about Harry's death and only privately spoke of it to her family. Or whatever she might have written was censored by Madeline and removed from the collection of archived letters. The latter is a possibility, because Madeline regularly blacked out sentences or words in letters that she felt were inappropriate or harmful; and because there are very few letters from Norah in the files written between May and the end of June 1939.

314 This amount fluctuated between £100 and £300 per year depending upon the income generated by the securities portfolio.

315 A reference to the fact that the local families were taking in the London relatives of their servants. In the case of Norah this referred to the relatives of her maid, cook, and gardeners, the Dentons and the Alstons.

316 NL/MW September 5, 1939.

317 NL/MW September 16, 1939.

318 Joseph P. Kennedy, Sr. (1888–1969), U. S. Ambassador to Britain (1938–1940). See Biographical Notes. The speech probably refers to an interview that Kennedy had with British reporters after Britain went to war in 1939 that stated: 'The Democratic Party policy of the United States is a Jewish production,' and added confidently that Roosevelt would 'fall' in the 1940 presidential elections. Kennedy resigned his ambassadorship just weeks after FDR's overwhelming triumph at the polls.

319 NL/MW December 25, 1939.

320 NL/MW June 1940.

321 NL/MW June 6, 1940.

322 NL/MW June 23, 1940.

323 NL/MW July 8, 1940.

324 NL/MW September 28, 1940.

325 Norah had obviously gained weight.

326 Madeline Whitbread diary entry. MBW Letters, October 11, 1940.

327 NL/MW April 1941.

328 NL/MW June 2, 1941.

329 NL/MW July 1941.

330 NL/MW April 1942.

331 NL/MW June 1942.

332 NL/MW May 1942.

333 NL/MW August 12, 1942.

334 Ruthven Castle is in Scotland, but Norah's letter states that 'Nancy Tree has gone to Ruthven Castle, that clinic in Wales.' NL/MW August 19, 1942.

335 NL/MW August 19, 1942.

336 NL/MW August 18, 1942.

337 NL/MW September 1942.

338 Madeline Whitbread to Humphrey Whitbread. MBW Letters, Southill

Park Archives. [Henceforward **MW/HW**] September 20, 1942.

339 NL/MW October 1942.

340 NL/MW October 28, 1942.

341 NL/MW February 1942.

342 Lees-Milne, James. *Ancestral Voices*, pp. 152–153.

343 MW/HW June 10, 1943.

344 Mrs. Drummond had worked for Norah for a short time as housekeeper.

345 Vita Sackville-West to Madeline Whitbread. MBW Letters, December 15, 1943. Southill Park Archives.

346 Violet (Letty) Benson to Madeline Whitbread. MBW Letters, June 4, 1944. Southill Park Archives.

347 MW/HW June 27, 1944.

348 Anne Poynder (Lady Islington) to Madeline Whitbread. MBW Letters, August 20, 1944. Southill Park Archives.

349 MW/HW November 10, 1944.

350 MW/HW December 10, 1944.

351 NL/MW December 10, 1944.

352 MW/HW January 19, 1945.

353 NL/MW January 15, 1945.

354 NL/MW March 15, 1945.

355 NL/MW September 18, 1945.

356 In Norfolk.

357 NL/MW September 21, 1945.

358 NL/MW October 1, 1945.

359 Vita Sackville-West to Madeline Whitbread. MBW Letters, July 11, 1946. Southill Park Archives.

360 NL/MW August 1946.

361 NL/MW March 1947.

362 NL/MW April 1947.

363 NL/MW April 9, 1947.

364 NL/MW May 1947.

365 NL/MW May 25, 1947.

366 NL/MW June 1947.

367 NL/MW October 1947.

368 Madeline Whitbread Diaries. MBW Letters, 1948. Southill Park Archives.

369 Victor Cunard to Madeline Whitbread. MBW Letters, February 27, 1948. Southill Park Archives.

370 Norah Lindsay death certificate, registered on June 21, 1948, City of Westminster.

371 Nigel Bourke to Madeline Whitbread. MBW Letters, June 22, 1948. Southill Park Archives.

372 Norah Lindsay, Probate Registry registered on December 16, 1948.

373 *Chips, The Diaries of Sir Henry Channon*, *op. cit.* pp. 426–427.

374 *Ibid.* p. 384.

375 Tilden, Philip, *True Remembrances*, pp. 33–34.

376 In 1939 the words were published in Edward Marsh's book, *A Number of People: A Book of Reminiscences*, pp.194–196. The quote is from John Milton: *Paradise Lost*. Book iii. Line 337.

CLIENT LIST OF NORAH LINDSAY

CLIENT NAME	ESTATE NAME	COUNTRY	DATES WORKED	SCOPE OF WORK
Alington, Baron (Naps)	Crichel, Falconers Cottage	England/Dorset	1932–1936	a small cottage garden
Allendale, Viscount & Violet (Vi)	Bretton Park	England/Yorkshire	1935–1938; 1944; 1946	herbaceous borders, bulbs in woodlands and lawns, shrub garden
Ashford	unknown	England	1945	£10 per visit beginning in September 1945
Princess Aspasia	Eden's Garden	Italy/Venice	1930	herbaceous garden plantings and sea terraces
Astor, Waldorf & Nancy	Cliveden	England/Berkshire	1924–1933; 1938	Long Garden; Water Garden; Japanese Garden; Forecourt Gardens; Terrace Shrub Gardens
Astor, Waldorf & Nancy	Rest Harrow	England/Kent	1928	borders along the long fence by the shrub garden
Balsan, Consuelo & Jacques	Lou Sueil	France/Eze	1924–1925; 1930	herbaceous and shrub plantings
Balsan, Consuelo & Jacques	St. Georges-Motel	France/Normandy	1930–1935	herbaceous and shrub plantings
Baron, Sir Louis	Holmbury House	England/Surrey	1930–1935	swimming pool gardens and herbaceous borders
Beatty, Peter	The Priory, Reigate	England/Surrey	1938	'a spot of advice for 2 days'
Beatty, Peter	Astrop Park	England/Oxfordshire	1947	tulip borders, bulbs, shrubs, roses
Belmont, Mrs. William (Alva)	d'Augerville-la-Rivière	France	1927–1929	'helped with the plantings'
Benoit d'Azy, Charles Vicomte	unknown	France/Nevers	1938	'planned the garden for Charles and his wife Catherine'
Benson, Guy & Violet	Compton Bassett House	England/Wiltshire	1946	planting in rose gardens
Berners, Gerald	Faringdon	England/Oxfordshire	1930–1935	herbaceous gardens, wild garden
Bous, Mrs.	unknown	England	1944	referral of Barbie Wallace; £5 fee per visit
Bounardel, Mme. Minon (Comtesse de Montgomery)	unknown	France/Normandy	1936	'hired to make an English garden in Normandy'
Boussac, Mr.	Château de Mivoisin	France/Coligny	1937–1938	herbaceous gardens, shrubs, roses
Cavendish-Bentinck, Henry	Underley Hall	England/Cumbria	1929	consultation fees for two days suggesting plants and changes
Cazalet, Victor (Teeny)	Great Swifts	England/Kent	1936–1939	herbaceous garden plantings
Chapman, Fitzroy	Ashdown Place	England/Sussex	1931	herbaceous borders
Chapman, Spencer	unknown	England	1926	herbaceous garden plans
Churchill, Ivor	The Mill House	England/Hampshire	1938	herbaceous garden plantings

CLIENT NAME	ESTATE NAME	COUNTRY	DATES WORKED	SCOPE OF WORK
Cunard, Victor	Pertenhall	England/Bedfordshire	1936–1938	herbaceous borders in the walled garden
Davis, Henriette	117 Rue de la Faisanderie	France/Paris	1936	small roof garden
de Behague, Martine	123 Rue St. Dominique	France/Paris	1937	herbaceous garden plantings
de Ganay, Mme.	Château de Courances	France/Seine-et-Oise	1937	herbaceous garden planting consultation for a fee
Dentice di Frasso family	Villa Madama	Italy/Rome	1929	herbaceous garden plantings
Dowager Duchess of Norfolk	unknown (located next to Mulgrave Castle)	England/N. Yorkshire	1939	herbaceous garden plantings
Dudley, Eric	Himley Hall	England/Staffordshire	1933–1934	herbaceous garden plantings
Duff, Juliet	Bulbridge House	England/Salisbury	1934	herbaceous garden plantings 'for a small fee'
Duff, Michael	Vaynol	Wales/Gwyndd	1935–1946	herbaceous garden plantings
Edward, Prince of Wales	Fort Belvedere (later Edward VIII)	England/Berkshire	1930–1935	herbaceous border along the battlement wall, lily pool, iris walk, shrubs along tennis court, wild woodland plantings
Esher, Reginald Brett	Esher Place	England/Surrey	1930	laid out forecourt with herbaceous plantings, shrubs and roses
Falk, Mr. & Mrs.	Stockton House	England/Wiltshire	1928	the Falks let her 'use all my ideas – stone terraces, silent pools, dark pointed cypress'
Fauchier-Magnan, Mr. & Mrs.	unknown	France/Neuilly-sur-Seine	1930	'quite extensive' herbaceous gardens, shrubs, roses
Fellowes, Daisy	Les Zoraides	France/Cap Martin	1926	herbaceous garden plantings
Feversham, Charles (Sim)	Duncombe Park	England/Yorkshire	1929–1935	herbaceous garden plantings
Field, Audrey & Marshall Field III	Regent's Park	England/London	1930–1936	herbaceous garden plantings
Fould, Mrs.	Parvis Saint Firmin	France/Montreuil-sur-Mer	1931	herbaceous garden plantings
Friend of Heather Muir	Kineton	England/Warwickshire	1938	'a smallish villa garden'
Gage, Henry George	Firle Place	England/Sussex	1930–1935	herbaceous garden planting
Glyn, Sibell (for her son, David Long)	South Wraxall Manor	England/Wiltshire	1938	'cast a small professional eye on it for Sibell Glyn's son'
Grigg, Joan	Port Ledge	England/Devon	1929	herbaceous garden plantings
Guinness, Bridget	L'Avenue Charles Flouquet	France/Paris	1930; 1937	'I have to arrange her tiny garden'
Herbert, Aubrey & Mary	Pixton Park	England/Somerset	1932	herbaceous garden plantings
Hood, Samuel & Myrtle (née Baron)	unknown	England/Gloucestershire	1945	'small job – but still a job'
Horner, John & Frances	Mells Manor House	England/Somerset	1924–1930	herbaceous gardens, shrubs and roses

CLIENT NAME	ESTATE NAME	COUNTRY	DATES WORKED	SCOPE OF WORK
Howard de Walden, Margherita	Chirk Castle	Wales/Denbighshire	1924–1936	herbaceous borders, shrub garden, topiary proportion
Hudson, Hannah	Fyfield Manor	England/Wiltshire	1941	herbaceous garden plantings
Islington, John and Anne Poynder	Rushbrooke Hall	England/Suffolk	1924–1926	herbaceous garden plantings
Kerr, Philip, Marquess of Lothian	Blickling Hall	England/Norfolk	1932–1939	herbaceous borders on terraces and in Parterre Garden, Temple Walk, and Wild Garden
Kerr, Philip Marquess of Lothian	Monteviot	Scotland	1938–1939	herbaceous garden plantings
Lambert, Baroness Hausi	24 Avenue Marnix	Belgium/Brussels	1937–1938	herbaceous gardens, shrubs, roses
Lambton, Katherine (Kitty)	Sissinghurst Place	England/Kent	1932	herbaceous garden plantings
Lazard family	unknown	France/Paris	1933	herbaceous garden plantings
Leconfield, Violet Wyndham	Petworth House	England/Sussex	1929	herbaceous garden plantings
Lucas, Nan	Woodyates Manor	England/Wiltshire	1930–1932; 1937	water gardens, herbaceous borders
Macintosh, Alastair	Sunninghill Park	England/Berkshire	1930–1933	herbaceous gardens, shrubs, roses
Maidstone, Margherita	Sherfield Manor	England/Hampshire	1928	herbaceous gardens, water garden, shrubs, roses
Maugham, Syrie	Chelsea	England/London	1936	herbaceous garden plantings
Menzies, Charles	Bampton Manor	England/Oxfordshire	1939–1940	herbaceous garden plantings
Metcalfe, Alexandra (Baba) & Fruity	Little Compton House	England/Oxfordshire	1946	herbaceous garden plantings
Meyers, Lady	unknown	England	?–1935	one of her 'largest and longest term projects' – but no details of the gardens mentioned in her letters
Mosley, Oswald (Tom) & Cynthia (Cimmie)	Savehay Farm	England/ Buckinghamshire	1928; 1933	herbaceous borders; plans and plantings for Cimmie's Memorial Garden in 1933
Normanby, Oswald	Mulgrave Castle	England/N. Yorkshire	1938–1939; 1943–1944	'to give advice in 1938'; planned and planted herbaceous gardens, shrub and rose gardens between 1938–1944
Paul of Yugoslavia, Prince	Brdo Castle	Yugoslavia	1935–1936	herbaceous gardens, shrubs and roses
Paul of Yugoslavia, Prince	Bled Castle	Yugoslavia	1935–1936	herbaceous gardens, shrubs and roses
Peake, Osbert (Bushie)	Lownd Hall	England/Nottinghamshire	1939–1940	herbaceous borders; iris border; scarlet border
Philipps, Sir Laurence	Dalham Hall	England/Suffolk	1929–1930	herbaceous borders along front terrace wall, Sunk Walk, Rose Garden, Yew Walk, and walls of the Kitchen Garden

CLIENT NAME	ESTATE NAME	COUNTRY	DATES WORKED	SCOPE OF WORK
Philipson, Moyra	Encombe	England/Kent	1932	herbaceous borders, shrub gardens
Pisani, Contessa Lazzara	Villa Pisani	Italy/Stra	before 1937	herbaceous garden plantings
Ponsonby, Rea	Great Tangley	England/Surrey	1932	'a small job'
Poniatowski, Princess Francoise	Le Mont Bauny	France/Aisne	1937	consultation fees for herbaceous garden plantings
Prouvost. Jean	St. Jean	France/Loire Valley	1936–1939	four herbaceous borders, yew hedges, terrace gardens
Rhodes House	Rhodes House	England/Oxfordshire	1928–1929	herbaceous garden plantings along wall in Warden's Garden, and an avenue of yews
Romanov, Grand Duc Dmitri	Beaumesnil	France/Normandy	1933	planting plans for herbaceous gardens, fountains, water garden
Rothschild, Kitty Spottiswoode	unknown	France/Paris	1931	herbaceous city garden
Rothschild, Kitty Spottiswoode	unknown	Austria/Vienna	1930	'Kitty asked me to come do her garden in the fall of 1930'
Russell, Claud	Trematon Castle	England/Cornwall	1942	herbaceous garden plantings
Russell, Gilbert & Maud	Mottisfont Abbey	England/Hampshire	1935–1941	parterre garden, herbaceous plantings in walled garden
Sassoon, Sir Philip	Port Lympne	England/Kent	1927–1936	August- and September-blooming double herbaceous borders – Long Borders, front entrance, loggia, east, west and south terraces
Sassoon, Sir Philip	Trent Park	England/Hertfordshire	1924–1935	double herbaceous borders along bathing pool on east-facing façade of house; long borders to the lake at north front of house; woodland wild garden; water garden
Scott, Jervoise and Kathleen	Rotherfield Park	England/Hampshire	1928	herbaceous borders in walled garden, roses, shrubs, terraces
Shaw, Robert Gould III (Bobbie)	Chalk House	England/Kent	1933	herbaceous garden plantings
Stanley, Oliver and Maureen	Halecat House	England/Cumbria	1929	herbaceous gardens, shrubs and roses
Princess Stephanie of Belgium	Oroszvar	Hungary/Moson Megye	1928–1929	herbaceous gardens, shrubs and roses
Tennant, Edward	Innes House	Scotland/Morayshire	1936	herbaceous garden plantings
The Gleneagles Hotel	The Gleneagles Hotel	Scotland/ Perth and Kinross	1938	herbaceous borders, terrace gardens
Thomas, Lloyd	unknown	England/Wiltshire	1925	herbaceous garden plantings
Thyniski, Audrey	unknown	France/Paris	1938	herbaceous garden plantings

CLIENT NAME	ESTATE NAME	COUNTRY	DATES WORKED	SCOPE OF WORK
Towle, Mr. & Mrs. (Marjorie Lawrence)	Welcombe Hotel	England/Warwickshire	1936–1937	herbaceous borders, shrub garden, wild garden
Tree, Ronald & Nancy	Kelmarsh Hall	England/ Northamptonshire	1928–1933	double herbaceous borders; Fan Rose Garden; the Long Border and Lavender Garden; bulbs and shrubs in Wilderness area and Oak Walk
Tree, Ronald & Nancy	Ditchley Park	England/Oxfordshire	1933–1946	herbaceous garden plantings: 'done a great deal of work here – planned a new herb garden, and big scheme of wallflowers'
Tritton, Robert & Elsie	Godmersham Park	England/Kent	1936–1947	herbaceous borders in swimming court; Stag Courtyard with shrubs, roses and herbaceous plantings; water garden, wild gardens, rose garden, kitchen garden, tennis court terraces
Tudor-Owen, Captain & Mrs. F.H.	Woodcote Manor	England/Hampshire	1927	herbaceous garden plantings
Unknown	Wingfield Castle	England/Norfolk	1945	moated garden around the old castle
von Bismarck, Prince Otto Christian	Freidrichsruh	Germany/Hamburg	1930	herbaceous garden plantings, wild garden, kitchen garden
von Hofmannsthal, Alice Astor	Hanover Lodge	England/London	1936–1938	two long herbaceous borders
Wallace, Barbi Lutyens	Lavington Park	England/Sussex	1940–1941	herbaceous garden plantings
Ward, Freda and Pempy	Regent's Park	England/London	1938	herbaceous garden plantings
Warre, Ginger	unknown	France/Paris	1936	herbaceous garden plantings
Watson, William & Bessie	Sulhamstead House	England/Berkshire	1934–1935	herbaceous garden plantings
Weymouth, Henry Frederick Thynne (Marquess of Bath)	Greenaway	England/Wiltshire	1929	herbaceous garden plantings, beech walk, yew arbour
Wooster, Frank & Mary (Mitzi)	1, Parvis Saint Firmin	France/Montreuil-sur-Mer	1933–1934; 1937	seven large herbaceous borders

INFLUENCED BY NORAH LINDSAY, THOUGH NOT PAYING CLIENTS

NAME	ESTATE NAME	COUNTRY	DATES WORKED	SCOPE OF WORK
unknown	Melplash Court	England/Dorset	unknown	onsulted on the garden plantings
unknown	Parnham House	England/Dorset	unknown	consulted on the garden plantings
Cooper, Reginald	Cothay Manor	England/Somerset	1931	influenced his plantings
de Noailles, Charles	St. Bernard	France/Hyères	1938	influenced his plantings
de Trafford, Mrs. Rudy	Buttersteep House	England/Oxfordshire	1942	scheduled to work, made plans and gave her suggestions, but cancelled due to the war
Halphen, Mr.	unknown	France	1937	prospect only, never hired – gave him suggestions, referral of Mr. Boudin
Johnston, Lawrence (Johnny)	Hidcote Manor	England/Gloucestershire	1925–1947	consulted and advised on various aspects of the gardens – they worked together very closely planning and planting
Johnston, Lawrence (Johnny)	Serre de la Madone	France/Menton	1930–1947	consulted and advised on various aspects of the gardens – they worked together very closely planning and planting
Londonderry, Edie	Mount Stewart	Ireland/Co. Down	1929	influenced and advised on the plantings in the gardens; showed the gardeners how to lay a brick patio in the rose garden
Mallet, Louis	Les Marroniers	France/Grasse	1925	consulted and advised on various aspects of the gardens
Mallet, Louis	Mortefontaine	France/Alpes Maritimes	1930	consulted and advised on various aspects of the gardens
Portland, Duke & Duchess of	Welbeck Abbey	England/Nottinghamshire	1925–1944	consulted and advised on various aspects of the gardens
Schiff, Georgio	unknown	France/Paris	1937	prospect only, never hired – gave him suggestions, referral of Mr. Boudin
Wharton, Edith	Sainte Claire le Château	France/Hyères	1930–1937	visited each other's gardens frequently – shared ideas and advice
Whitbread, Howard & Madeline	Southill Park	England/Bedfordshire	1904–1944	Norah's sister – they shared ideas and advice
Woodhouse, Violet Gordon	Nether Lypiatt Manor	England/Gloucestershire	c.1930s	consulted and advised on various aspects of the gardens

BIOGRAPHICAL NOTES
NORAH LINDSAY'S CIRCLE OF FRIENDS

Aberconway, Henry McLaren, 2nd Baron (1898–1977) Politician, industrialist and horticulturalist who developed the garden at Bodnant House. He married Christabel MacNaghten in 1910.

Agar, Herbert (1897–1980) American writer, who won the Pulitzer Prize in 1934. He married Barbi Wallace.

Aitken, William Maxwell (Max) 1st Baron Beaverbrook (1879–1964) Canadian-British politician and owner of the newspaper empire that included the *Daily Express* and the London *Evening Standard*. His son, **Sir Max Aitken** (1910–1985), married Peter Lindsay's ex-wife, Janie Kenyon-Slaney, in 1946.

Allendale, Vi (born Violet Lucy Emily Seely), Viscountess Allendale (1892–1979) She married Wentworth Henry Canning Beaumont, 2nd Viscount Allendale, in 1921. Norah designed gardens at Bretton Park where they lived with their six children.

Alston, Daisy (born Doris Gibbon) (1908–1991) Norah's devoted personal maid. Daisy's mother was Norah's cook, the unmarried Annie Gibbon, who later married Norah's gardener, Frederick Denton, ten years her junior, in 1910. Daisy married William Alston in 1933. They had a child, Norah Janet in 1937 (named after Norah). When her daughter was three years old, Daisy left her and her husband to travel with Norah. After Norah's death, Daisy worked for Billy Wallace, grandson of Edwin Lutyens. Daisy remarried in 1956 to Thomas Patrick Hart, a chauffeur. Daisy reconnected with her daughter Norah Janet in 1964. They reconciled and remained in regular contact until Daisy's second husband's death in the late 1970s. Daisy became ill in the 1980s and went to live with Norah Janet until her death in 1991.

Aspasia, Princess of Greece and Denmark (born Aspasia Manos) (1896–1972) Married in 1919 to Alexander I, King of the Hellenes (1893–1920) who ruled Greece from 1917–1920. Because she was a commoner, she was called Princess Aspasia of Greece and Denmark rather than Queen Aspasia of Greece. There was a controversy over the King's death one year after he married Aspasia which centred on whether he died from a bite from his pet monkey or if he was assassinated. Norah designed plantings for her Eden Garden in Venice.

Asquith, Anthony (Puffin) (1902–1968) Film director; youngest son of H.H. Asquith and his second wife, Margot. At the age of seventeen, he went to Hollywood and lived with Mary Pickford and Douglas Fairbanks. His many successful films include *The Importance of Being Earnest, The VIPs,* and *The Yellow Rolls-Royce*. Like his father, he is buried in the churchyard at Sutton Courtenay.

Asquith, Herbert Henry, 1st Earl of Oxford and Asquith (1852–1928) Liberal Prime Minister 1908–1916. He married, first, Helen Melland with whom he had five children, and second, in 1894, Margot Tennant with whom he had two children. Lived next door to Norah in Sutton Courtenay at their home called The Wharf. Like Norah, H. H. Asquith is buried in the churchyard at Sutton Courtenay. His grandson is the current owner of Mells Manor House.

Asquith, Margot (born Margaret Tennant) (1864–1945) Political hostess and diarist; Married to Herbert Henry Asquith, 1st Earl of Oxford and Asquith. She bought The Wharf in Sutton Courtenay, next door to Norah, in 1911, and is buried at the churchyard.

Asquith, Lady Cynthia (née Charteris) (1887–1960) Daughter of Hugo, 11th Earl of Wemyss and Mary Wyndham, both members of The Souls. She was married in 1910 to Herbert Asquith (1881–1947), son of H. H. Asquith by his first wife, Helen.

Asquith, Raymond (1878–1916) Scholar and army officer; son of British Prime Minister H.H. Asquith and his first wife Helen. He married, in 1907, Katharine Horner, daughter of Sir John and Lady Horner. He was killed during the First World War.

Astor, David (1912–2001) Editor of *The Observer* for 27 years; son of Waldorf and Nancy Astor. He was a close and life-long friend of Norah, and purchased the Manor House of Sutton Courtenay from Peter Lindsay in the early 1950s, retaining it as his country home until his death. David Astor is buried in the churchyard at Sutton Courtenay, like Norah.

Astor, Nancy Langhorne, Viscountess Astor (1879–1964) American-British society hostess and politician. She married Waldorf Astor in 1906. She was elected as a Conservative MP and became the first woman to sit in Parliament in 1919. Norah designed extensive gardens for her at two of her houses, Cliveden, Berkshire, and Rest Harrow, Kent.

Astor, Waldorf, 2nd Viscount (1879–1952) Businessman and politician. Owner of *The Observer* newspaper, and Conservative MP 1910–1919. His father, William Waldorf Astor, gave him the family estate, Cliveden, as a wedding gift.

Baker, Sir Herbert (1862–1946) Architect. He was the central figure in the architecture of southern Africa from 1892–1912, and collaborated with Edwin Lutyens in designing New Delhi. He designed Port Lympne, Kent, for Philip Sassoon and Rhodes House in Oxford.

Baldwin, Stanley, 1st Earl Baldwin of Bewdley (1867–1947) British Prime Minister, 1923–1924; 1924–1929; and 1935–1937. He was a cousin of the author Rudyard Kipling, and nephew of Edward Burne-Jones.

Balfour, Arthur James (A.J.), 1st Earl Balfour (1848–1930) British Prime Minister 1902–1905.

Balsan, Consuelo, (née Vanderbilt) (1877–1964) Married Charles Spencer-Churchill, 9th Duke of Marlborough (1871–1934) in 1896. They had two sons and divorced in 1921; the marriage was annulled in 1926. She married Jacques Balsan in 1921, and had homes in France at Lou Sueil, St. Georges-Motel, and in the United States in Florida. Norah was a friend of Consuelo's and designed gardens at Lou Sueil and St. Georges-Motel.

Balsan, Jacques (1868–1956) French pilot and textile manufacturing heir.

Baring, Maurice (1874–1945) Author, poet, and journalist.

Beatty, Peter (1910–1945) Second son of David, 1st Earl Beatty, and Ethel Field; half-brother of Ronald Tree. Norah designed gardens at his home Astrop Park in Oxfordshire.

Beecham, Sir Thomas (1879–1961) British conductor. He founded the London Philharmonic and the Royal Philharmonic Orchestras.

Beit, Sir Alfred (1903–1994) Financier and philanthropist.

Bell, Clive (1881–1964) Art critic, associated with the Bloomsbury Group, who helped set up the first Post-Impressionist show in London in 1910. He married, in 1907, Vanessa Bell, the artist (and sister of Virginia Woolf), though they lived amicably apart for some time.

Belloc, Hilaire (1870–1953) British writer and poet. Norah and Hilaire enjoyed a close, intimate friendship with each other after the death of Belloc's wife Elodie in 1910. Several letters written by Belloc to Norah exist in the archives.

Belmont, Alva Erskine Vanderbilt (1853–1933) American socialite and supporter of women's suffrage both in the United Kingdom and United States. She married William Kissam Vanderbilt, the American railroad millionaire, in 1875. She divorced William Vanderbilt and married Oliver Belmont in 1896. In the 1920s she moved to France to be nearer her daughter, Norah's friend and client, Consuelo Balsan, and to work for international women's suffrage. Norah designed gardens for her at her château at d'Augerville-la-Rivière.

Benson, Letty (born Lady Violet Catherine Manners; she became Violet Charteris, then Lady Elcho and later Lady Violet Benson) (1888–1971) She was Harry Lindsay's niece, the second daughter of the 8th Duke of Rutland and Violet, Duchess of Rutland. She was married in 1911 to Hugo (Ego) Francis Charteris, later Lord Elcho (1884–1916), the eldest son of 11th Earl of Wemyss; and secondly, in 1921, to Guy Holford Benson (1888–1975).

Berners, Gerald, Gerald Hugh Tyrwhitt-Wilson, 14th Baron Berners (1883–1950) Composer, novelist, and painter. He lived not far from Sutton Courtenay in the manor house in Faringdon, kept a flock of pastel-dyed pigeons, entertained with very strange parties (he brought a horse into the living room during one of his teas), and travelled extensively around Europe, often with Norah as a companion. In *The Pursuit of Love*, Nancy Mitford portrayed him as Lord Merlin, who would dip his pigeons into basins of magenta, green, and ultramarine so that when released they resembled, as Mitford wrote, 'a cloud of confetti in the sky'. As a composer, he collaborated with Sacheverell Sitwell, Gertrude Stein, and Serge Diaghilev. He and Norah remained friends for over forty years. She designed herbaceous borders and spring-bulb-filled woodlands at his home at Faringdon, and spent hours playing music with him at Faringdon and Sutton Courtenay. The flock of pigeons continues to be dyed each year and can be seen flying through the town square before returning to the lawns of Faringdon for their afternoon meal.

Bismarck *see* **von Bismarck-Schonhausen**

Bonham-Carter, Violet (born Helen Violet Asquith), Baroness Asquith of Yarnbury (1887–1969) British politician. Daughter of H.H. Asquith and his first wife, Helen. Married Maurice Bonham-Carter (Bongie) in 1915. She was President of the Women's Liberal Federation from 1923–1925 and 1939–1945, and President of the Liberal Party from 1945–1947.

Boudin, Stéphane (1888–1967) Influential French interior decorator with Maison Jansen in Paris. His clients included Jean Prouvost, Audrey Field, Prince Paul of Yugoslavia, Ronnie Tree at Ditchley, Chips Channon in London, and the Duke and Duchess of Windsor at their home, The Mill, near Boulogne. He was a driving force in the 1960s when, as the Director and President of the House of Jansen [Maison Jansen] in Paris, he was hired by Jacqueline Kennedy to help with the redecoration of the White House.

Bourke, Cecil Richard Fonoughmore (1875–1884) Norah's younger brother who died in London when he was nine years old.

Bourke, Edward Roden (1835–1907) Norah's father; Major in the 3rd Hussars, sixth son of the 5th Earl of Mayo. He married Emma Mary Augusta Hatch in 1872. They had five children: Anne, Norah, Cecil Richard, Madeline, and Nigel. Edward served as Postmaster General of Madras, and as Military Secretary to his older brother, Richard, Governor-General and Viceroy of India. In 1875 he returned to London after the assassination of the Viceroy to work for his younger brother Harry, at Brunton, Bourke & Company.

Bourke, Emma (Emmie) Mary Augusta (née Hatch) (1855–1935) Norah's mother. The daughter of Lieutenant-General George Cliffe Hatch, she was raised in India and sent to the Brussels Conservatoire to study the piano. At the age of 17 she married the 37 year-old Edward Roden Bourke. Major Bourke died in 1907, and in 1908 Emmie married the 5th Earl of Clarendon as his second wife, becoming Countess of Clarendon. They lived at The Grove until Lord Clarendon died in 1914. Emmie was beautiful and musically talented. She was a friend of Edward VII with whom she corresponded for many years.

Bourke, Henry (Harry) Lorton (1840–1911) Norah's uncle. Son of the 5th Earl of Mayo. Edward Roden Bourke's younger brother, for whom he worked at Brunton & Bourke. He lived at Wootton Hall, Ashbourne, Derbyshire.

Bourke, Nigel Edward Jocelyn (1886–1970) Norah's youngest brother. He and his wife Doris lived in British Columbia, Canada. They had four children: Josslyn, Alice, Deborah, and Susan.

Bourke, Richard Southwell, 6th Earl of Mayo (1822–1872) The older brother of Norah's father, Edward. Irish statesman. Chief Secretary for Ireland in 1852, 1858, and 1866. In 1869 became Governor-General and Viceroy of India. He was assassinated in 1872.

Brand, Robert (Bob) Henry, 1st Baron Brand (1878–1963) British banker and public servant. In 1917 he married Phyllis Langhorne, sister of Nancy Astor.

Brownlow, Perry, Peregrine Cust, 6th Baron Brownlow (1899–1978) A close friend of Edward VIII. He accompanied Wallis Simpson to France when she and the Duke went into exile.

Bullock, Sir Malcolm, 1st Baronet (1890–1966) Diplomat and Conservative MP. He married Victoria Stanley, daughter of 17th Earl of Derby.

Burne-Jones, Sir Edward Coley (1833–1898) British artist known for his association with the Pre-Raphaelite Brotherhood (a group of English painters, poets and critics, founded in 1848 by John Millais, Dante Gabriel Rossetti and William Holman Hunt). Frances Horner was a close friend and frequently posed for him.

Burns, John Eliot (1858–1943) Elected to Parliament in 1892. President of the Board of Trade, 1914.

Burroughes, Anne Kathleen Julia (née Bourke) (1872–1935) Norah's older sister. She married George Burroughes in 1893. They had 3 children, Pamela, Randall and Stephen, and lived in Cobham, Surrey. After Anne died, her husband moved back to his family home in Blakeney, Norfolk.

Carlisle, George Howard, 11th Earl (1895–1963).

Carter, Lily (née Head) (1912–2004) Norah's parlourmaid and the wife of her under-gardener, Walter Carter. Lily went into service at Sutton Courtenay

in 1928, recommended by Frances, Lady Horner. She worked at Sutton Courtenay from 1928–1932, and remembered Norah as having been temperamental and demanding. She also remembered that people came to look at the Sutton Courtenay garden and the special plants that Norah grew, especially the blue poppies.

Carter, Walter Charles (1908–1940) Norah's gardener, starting at the age of thirteen, from 1921–1938. Married Norah's parlour maid Lily Head in 1934. In 1938 he went on to Little Wittenham and worked as the head gardener for Major Herapath. Carter went into the army in 1939 and was killed at Dunkirk in 1940.

Cavendish-Bentinck, Lord (Francis) Morven (1900–1950) Son of the 6th Duke of Portland and Winnie, Duchess of Portland.

Cavendish-Bentinck, William *see* **Portland**

Cazalet, Victor (Teeny) (1896–1943) Politician. Conservative MP and director of the company that owned The Dorchester Hotel. He was killed in 1943, with the Polish leader General Wladyslaw Sikorski, when their plane from Gibraltar to Britain crashed seconds after take-off.

Chamberlain, Sir (Joseph) Austen (1863–1937) British statesman. He was Chancellor of the Exchequer in 1903, Secretary of State for India in 1915–1917, a member of the War Cabinet in 1918 and Secretary of State for Foreign Affairs 1924–1929. Shortly after his death in 1937, Austen's half-brother, Neville Chamberlain, became Prime Minister.

Channon, Chips (Sir Henry) (1897–1958) American, naturalized British, politician and author, known for his diaries. Conservative MP 1935–1958. Married Lady Honor Guinness (1909–1976) in 1933. They divorced in 1945.

Chaplin, Alvilde (née Bridges) (1909–1994) Garden designer and author. She first married Anthony Freskin Charles Hamby Chaplin, 3rd Viscount Chaplin (1906–1981); they divorced in 1950. Her second marriage to James Lees-Milne was complex as both were bisexual. James had an affair with Harold Nicolson in the 1930s, and years later in the 1950s Alvilde had an affair with Vita Sackville-West, Harold Nicolson's wife.

Chaplin, Charlie (Sir Charles Spencer Chaplin) (1889–1977) English comedy actor and film star. He married four times: in 1918, Mildred Harris (divorced in 1920); in 1924, Lita Grey, with whom he had two sons (divorced in 1928); a (probable common-law) marriage to Paulette Goddard from 1932–1940; in 1943 he married Oona O'Neill, daughter of playwright Eugene O'Neill, with whom he had eight children.

Charteris, Sir Evan (1864–1940) Author, biographer of John Singer Sargent. The son of the 10th Earl of Wemyss, he married Dorothy Margaret Browne, daughter of Sir Valentine Charles Browne, 5th Earl of Kenmare in 1930.

Churchill, Lady Gwendoline (Goonie) (née Bertie) (1885–1941) Married Major John Churchill in 1908. Winston Churchill's sister-in-law.

Churchill, Clementine (Clemmie) (née Hozier) (1885–1977) Wife of Sir Winston Churchill.

Churchill, Sir Winston Leonard Spencer (1874–1965) British statesman and world leader; Prime Minister 1940–1945 and 1951–1955 and holder of numerous government posts in his 60-year political life. He married Clementine Hozier (Clemmie) in 1908. He was a friend of Norah through their associations with his private secretary, Edward Marsh, and her close friends Ronnie and Nancy Tree.

Clarendon, Edward Villiers, 5th Earl (1846–1914) In 1876 he married Lady Caroline Agar; they had two children. After her death he married Norah's mother, Emma Bourke, in 1908. Known as Lord Hyde or Hydie, he lived at The Grove in Watford.

Coates, Audrey *see* **Field**

Coats, Peter (1910–1990) ADC to Lord Wavell as Viceroy of India, and, later, a garden designer and writer. He was known as 'Petticoats'.

Colefax, Sybil (née Halsey) (1874–1950) Married to Sir Arthur Colefax (1886–1936). A prominent London hostess, she was co-founder, with her partner John Fowler, of the interior design firm Colefax and Fowler.

Cooper, George Frederick Paston (1861–1895) Son of the 3rd Baronet Cooper of Gadebridge. He served in the 4th Battalion Bedfordshire Regiment, and courted Norah at the same time as Harry Lindsay. He died unmarried, shortly before Norah and Harry's wedding.

Cooper, Lady Diana Olivia Winifred Maud (née Manners) (1892–1986) Actress, society hostess, and author. She married Alfred Duff Cooper (1890–1954), later Viscount Norwich, in 1919. She was the daughter of the 8th Duke of Rutland (although her biological father was said to be the writer and politician Harry Cust) and Violet, Duchess of Rutland, and was Harry Lindsay's niece.

Cooper, Lt. Col. Reginald A., (1885–1965) Diplomat, garden designer and restorer of country houses. A close friend of Norah and Lawrence Johnston, he lived at Cothay Manor, Somerset. Advised his great friend, Harold Nicolson, on the layout of the bowling green at Sissinghurst.

Cunard, Maud (Emerald) Burke (1872–1948) Changed her name to 'Emerald' in about 1927 because of her love for wearing massive amounts of the gem. She was an American from San Francisco and a famed society hostess who in 1895 married Sir Bache Cunard (1851–1925), heir to the shipping fortune. She was originally a friend of Emmie Bourke, but later a close friend of Norah.

Cunard, Victor (1898–1960) Diplomat. Norah designed his gardens at Pertenhall, Bedfordshire. They were close friends and often travelled together.

Curzon The three daughters of George Nathaniel Curzon, 1st Marquess Curzon (1859–1925), were: **(Mary) Irene** (1896–1966), later Baroness Ravensdale; **Cynthia (Cimmie)** (1898–1933), the first wife of Sir Oswald Mosley; and **Alexandra (Baba)** (1904–1995) who married in 1925 Edward 'Fruity' Metcalfe, one of Edward VIII's closest friends.

Dalkeith, Walter, (Walter Montagu-Douglas-Scott, 8th Duke of Buccleuch, 10th Duke of Queensberry) (1894–1973) Politician. As Earl of Dalkeith, he was a Scottish Unionist MP from 1923–1935. He was married in 1921 to Vreda Esther Mary (Molly) Lascelles (1900–1993), granddaughter of the 10th Duke of St. Albans.

Davidoff, Basil, Consuelo Balsan's Russian major-domo at Lou Sueil and St. Georges-Motel. He was an excellent tennis player; one of his duties was to set up and play in matches with guests in tennis, golf, and bridge.

Davis, Henriette Long-time friend of both Norah and Madeline. She lived in Paris, and often sent Norah her cast-off clothing.

de Ganay, Hubert, Marquis (1888–1974) Owner of the Chateau de Courances and its celebrated garden.

de Noailles, Charles, Vicomte (1891–1981) Patron of art, music and literature in France. His château was adjacent to Edith Wharton's in Hyères, France, and he often spent time with Norah and Johnny Johnston at Johnston's home, Serre de la Madone, Menton, France.

d'Erlanger, Catherine, Baroness (d. 1959) Society hostess. She was born Marie-Rose Catherine d'Aqueria, daughter of the Marquis de Rochegude. She married the Anglo-French banker Baron Emile d'Erlanger (1866–1939) in 1896.

de Rothschild, Lionel (1882–1942) British banker and heir to N.M. Rothschild & Sons banking fortune. He was the creator of Exbury Gardens, Hampshire, famous for the Rothschild collection of rhododendrons, azaleas and camellias, and sponsored plant-hunting expeditions to the Himalayas. He was a good friend of Lawrence Johnston and Reginald Cooper.

Dentice di Frasso, Dorothy Taylor (1888–1954) Wealthy American married to Conte Carlo de Frasso. She was a close friend of Barbara Hutton and Cary Grant. The Dentice di Frasso family purchased Villa Madama in Rome in 1925. Norah designed gardens for the villa. In 1937 the villa was leased to the Italian Ministry for Foreign Affairs and was purchased by the Italian State in 1941.

Denton, Annie (née Gibbon) (1875–1954) Norah's cook and the mother of Norah's personal maid, Daisy Alston. She married Norah's gardener Frederick Denton in 1910.

Desborough, Ettie, Lady (Ethel Anne Priscilla Grenfell, neé Fane) (1867–1952) Society hostess and member of The Souls. She married William, 1st Baron Desborough, in 1887; they lived at Taplow Court. Her children were the poet Julian Genfell who, with his brother Billy, was killed in World War I, Ivo, who died in a car crash in 1925, Monica and Imogen. Ettie was a great friend of Norah and her mother, Emmie.

Doubleday, Frank Nelson (1862–1934) U.S. publisher; founder of Doubleday & McClure Company, in 1897. The firm became Doubleday, Page & Co. in 1899. His first wife was Neltje Blanchan (1865–1918), a nature writer, with whom he visited Sutton Courtenay.

Drian, Adrien Etienne (1890–1965) Painter, fashion magazine illustrator, and costume designer.

Dudley, Eric (William Humble Eric Ward, 3rd Earl of Dudley) (1894–1969) Norah designed gardens for him at Himley Hall and Park where the landscapes were originally designed by Capability Brown. In 1934 the Duke and Duchess of Kent honeymooned at Himley. Edward VIII spent his last weekend there before his abdication.

Dudley Ward, Freda (born Winifred May Birkin) (1894–1983) Textile heiress. First married William Dudley Ward, a Liberal MP; they divorced in 1931. She then married Pedro, Marqués de Casa Maury, a racing driver. She met Edward, Prince of Wales, in 1918 and became his mistress for many years.

Duncan, Isadora (1878–1927) American dancer. Her style of free movement greatly influenced modern dance.

Eden, Sir Anthony, 1st Earl of Avon (1897–1977) Foreign Secretary for three periods between 1935 and 1955, including World War II. Prime Minister 1955–1957.

Edward VII (Albert Edward) (1841–1910) King of the United Kingdom from 1901–1910. The son of Queen Victoria, before his accession to the throne, he held the title of Prince of Wales for 60 years.

Edward, Prince of Wales (Edward Albert Christian George Andrew Patrick David) later Edward VIII; from 1937 Duke of Windsor (1894–1972) King of the United Kingdom from January 20, 1936 until his abdication on December 11, 1936. He married Wallis Simpson in 1937. Norah helped design his gardens at Fort Belvedere, Windsor Great Park.

Fellowes, Daisy (born Marguerite Séverine Philippine Decazes) (1887–1962) Society beauty and writer. Her mother was Isabelle Singer, the sewing-machine heiress, her father the 3rd Duc Decazes, and she was partly raised by her aunt Winaretta, Princess de Polignac (née Singer). She married the Hon. Reginald Fellowes (1884–1953) in 1919. Norah designed the gardens at her estate Les Zoraides on Cap Martin, France.

Fenwick, Mark (1860–1945) Heir to a banking fortune, he later became Managing Director of the Consett Iron Co. Ltd. In 1902 he hired architect Sir Edwin Lutyens to make extensive alterations to his house and formal gardens at Abbotswood, near Stow-on-the-Wold. He was an accomplished gardener and a close friend of Lawrence Johnston with whom he exchanged plants and ideas.

Feversham, Sim (Charles William Slingsby Duncombe, 3rd Earl of Feversham) (1906–1963) Married to Anne, daughter of Lord Halifax. Norah helped design some his gardens at Duncombe Park, North Yorkshire.

Field, Evelyn (Evy) Marshall, First wife of Marshall Field III whom she married in 1915 and divorced in 1930.

Field, Audrey James Coates (1902–1968) Widow of British textile owner Capt. Dudley Coates. She was the second wife of Marshall Field III (they married in 1930, divorced 1934) She was a great friend of Edward, Prince of Wales, before his marriage to Wallis Simpson.

Field, Marshall III (1893–1956) Head of the Chicago brokerage firm Field, Glore & Co., and heir to the Marshall Field department store chain. He was President of Field Enterprises, Inc., published *Chicago Sun-Times*, owned Simon and Schuster, Inc., and Pocket Books, Inc., and operated radio stations.

Fielden, Capt. Edward Hedley ('Mouse') (1903–1976) Pilot for the royal family, and personal pilot for Edward, Prince of Wales, in the 1930s.

Flandin, Pierre-Etienne (1889–1958) Prime Minister of France 1934–1935.

Gage, Henry Rainald 6th Viscount Gage (1895–1982) Married in 1931 to Imogen 'Mogs' Grenfell (d.1969) (daughter of Ettie Desborough). Norah designed his gardens at Firle Place, Sussex.

George V (George Frederick Ernest Albert) (1865–1936) King of the United Kingdom(1910–1936). The son of Edward VII, he married, in 1893, Princess Mary of Teck, who became **Queen Mary** (1867–1953), and was the father of Edward VIII and George VI.

George VI (Albert Frederick Arthur George) (1895–1952) King of the United Kingdom(1936–1952). On the death of his father, George V, he became Duke of York, and King upon the abdication of his brother, King Edward VIII. He was King during the Second World War, and father of the present Queen.

George, Duke of Kent (Prince George) (1902–1942) Edward VIII's younger brother. Married Princess Marina of Greece in 1934.

Gilmour, Mary Cecilia Rhodesia (née Hamilton) (1896–1984) Daughter of 3rd Duke of Abercorn. She married, firstly, Maj. Robert Kenyon-Slaney (divorced in 1930) and secondly Sir John Gilmour, 2nd Bt. She was the mother of Janie Kenyon-Slaney, Peter Lindsay's first wife.

Glyn, Sibell (1881–1958), daughter of 2nd Baron Derwent. In 1910 she married Brig. Gen. Hon. Walter Long (who was killed in action in 1917); their son David Long (1911–1944) was also killed in action. In 1921 she married Ralph Glyn (Baron Glyn). Norah designed gardens under Lady Glyn's direction for her son David, at South Wraxall Manor, Wiltshire.

Goddard, Paulette (born Pauline Marion Levy) (1910–1990) Actress. She was at the height of her career in the mid-1940s when Norah knew her. She married four times: Edgar James (1927–1931); Charlie Chaplin (1936–1942); Burgess Meredith (1944–1950); Erich Maria Remarque (1958–1970).

Grenfell *see* **Desborough**.

Granby *see* **Rutland**.

Grigg, Joanie (born Joan Dickson-Poynder) (1897–1987) Organizer of maternity and nursing services in Africa. Married in 1923 to Edward Grigg, 1st Baron Altrincham (1879–1955), Special Adviser to the Prince of Wales 1919–1920, and Governor of Kenya 1925–1930. She was the daughter of Anne, Lady Islington, one of Norah's closest friends. Norah designed gardens for her at Port Ledge, Devon.

Gubbay, Hannah (née Ezra) (d.1968) First cousin of Philip Sassoon. She often acted as his hostess, and inherited Trent Park from him. She sold the estate in 1951 to Middlesex County Council and it became a teacher training college, Trent Park College.

Hamilton, Gen. Sir Ian (1853–1947) Distinguished army officer whose career was ended by his failure as Commander-in-Chief of the Mediterranean Expeditionary Force in the campaign against Turkey at Gallipoli in 1915. Sir Ian and his wife **Jean** (née Muir) (1861–1941) were close friends of Norah, who often stayed at Jean Hamilton's London flat when Sutton Courtenay was being rented out.

Hearst, Millicent (1903–1951) Wife of the famous newspaper owner William Randolph Hearst.

Herbert, Sydney (1890–1939) Son of Sir Michael Herbert who was Ambassador to the U.S. from 1902–1903.

Hillier, Edwin Lawrence (1865–1944) Owner of Hillier's plant nursery in Hampshire. Norah often consulted him directly, when making her plant selections.

Hoare, Samuel John Gurney, 1st Viscount Templewood (1880–1959) British Conservative politician. As Foreign Secretary in 1935 he was instrumental in developing the Anglo-French agreement, infamous as the Hoare-Laval pact, which would have granted Italy territorial rights in Ethiopia. The public uproar against this decision led to Hoare's resignation as Foreign Secretary. He was ambassador to Spain from 1940–1944.

Hofmannsthal *see* **von Hofmannsthal**

Hood, Myrtle (d.1982) Married in 1937 to Samuel Brian Digby (Sammy) Hood, 6th Viscount Hood (1910–1988), Counsellor in Paris 1948–1951. Myrtle was the daughter of Norah's clients the Barons. Her husband was a close friend of Norah's nephew, Humphrey Whitbread. Norah designed gardens for her residence in Gloucestershire.

Horner, Frances, Lady (née Graham) (1858–1940) Hostess and patron of the arts; a member of The Souls, and friend of the painter Edward Burne-Jones. She married **Sir John Francis Fortescue Horner** (1842–1927) in 1883. She was a lifelong friend of Norah and her first paying client. Norah designed gardens for the Horners at Mells Manor House.

Howard de Walden, Thomas Evelyn Scott-Ellis, 8th Baron (1880–1946) Writer, sportsman, and patron of the arts. He leased Chirk Castle from the Myddelton family from 1911–1946. In 1912 he married **Margherita** (b.1890), the daughter of Charles van Raalte, an important collector of musical instruments. They had six children. She was very socially conscious and committed to charitable work in child welfare. Margherita, Lady Howard de Walden, was a close friend of Norah's for more than forty years. Norah redesigned the topiary, herbaceous borders, and shrub borders at Chirk Castle.

Hudson, Edward (1854–1936) Founder of *Country Life* magazine in 1897. Owner of Lindisfarne Castle and Deanery Garden.

Hudson, Nan (1869–1957) British artist. She was the partner of Ethel Sands, and cousin of Lawrence 'Johnny' Johnston.

Hughes, Alice (1857–1939) Society and court portrait photographer, known for her covers for *Country Life* magazine and for her work for the royal family. She was the daughter of portrait painter Edwin Hughes, and worked from her home in Gower Street, London.

Hussey, Christopher Edward Clive (1899–1970) Architectural historian. He was Adviser to, and later Architectural Editor of, *Country Life*. Author of a series of books on British architecture.

Hutton, Barbara (1912–1979) American heiress and socialite; daughter of Frank W. Woolworth, founder of the Woolworth department store chain. She was in the company of her fiancé Alexis Mdivani (the first of her seven husbands) when Norah saw them at The Gleneagles Hotel.

Islington, Anne Dickson-Poynder, **Lady** (neé Beauclerk Dundas) (d.1958) One of Norah's early clients and a very close friend. In 1896 she married John Dickson-Poynder, 1st Baron Islington (1866–1936), British politician and Governor of New Zealand (1910–1912) Norah designed her gardens at Rushbrooke Hall.

Ismay, Hastings Lionel, 1st Baron Ismay (1887–1965) British soldier and diplomat. Chief of Staff to Winston Churchill in World War II. In 1952 became the first Secretary General of NATO. Nicknamed Pug.

Jekyll, Gertrude (1843–1932) British garden designer and garden writer, famous for her artistic or painterly approach to plantings in the garden, especially her subtle use of colour and for planting in long flowing drifts of plants. Her planting style in herbaceous borders has been copied for decades. She was a strong influence on the garden design of Norah Lindsay.

Jellicoe, Sir Geoffrey (1900–1996) British architect, town planner, and influential landscape architect. His book *Italian Gardens of the Renaissance* (1925) influenced Ronnie and Nancy Tree to hire him to work at Ditchley Park.

Johnston, Lawrence Waterbury (Johnny) (1871–1958) American/naturalized-British garden designer and plantsman. He created famous gardens at Hidcote Manor in Gloucestershire and Serre de la Madone in Menton, France. He joined the British Army, fighting in the Boer War and throughout World War I, despite being 43 when the war began and being injured in the first year, only retiring in 1922. A close personal friend of Norah, who often stayed with him at Hidcote and Serre de la Madone, he left the latter to Norah's daughter, Nancy.

Kennedy, Joseph P., Sr. (1888–1969) Ambassador to Britain (1938–40) He was the father of John F. Kennedy (1917–1963), President of the United States (1961–1963).

Kenyon-Slaney, Janie (Ursula Jane) (b.1920) Married Norah's only son Peter in 1940; they divorced in 1945. Secondly, she married in 1946 Sir Max Aitken, son of Lord Beaverbrook; they divorced in 1950.Thirdly she married Robert Edward John [Robin] Compton in 1951.

Keppel, Alice (née Edmonstone) (1868–1947) Married Hon. George Keppel (1865–1947) in 1891. She was the mistress of Edward VII from 1898 until his death in 1910 and was a good friend to Norah and her mother, Emmie.

Kerr, Philip Henry, 11th Marquess of Lothian (1882–1940) Writer, politician and diplomat. Private secretary to the Prime Minister, Lloyd George, (1916–1922), he drafted the Preface to the Treaty of Versailles in 1919. He became Secretary of the Rhodes Trust in 1921, and in the 1930s was made Under-Secretary of State for India. He was Ambassador to the United States from 1939–1940. Norah designed his gardens at Blickling Hall, Norfolk.

Kingdon-Ward, Capt. Francis (Frank) (1885–1958) Plant explorer and author.

Knox, Collie (1899–1977) Author and journalist. Editor of a column called 'Collie Knox Calling' in the *Daily Mail*.

Kommer, Rudolf (1885–1943) Agent for producer Max Reinhardt in the United States. He was also a correspondent for German newspapers, and a German translator of American plays.

Korda, Sir Alexander (1893–1956) Hungarian-born British filmmaker and noted producer in Britain and the United States. He married film actress Merle Oberon in 1939.

Lambert, Baronne. Scion of a Jewish banking dynasty in Belgium, Banque Bruxelles Lambert. Norah designed gardens for his residence in Belgium.

Lancaster, Nancy (formerly Nancy Tree, born Nancy Keane Perkins) (1897–1994) American society hostess and interior designer. A niece of Nancy Astor, she married Ronald Tree in 1920. The Trees leased Kelmarsh Hall, Northamptonshire, and later bought Ditchley Park, Oxfordshire; they divorced 1947. She married **Colonel Claude (Juby) Lancaster** (1899–1977), the owner of Kelmarsh Hall in 1948. In 1945, Ronnie Tree bought out Sybil Colefax's share of the interior design firm Colefax & Fowler for Nancy, and she became an influential decorator, known for her Country House Style. Norah designed gardens for Nancy, when she was married to Ronnie Tree, at Kelmarsh and Ditchley.

Landsberg, Albert Clinton (Bertie) (d.1965) Son of the financial adviser to the Emperor of Brazil. Pablo Picasso painted a portrait of Landsberg in 1921 which hangs in the Fitzwilliam Museum, Cambridge, UK. He owned the Villa Malcontenta in Venice where Norah often stayed as a paying guest.

Lascelles, Henry George Charles, 6th Earl of Harewood (1882–1947) In 1922 he married HRH Princess Mary, the Princess Royal (1897–1965), the only daughter of George V.

Lathom, Ned, Edward William Bootle-Wilbraham, 3rd Earl of Lathom (1895–1930) Playwright, Noel Coward's first patron and friend of Ivor Novello, both of whom Norah socialised with through Ned. He and Norah travelled to the United States in the spring of 1919. Handsome, intelligent, charismatic and wealthy, Ned Lathom lived the last few years of his life extravagantly and happily, spending his great wealth on the theatre. Norah was greatly saddened when he died in 1930, bankrupt, in a flat in London.

Laval, Pierre (1883–1945) Prime Minister of France. Pro-Nazi during World War II, he was found guilty of high treason after the war and executed.

Lavery, Sir John (1856–1941) British-Irish portrait painter.

Leconfield, Violet, Lady (Beatrice Violet Rawson Wyndham) (1892–1956) Married Sir Charles Henry Wyndham, 3rd Baron Leconfield in 1911.

Lees-Milne, James (1908–1997) British biographer, architectural historian and conservationist. For many years he was on the staff of the National Trust as Secretary of the Country House Committee and architectural consultant. Married Alvide Chaplin in 1951.

Legh, Piers (Joey) Walter, (later Lt.-Col. Sir Piers Legh) (1890–1955) British soldier; equerry to the Prince of Wales (Edward VIII) In 1941 he became Master of the Household.

Leigh, Vivien (1913–1967) Actress. Married Sir Laurence Olivier in 1940.

Leslie, Anita (1914–1985) Biographer. The daughter of Sir Shane (author and poet) and Marjorie Leslie, she married the Russian horseman Col. Paul Rodzianko, and had a distinguished war career driving ambulances behind enemy lines. Her grandmother was Winston Churchill's aunt.

Lindsay, Charles Hugh (1816–1889) Harry's father. Son of James Lindsay, 24th Earl of Crawford, he married Emilia Anne Browne, in 1851. He was Groom-in-Waiting to Queen Victoria, Lieutenant-Colonel of the Grenadier Guards and Colonel Commanding the St. Georges Rifles. From 1865 to 1874 he was MP for Abingdon.

Lindsay, Lt Col.(David Ludovic) Peter (1900–1971) Norah's son. Married in 1940 to Janie Kenyon-Slaney, they divorced in 1946. In 1950 he married Barbara Dunn, who died in 2003; they had three children: Jane, Sarah, and David.

Linlithgow, Doreen, Marchioness of (Doreen Maud Hope, née Milner) (1886–1965) Married, in 1911, Victor Hope, 2nd Marquess of Linlithgow, Viceroy of India (1936–1943).

Listowel, William (Billy) Hare (1906–1997) 5th Earl. Politician.

Lloyd, Mary Helen Wingate (1868–1934) Married to Horatio Gates Lloyd, a financier and President of the Commercial Trust Company of Philadelphia, Pennsylvania. Lived at Allgates, their estate in Haverford, near Philadelphia. Active in the campaign for women's suffrage and organized one of the founding clubs of the Garden Club of America (GCA). Served for many years as the editor of the Plant Material department of the GCA *Bulletin*. She served as Director of GCA from 1928–1933, and held the position of First Vice-President until her death. Active in many plant societies, including the Pennsylvania Horticultural Society and a charter member of the American Iris Society. Mrs. Lloyd organized the tour of American gardeners who visited Sutton Courtenay and Cliveden in 1929.

Lutyens, Sir Edwin Landseer (1869–1944) British architect known for the country houses he designed, his collaboration with the British garden designer Gertrude Jekyll, and as the planner and co-architect of New Delhi.

Lygon, Lady Mary, Baroness Ampthill (1874–1957) Married Arthur Oliver Villiers Russell, 2nd Baron Ampthill. A Lady of the Bedchamber to HM Queen Mary, she was invested as a Dame Grand Cross, Order of the British Empire in 1918 and Dame Grand Cross, Royal Victorian Order in 1946.

Lytton, Pamela, Countess of (born Pamela Chichele-Plowden) (1874–1971) Married, in 1902, to Victor Bulwer-Lytton, 2nd Earl (1876–1947), politician and colonial administrator, and Chairman of the League of Nations Commission on Manchuria in 1932. She lived at Knebworth, Hertfordshire, and was a good friend of her brother-in-law, Sir Edwin Lutyens, who advised her on the many alterations to Knebworth. Pamela was a childhood friend of Norah's and they remained close for their entire lives.

MacCarthy, Sir Desmond (1877–1952) Writer and critic.

Mackintosh, Alastair (b.1889) Author. Wrote *No Alibi* in 1961. Norah designed gardens for his estate at Sunninghill Park, Berkshire.

Maddison, Adela (née Tindall) (1862/3–1929) Accomplished composer and musician. In 1883 she married the barrister Frederick Brunning Maddison (1850–1906), a director of Metzler, the firm who published her music. The Maddisons were responsible for bringing the French composer Gabriel Fauré's (1845–1924) music to England. Adela translated some of his songs into English, and Fauré dedicated his Seventh Nocturne to her.

Mann, Harrington (1865–1937) A specialist in portrait painting, he studied at the Glasgow School of Art and the Slade under Legros, followed by a period at the Academie in Paris. His daughter was Cathleen Mann, Marchioness of Queensberry. He painted the portrait of Norah (on the frontispiece) early in her marriage.

Manners *see* **Rutland**

Marsh, Sir Edward (Eddie) Howard (1872–1953) Civil servant, classicist, translator, and patron of poetry and painting. In 1906 became the private secretary to Winston Churchill, a post which he held for almost 25 years. He was a close friend of Rupert Brooke, with whom he edited four volumes of poetry, including the works of Walter de la Mare and D.H. Lawrence. He remained a close friend of Ivor Novello for more than two decades. Under the name Edward Moore, Eddie Marsh wrote the words to Ivor Novello's song 'The Land of Might Have Been'. Eddie was a frequent guest at Sutton Courtenay. Norah considered him a good friend for more than thirty years.

Masefield, John (1878–1967) Poet, novelist, dramatist and journalist. His plays included: *The Coming of Christ* and *The Tragedy of Nan*.

Maugham, Syrie (formerly Syrie Wellcome, née Barnardo) (1879–1955) Interior designer. Famous for promoting the all white look in decoration in the 1920s and 1930s. In 1916 she married the novelist Somerset Maugham (1874–1965); they divorced in 1927. Norah designed her London garden.

Maxwell, Elsa (1883–1963) International hostess and socialite.

Maze, Paul (1887–1979) French Artist.

Menzies, Charles Cuthbert (1905–1951) Vice-Chairman of the John Menzies Publishing Company in Edinburgh. Norah designed his gardens at Bampton Manor, Oxfordshire.

Meredith, Burgess (1907–1997) American actor, whose third wife was Paulette Goddard.

Messel, Oliver (1904–1978) Artist, stage designer and costume designer.

Metcalfe, Lady Alexandra (Baba) *see* **Curzon**

Mitford: The children of David (Freeman-) Mitford, 2nd Baron Redesdale, included the writers **Nancy** (1904–1973) and **Jessica** (1917–1996), **Diana** (1910–200) who married Sir Oswald Mosley, and **Tom** (1909–1945), who never married.

Molyneux, Edward (1891–1974) Irish couturier who worked in Paris between the wars. Diana Cooper and Molyneux had an arrangement whereby she could have any dress she liked at no cost as an advertisement.

Mosley, Cimmie *see* **Curzon**

Mosley, Sir Oswald (Tom) (1896–1980) Politician and founder, in 1932, of the British Union of Fascists. When his first wife Cimmie died in 1933 Norah was asked to design and plant a memorial on their property, Savehay Farm, Buckinghamshire in Cimmie's honour. In 1936 he married Diana Guinness, née Mitford. Hitler was in attendance at the ceremony.

Morrell, Lady Ottoline (née Cavendish-Bentinck) (1873–1938) Society hostess and patron of writers and artists. In 1902 she married Philip Morrell, MP; they lived at Gardsington Hall, Oxfordshire, and she was a frequent visitor at Sutton Courtenay. She was the half-sister of the Duke of Portland.

Muir, Heather. Owner and creator, in the 1920s of the gardens at Kiftsgate Court, Gloucestershire, which are next to Hidcote Manor.

Myddelton, Lady Margaret (born Mary Margaret Elizabeth Petty-FitzMaurice) (1910–2003) She married Lt. Col. Ririd Myddelton in 1931,

and lived at Chirk Castle until her death. Although the Myddleton family owned and mostly lived at Chirk Castle from 1595 until 2004, during the 1930s Thomas, 8th Baron Howard de Walden, and his family lived at the castle which they leased from the Myddelton family.

Niven, David (1910–1983) Actor and author. Married to Primula Rollo in 1940.

Normanby, Oswald Phipps, 4th Marquess of (1912–1994) Norah designed his gardens at Mulgrave Castle, Yorkshire where Repton had originally laid out extensive parklands.

Norris, May (d.1938) American interior decorator who transformed the old château at Gourdon into a spectacular destination for her American and British friends. Mary Norris was a close friend of Cole Porter, Sibyl Colefax, Johnny Johnston, Edith Wharton, and Norah Lindsay. Norah holidayed at Gourdon on more than one occasion with Miss Norris.

Norton, Robert. English watercolour artist, who also wrote nature and love poems. He was a close friend of Edith Wharton.

Novello, Ivor (born David Ivor Davies) (1893–1951) Actor, composer, and playwright, one of Britain's greatest geniuses on the musical stage. In 1914 he wrote the song 'Keep the Home Fires Burning', which became the most popular song amongst British soldiers. He appeared on stage in the West End in musical shows of his own devising, the best known being *The Dancing Years* (1939) He also went to Hollywood and appeared in films such as *The White Rose* (1923) and *The Vortex* (1928). Ivor frequently visited Sutton Courtenay with his friends Ned Lathom and Eddie Marsh.

Oberon, Merle (born Estelle Merle O'Brien Thompson) (1911–1979) Actress. Married to Sir Alexander Korda from 1939–1945. At the time that she attended Harry Lindsay's funeral she was starring in the film *Wuthering Heights* as Cathy Linton.

Ogilvy, Mabell, Countess of Airlie (née Gore) (1866–1956) Writer and courtier. She married David Ogilvy, 11th Earl of Airlie in 1886. She became Lady-in-waiting and Lady of the Bedchamber to her friend Queen Mary from 1902. Discreet insights into royal life appear in *Thatched with Gold: The Memoirs of Mabell, Countess of Airlie*.

Olivier, Laurence (Lord Olivier) (1907–1989) Eminent actor and director.

Page, Russell (1906–1985) Landscape architect. He went into partnership with Geoffrey Jellicoe in 1935. He worked for Ronnie and Nancy Tree at Ditchley Park.

Palewski, Col. Gaston (1901–1984) French soldier and politician. Charles de Gaulle's chief of staff. The novelist Nancy Mitford fell in love with him in 1942, portraying him as Fabrice in *The Pursuit of Love*.

Paul of Yugoslavia (Prince Paul of Serbia; became Prince Paul of Yugoslavia after 1919) (1893–1976) Married to Princess Olga of Greece and Denmark (1903–1997) in 1923. From 1934–1941 was Prince Regent for his nephew King Peter II of Yugoslavia. Norah designed his gardens at Bled, near Belgrade and Brdo (in present-day Slovenia).

Peake, Osbert, 1st Viscount Ingleby (1897–1966) Politician.

Philipp, Prince of Hesse-Kassel (1896–1980) Head of the Electoral House of Hesse from 1940–1980. In 1923 he was in Rome, established as a successful interior designer, where Norah became friendly with him and when he accompanied her to the coronation of Pope Pius XI. He joined the Nazi party in 1930; from 1933–1944 he served as Nazi Governor of Hesse-Nassau and was complicit in vile acts committed by the Nazi regime. But when Philipp's father-in-law, King Victor Emanuel III of Italy, arrested Mussolini in 1943 Philipp was arrested, and sent to Flossenburg concentration camp. His wife, Princess Mafalda of Savoy, was sent to Buchenwald where she died. In 1945 Philipp was transferred to Dachau concentration camp, then on to Villabassa in the Italian Dolomites. In 1945 American troops took over the camp and he was freed. He died in Rome.

Philipps, Sir Laurence Richard, 1st Baron Milford (1874–1962) Shipping magnate and horse-racing enthusiast. He and his wife Ethel (née Speke) (1879/80–1971), bought Dalham Hall near Newmarket in 1928, and established the Dalham Hall Stud. Norah designed the gardens at Dalham Hall for the Philipps.

Phipps, Nora Langhorne (1890–1955) Sister of Nancy Astor and aunt of Nancy Lancaster. She married the British architect, Paul Phipps. They had one daughter, the actress and comedienne Joyce Grenfell (1910–1979). Nora later married the silent movie actor, Maurice 'Lefty' Flynn, a football player at Yale (who earned his nickname because he kicked with his left foot).

Piacentini, Marcello (1881–1960) Italian architect, designer of the Italian pavilion at the 1910 World Exposition in Brussels. During the regime of Mussolini in the 1930s, he became known for his many government commissions in Rome, Milan and Livorno.

Pinsent, Cecil (1884–1963) British architect known for the villas and gardens he built in Tuscany, often for British and American expatriates.

Polden, Mrs. Norah's cook from the late 1920s through the 1930s.

Ponsonby, Arthur (1871–1946) Diplomat 1894–1902. Labour MP for Sheffield (1922–1930). Under-Secretary of State at the Foreign Office in 1924. In 1898 he married Dorothea (Dolly) Parry (1876–1963).

Pope-Hennessy, James (Jamesy) (1916–1974) Author and historian. His many books include biographies of Queen Mary and Robert Louis Stevenson, and *London Fabric*, a poetic, personal view of places and landmarks in London.

Pope Pius XI (born Ambrogio Damiano Achille Ratti) (1857–1939) Italian. Reigned as Pope from February 6, 1922 until February 10, 1939.

Portland, Winnie Cavendish-Bentinck, Duchess of, (born Winifred Anna Dallas-Yorke) (1863–1954) She was a very close friend of Norah's, and a member of The Souls. She married William John Arthur Cavendish-Bentinck, 6th Duke of Portland (1857–1943); they lived at Welbeck Abbey.

Potocki, Alfred (1886–1958) Polish count. Son of Count Roman Potocki and Princess Elizabeth Radziwill. He married Izabela Narkiewicz-Jodko.

Poynder, Anne *see* **Islington**

Prouvost, Jean (1885–1978) Industrialist and media magnate. He founded *Paris-Soir* in 1931, *Marie Claire* in 1937 the first magazine aimed at women, and *Paris-Match* in 1938. In the 1950s he acquired *Le Figaro*. Norah designed gardens at his estate in St. Jean, France. While she was there Prouvost was holding the initial meetings for the formation of *Marie Claire*. Norah was intrigued and interested in the process and often wrote about the meetings and the people involved.

Queen Mary *see* **George V**

Rhodes, Cecil John (1853–1902) British born South African businessman and politician; Prime Minister of Cape Colony and founder of Rhodesia. He founded the De Beers diamond company, and with the profits of his southern African enterprises established the Rhodes Scholarships, enabling students from territories (formerly) under British rule, or from Germany, to study at the University of Oxford.

Rollo, Prim (Primula Niven) (1918–1946) Married the actor David Niven in 1940. At a party at Tyrone Power's house in California she fell down a flight of stairs and died from a fractured skull at the age of 28. David Niven raised their two sons, David Jr. and Jamie.

Romanov, Grand Duke Dmitri (1901–1980) Secretary of the Travellers' Club in Paris. Norah designed gardens for the Duke and his wife, the American Audrey Emery, at Beaumesnil, Normandy, France.

Rothschild *see* **de Rothschild**

Russell, Sir Claud (1871–1959) Minister to Abyssinia 1920–1925, and Switzerland 1928–1931; Ambassador to Portugal 1931–1935. Norah planted his gardens at Trematon Castle, Cornwall.

Russell, Gilbert (1875–1942) and **Maude** (d.1972) Lived at Mottisfont Abbey where Norah designed the gardens.

Rutland, Henry John Brinsley Manners, 8th Duke of (1852–1925) Private Secretary to the Prime Minister 1885–1886; Col. 3rd and 4th Battalions Leicester Regiment; Member of Parliament 1888–1895. In 1882 he married Harrys Lindsay's sister, Violet. They lived at Belvoir Castle.

Rutland, Violet Manners, Duchess of (born Marion Margaret Violet Lindsay; Marchioness of Granby from 1888–1906) (1856–1937) Harry Lindsay's sister. She married Henry, 8th Duke of Rutland, in 1882. A talented artist and member of The Souls, she introduced Norah and Harry.

Sackville-West, Edward (Eddy) Charles (1901–1965) 5th Baron Sackville. Novelist. Cousin of Vita Sackville-West.

Sackville-West, Vita (1892–1962) Novelist and poet. The daughter of the 3rd Lord Sackville, she married the politician and diplomat Harold Nicolson (1986–1968) in 1913. She looked to Norah for advice on her famous garden at Sissinghurst, and visited Sutton Courtenay for gardening ideas.

Sandeman, Christopher (Kit) (1882–1951) Naturalist and author. Found new species of Peruvian and Colombian *Piperaceae* in 1942 and 1943. Wrote about his eight years of exploration (1938–1946) in the book, *A Wanderer in Inca Land* (1948).

Sands, Ethel (1873–1962) American/naturalized British artist. Her circle of friends included Henry James, Virginia Woolf, and Clive Bell. Ethel went to Paris in 1894 to study painting and met Nan Hudson, who became her companion for life. In 1913 she and Hudson became founding members of the London Group. She lived and worked in England and France.

Sangro, Lydia Contessa Lydia di Sangro di Buccino of Florence.

Sargent, John Singer (1856–1925) American portrait and landscape painter, who lived most of his life in Europe.

Sassoon, Philip Albert Gustave David, 3rd Bt. (1888–1939) Politician, art collector, society host; MP for Hythe 1912–1939. He was private secretary to Field Marshal Haig in World War I, Parliamentary Private Secretary to David Lloyd George in 1920, Under-Secretary of State for Air between 1924–1929 and 1931–1937, and in 1937 became First Commissioner of Works. Descended from the Sassoon and Rothschild families, his sister **Sybil** (1894–1989) was the Marchioness of Cholmondeley. He owned homes in London on Park Lane, at Trent Park, North London, and Port Lympne, Kent. One of Norah's best friends, she designed gardens for him at Trent Park and Port Lympne.

Scott, Sir Jervoise Bolitho, Bt. (1892–1965) Married to Kathleen Walter (1898–1987) of Malshanger in 1924. Norah designed their gardens at Rotherfield Park, Hampshire.

Sefton, Hugh Molyneux, 7th Earl of (1898–1972) A close friend of Edward, Prince of Wales.

Shaw, George Bernard (1856–1950) Playwright. Often referred to as G.B.S. A frequent house-guest at Sutton Courtenay and at the weekend parties that Norah attended at Cliveden and Blickling Hall.

Shaw, Robert Gould Shaw III (Bobbie) (1898–1970) Nancy Astor's son by her first marriage in 1897 to Robert Gould Shaw II (they divorced in 1903). Norah designed gardens for him at Chalk House, Kent.

Simpson, Wallis (Duchess of Windsor; born Bessie Wallis Warfield) (1896–1986) American socialite. She married, first, in 1916 Earl 'Win' Spencer, and second, banker Ernest Simpson in 1928. She moved to London, established herself as a society figure, and became the mistress of the Prince of Wales whom, as Duke of Windsor, she married in 1936.

Sitwell, Sir Osbert (1892–1969) Poet, essayist and novelist. Brother of the poets and writers **Edith** (1887–1964) and **Sacheverell** (1897–1988).

Spencer-Churchill, Charles, 9th Duke of Marlborough (1871–1934). Known as 'Sunny', he married Consuelo Vanderbilt in 1896. They lived at Blenheim Castle, and had two sons: **John**, 10th Duke (1897–1972) and **Ivor** (1898–1956). They divorced in 1921 and the marriage was annulled in 1926.

Squith Nickname for H.H. Asquith.

Stanley, Oliver Frederick George (1896–1950) Conservative MP, Minister of various departments of government from 1933–1945. He married Maureen Helen Vane-Tempest-Stewart (1900–1942), daughter of 7th Marquess of Londonderry, in 1920. Norah designed their gardens at Halecat House, Cumbria.

Stanley of Alderley, Sylvia, Lady (Sylvia Ashley; born Edith Louisa Hawkes) (1904–1977) Actress, model, and society beauty. She married five times: first, in 1927, Anthony, Lord Ashley, divorced 1934; second, in 1936 Douglas Fairbanks (Sr.) he died 1939; third, in 1944, Edward John**,** 6th Baron Stanley of Alderley (who was himself married four times), divorced 1948; fourth, in 1949, Clark Gable, divorced 1952; fifth, in 1954, racing-car driver Prince Dimitri Djordjadze.

Stark, Dame Freya (1893–1993) Writer and Middle East explorer and traveller.

Stephanie, Princess of Belgium (1864–1945) Daughter of Leopold II, King of Belgium; married Crown Prince Rudolf (1858–1889), only son of Emperor Franz Joseph I of Austria in 1881. The marriage was unhappy, producing only one child, Archduchess Elisabeth (1883–1963). In 1889, Prince Rudolph (aged 31) committed suicide after killing his mistress, the beautiful young Baroness Mary Vetsera (aged 16) on January 30, 1889 at the royal hunting lodge in Mayerling. The murder/suicide or suicide/suicide was a mystery then and, to a large degree, remains so. Princess Stephanie married for a second time in 1900 to the Hungarian aristocrat, Count Elemer Lonyay de Nagy-Lonya et Vasaros-Nameny (1863–1946), Ambassador for Austro-Hungary in Paris. Norah designed gardens for the Princess at her castle Oroszvar, Hungary.

Stone, Marcus (1840–1921) Influential genre painter known for graceful, pretty, restful portraits.

Storrs, Sir Ronald (1881–1959) Close friend of T. E. Lawrence (Lawrence of Arabia) during the Arab Revolt 1914–1917. Governor of Jerusalem 1920–1926. Governor of Cyprus 1926–1932. Governor of Northern Rhodesia 1933–1934. Middle East Commentator and Lecturer 1934–1950.

Sykes, Christopher (1907–1986) English novelist, friend and biographer of Evelyn Waugh and Nancy Astor.

Thomas, Lloyd Norah designed his gardens near Swindon, Wiltshire.

Thynne, Henry Frederick, 6th Marquess of Bath (1905–1992) Married in 1927 to Daphne, daughter of 4th Baron Vivian. They divorced in 1953. Secondly married Virginia Parsons, daughter of Viola Tree. When Henry and Daphne – then Viscount and Viscountess Weymouth – were first married they lived at Greenaway where Norah designed the gardens. They then moved to Sturford Mead and lived on the property at Longleat.

Tilden, Philip (1887–1956) British architect. He executed Philip Sassoon's design for the fountains and terraces in the gardens at Port Lympne, Kent. He is known for his work at Chartwell, the home of Winston Churchill.

Tree, Ronald (1897–1976) American/British politician. Conservative MP 1933–1945. He was Marshall Field's first cousin. He married, first Nancy Perkins (*see* Nancy Lancaster), and second Marietta Peabody (1917–1991), in 1947. While married to Nancy, Tree leased Kelmarsh Hall, Northamptonshire, from Nancy's future husband, Juby Lancaster, and later bought Ditchley Park, Oxfordshire. Norah designed his gardens at Kelmarsh Hall and Ditchley Park.

Tree, Iris (Iris Moffat, Countess Ledebur) (1897–1968) Actress and poet. She was the daughter of actor-manager Sir Herbert Beerbohm Tree (1852–1917), and sister of Viola Tree.

Tree, Viola (Viola Parsons) (1884–1938) Stage and screen actress, best known for her portrayals of Shakespearean heroines. She was the oldest daughter of Sir Herbert Beerbohm Tree, and married Alan Parsons (1887–1933), drama critic and gossip columnist for the *Daily Sketch* and *Daily Mail*. Their daughter, Viola Parsons, became the second wife of the 6th Marquess of Bath.

Trefusis, Violet née Keppel (1894–1972) Writer. The daughter of Alice Keppel, she married Denys Trefusis in 1919 at the same time that she was having an affair with Vita Sackville-West.

Tritton, Robert Noted collector of fine art and antique furnishings. With his wife Elsie, he lived at Godmersham Park, Kent, an estate once owned by Jane Austen's brother, Edward Knight. Norah designed the gardens at Godmersham Park.

Trotter, Brig.-Gen. Gerald Frederic (b.1871) Known as 'G'. Trotter. Groom-in-Waiting and Extra Equerry of Edward VIII.

Tudor-Owen, Frederick Herbert Gordon Norah designed the gardens at Woodcote Manor, Hampshire for Captain Tudor-Owen and his wife, Elvira Maude.

Valery, Paul (1871–1945) Eminent French writer and poet.

Vanderbilt, Grace (1871–1953) Society hostess. Married to Cornelius Vanderbilt III, of the prominent American Vanderbilt family.

Vansittart, Robert Gilbert, Baron (1881–1957) Diplomat. Private Secretary first to Baldwin and then to Ramsay MacDonald 1928–1930; Permanent Under-Secretary in the Foreign Office, 1930–1938.

Villiers, Gerald Hyde (1882–1953) Diplomat. Nephew of Lord Clarendon, Emmie Bourke's second husband.

von Bismarck-Schonhausen, Otto Christian Archibald, Prince (1897–1975) German diplomat, grandson of the great German Chancellor; secretary to the German Embassy in London from 1928. He married Ann-Mari Tengbom with whom he had one child. Norah designed their gardens in Friedrichsruh, Germany.

von Hofmannsthal, Alice (born Ava Alice Muriel Astor) (1902–1956) American society hostess and patron of the arts. She was the only daughter of John Jacob Astor who was killed during the Titanic disaster, and was married four times, to: Prince Serge Obolensky, Czarist officer; Raimund von Hofmannsthal, Austrian writer; Philip Harding, British journalist; David Pleydell-Bouverie. She was a financial supporter and one of the few female lovers of Sir Frederick Ashton, who based a ballet on her character. Norah designed her gardens at Hanover Lodge, Regent's Park, London.

von Hofmannsthal, Raimund (1906–1974) Austrian writer who worked with the theatrical producer Max Reinhardt. He was the son of the poet Hugo von Hofmannsthal who wrote libretti for Richard Strauss. His first marriage was to Alice Astor; his second, in 1939 was to Lady Elizabeth Paget, daughter of the 6th Marquess of Anglesey.

Voronoff, Serge (1866–1951) Russian-born French experimenter in organ transplantation. His early experiments included transplanting thyroid glands from chimpanzees into humans with thyroid deficiencies. In 1920 his first 'monkeygland' transplantation took place with slices of chimpanzee testicles implanted into humans. He published a book, *Studies of Aging and Rejuvenation with Transplants* (1926) and by the early 1930s was treating thousands of men from around the world.

Wallace, Barbara (Barbi) (1898–1981) Daughter of Sir Edwin Lutyens. First married to Capt. the Rt. Hon. David Euan Wallace (1892–1941) in 1920. He became Minister of Transport in 1939. She later married Herbert Agar.

Wantage, Robert James Loyd-Lindsay, Baron (1832–1901) Philanthropist, who was awarded a VC in the Crimean War. He married heiress Sarah Loyd (1837–1920) in 1858. Lord Wantage was Harry Lindsay's cousin. His wedding gift to Harry was the deed to the Manor of Sutton Courtenay and his gift to Norah was £5,000.

Waugh, Evelyn (1903–1966) Novelist. Wrote *Brideshead Revisited* in 1945. Norah's long-time friend and frequent guest at her home at Sutton Courtenay.

Weir, William Douglas, 1st Viscount Weir (1877–1959). Scottish industrialist. During World War I produced explosive shells and in 1919 became Minister of Munitions. In 1925 he was appointed chairman of a committee to assess the United Kingdom's electrical power industry, whose conclusions led to the Electricity Act 1926 and the creation of the National Grid. He and his wife Alice, née MacConnachie (1879–1959), rented and lived in the Manor House of Sutton Courtenay in 1918.

Wellesley, Lord Gerald, 7th Duke of Wellington (1885–1972). Architect, diplomat and soldier; known for his expertise in the Regency period. He wrote Norah's obituary notice in 1948.

Weymouth *see* **Thynne**

Wharton, Edith née Jones (1861–1937) American novelist. Married in 1885 to Edward Wharton. Wrote *The Decoration of Houses* (1897), followed by 32 volumes of fiction, including the *House of Mirth* (1905), *Ethan Frome* (1911), and *The Age of Innocence* (1921). She had homes in New York, Massachusetts, and on the French Riviera at Hyeres. Norah and Edith shared common interests in books and gardening. Norah often spent time at Edith's home Sainte-Claire le Château in Hyeres. Edith wrote a portion of one of her novels while staying at Sutton Courtenay.

Whistler, Rex (Reginald John) (1905–1944) Celebrated mural and *trompe l'oeil* painter and book illustrator. He was painting both at Haddon Hall

when Harry was restoring the woodwork, and at Port Lympne and Mottisfont Abbey when Norah was working in those gardens. He was a welcome guest at Sutton Courtenay. He died leading his troop into action in Normandy.

Whistler, Sir Laurence (1912–2000) Rex Whistler's younger brother. Poet, architectural historian and glass engraver.

Whitbread, Humphrey (1912–2000) Barrister, son of Samuel Howard Whitbread and Madeline Bourke. Norah's nephew. He lived in London and owned a country house in Bedfordshire not far from his parents home at Southill Park.

Whitbread, Madeline Emmie Louisa née Bourke (1878–1961) Norah's younger sister. She saved all the letters that she received from her siblings and mother, had them transcribed, and bound in leather volumes each year. Madeline married (Samuel) **Howard Whitbread** (1858–1944), heir to the Whitbread brewery business, in 1904. He was an MP from 1892–1895 and from 1906–1910, Chairman of Bedfordshire County Council for 44 years, Lord Lieutenant of Bedfordshire 1912–1936, and Chairman Whitbread & Co. Ltd. 1916–1944. They lived at Southill Park in Bedfordshire.

Willmott, Ellen (1858–1934) Horticulturist, gardener, and author. Lived at Warley Place, Essex. She sponsored plant-hunting expeditions, and wrote the two volume *Genus Rosa* (1910–1914). She was awarded the Victoria Medal of Honour by the Royal Horticultural Society in 1897, and was admitted to the fellowship of the Linnean Society in 1905. She had many species of plant named after her, and had the habit of scattering seed of the silvery-blue *Eryngium giganteum* where she visited, earning the thistle the name of Miss Willmott's Ghost.

Wills, Sir Ernest Salter 3rd Bart. (1869–1958). Director of the family tobacco business firstly the H. O. Wills Company, then Imperial Tobacco Company.

Wimborne, Alice, Lady (born Alice Katherine Sibell Grosvenor) (1880 –1948) Married Ivor Churchill Guest, 1st Viscount Wimborne (1873–1939). She lived with famed British composer William Walton, 22 years her junior.

Winn, Elizabeth Susan (1925–) Nancy Lancaster's niece.

Woodhouse, Violet Gordon (born Violet Kate Eglinton Gwynne) (1871–1948) Leading harpsichord and clavichord player. Her salon included Picasso, Diaghilev, Rodin, and T. E. Lawrence. Norah advised on the plantings for her gardens at Nether Lypiatt Manor, Gloucestershire.

BIBLIOGRAPHY

MANUSCRIPT SOURCES CONSULTED

Alston Family Archives: Daisy Alston scrapbooks and photographs.

Bilecki Family Archives: Tritton family photographs.

British Library – Oriental and India Office Collections: Bourke records.

Carter Family Archives: Carter family scrapbooks and photographs.

Penelope Dare Family Collection: Bourke letters, diaries, and scrapbooks.

Gleneagles: archival photographs.

The Grove: archives and photographs.

Hampshire Records Office: Mottisfont Abbey Archives; Woodcote Manor Archives; Hillier Nursery Archives.

Hertfordshire Archives & Local Studies: Grenfell family; Desborough; Charteris Archives.

Houghton Hall Archives: papers of Philip Sassoon.

John F. Kennedy Library Foundation: photograph of Stéphane Boudin from the papers of Jacqueline Bouvier Kennedy.

King's College, London: Ian and Jean Hamilton personal correspondence.

Lindley Library of the Royal Horticultural Society: National Garden Schemes Collection; Hillier Nursery catalogues.

David Lindsay Family Collection: Lindsay letters, diaries, and scrapbooks.

Mells Manor House and Lord Oxford and Asquith Archives: letters, diaries, and scrapbooks.

John Menzies & Co., Archives: Charles Cuthbert Menzies and John Menzies papers.

National Portrait Gallery, London: Lady Ottoline Morrell Collection.

National Records Office, London – Wills, Birth, Death, Marriage Certificates: Lindsay, Bourke, Johnston.

National Trust, London: National Trust Photo Library.

Natural History Museum, London: herbarium specimens and travel logs – Nancy Lindsay.

Oxford University, Rhodes House: Rhodes House Archives.

Reading University: Nancy Astor Papers – personal correspondence.

Sir Jervoise and Lady Scott, Rotherfield Park Archives: Letters, diaries, and crapbooks.

Smithsonian Institution Archives and Manuscripts: Archives of American Gardens.

State Protocol Services of the Republic of Slovenia: Brdo Castle.

John Sunley, Esq., Godmersham Park: Current and archival photographs.

Samuel and Jane Whitbread, Southill Park Archives: Whitbread; Bourke; Lindsay; Letters, diaries, and crapbooks

Yale University Beinecke Rare Book and Manuscript Library, Yale Collection of American Literature: Edith Wharton Collection

SECONDARY SOURCES

Abdy, Jane and Charlotte Gere, *The Souls* (Sidgwick & Jackson, London, 1984).

Alsop, Susan Mar, *To Marietta from Paris 1945–1960* (Weidenfeld and Nicolson, London, 1976, and Doubleday & Company, Inc., New York, 1975).

A Memoir of Chirk Castle (Chirk: Chirk Castle, 1923).

Amory, Mark, *Lord Berners: The Last Eccentric* (Chatto & Windus, London, 1998).

Aronson, Theo, *The King in Love*, (HarperCollins, London, and Harper & Row, Publishers, New York, 1988).

Asquith, Cynthia, *Remember and Be Glad* (Weidenfeld & Nicolson, London, 1995, and Charles Scribner's Sons, New York, 1952).

Asquith, Margot, *Margot Asquith An Autobiography* (George H, Doran Company, New York, 1920).

Astor, Michael, *Tribal Feeling* (John Murray, London, 1964),

Balfour, Neil, and Sally Mackay, *Paul of Yugoslavia: Britain's Maligned Friend* (Hamish Hamilton, London, 1980).

Balsan, Consuelo Vanderbilt, *The Glitter and The Gold* (George Mann, Maidstone, 1973).

Bantock, G.H., *L.H. Myers A Critical Study,* (University College Leicester and Jonathan Cape, London,1956).

Beaton, Cecil, *The Glass of Fashion* (Weidenfeld and Nicolson, London, 1954).

Becker, Robert, *Nancy Lancaster: Her Life, Her World, Her Art* (Alfred A. Knopf, New York, 1996).

Bennett, Daphne, *Margot: A Life of the Countess of Oxford & Asquith* (Franklin Watts, New York, 1985).

Blanchan, Neltje, *Nature's Garden* (Doubleday, Page & Co., New York, 1901).

Blanchan, Neltje, *The American Flower-Garden* (Doubleday, Page & Company, New York, 1909).

Bloch, Michael, ed. *Wallis and Edward: Letters 1931–1937* (Summit Books, New York, 1986).

Bonham Carter, Mark, *The Autobiography of Margot Asquith* (Eyre and Spottiswoode, London, 1962, and Houghton Mifflin Company, Boston, 1963).

Boothby, Robert, *I Fight to Live* (Victor Gollancz Ltd., London, 1947).

Boyd, Lizzie Edmunds, *England: Her People and Her Gardens* (Bruce Humphries, Inc., Boston, 1940).

Bradley-Hole, Kathryn, *Villa Gardens of the Mediterranean* (Aurum Press, London, 2006).

Brock, Michael and Eleanor, ed. *H.H. Asquith, Letters to Venetia Stanley* (Oxford University Press, Oxford and New York, 1982).

Brown, Jane, *Eminent Gardeners: Some People of Influence and their Gardens 1880–1980* (Viking, London, 1990).

Burke's Peerage & Baronetage (Burke's Peerage Genealogical Books, Ltd., Switzerland, 1999).

Butler, Iris, *The Viceroy's Wife: Letters of Alice, Countess of Reading, from India, 1921–1925* (Hodder and Stoughton, London, 1969).

Chatfield, Judith, *The Classic Italian Garden* (Rizzoli International Publications, Inc., New York, 1991).

Chatfield, Judith *A Tour of Italian Gardens* (Rizzoli International Publications, Inc., New York, 1988).

Chisholm, Anne, *Nancy Cunard* (Sidgwick and Jackson, London, and Alfred A. Knopf, Inc., New York, 1979).

Chittenden, Fred J., and Patrick M. Synge, eds. *The Royal Horticultural Society Dictionary of Gardening* (Oxford University Press, Oxford, 1956).

Clarke, Ethne, *Hidcote* (Michael Joseph, London, 1989).

Coats, Peter, *Flowers in History* (The Viking Press, New York, 1970).

Coats, Peter, *Great Gardens of the Western World* (G. P. Putnam's Sons, New York, 1963).

Cooper, Diana, *The Light of Common Day* (Rupert Hart-Davis, London, 1959).

Cooper, Lady Diana, *The Rainbow Comes and Goes* (Rupert Hart-Davis, London, and Houghton Mifflin, Boston, 1958).

Cooper, Duff, *Old Men Forget: The Autobiography of Duff Cooper* (Rupert Hart-Davis, London, 1953).

Cornforth, John, *The Inspiration of the Past* (Viking in association with Country Life, London and New York, 1985).

Cornforth, John *The Search For A Style: Country Life and Architecture 1897–1935* (André Deutsch in association with Country Life, London).

Country Life Library, ed. *Gardens Old & New: The Country House & Its Garden Environment* (Country Life Ltd., London)

Crathorne, James, *Cliveden: The Place and the People* (Collins & Brown, London, 1995).

Curzon of Kedleston, Marquess, *A Viceroy's India: Leaves From Lord Curzon's Note-Book* (Sidgwick & Jackson, London, 1984).

Curzon of Kedleston, Marquess, *Tales of Travel* (Hodder and Stoughton, London, 1923).

De Courcy, Anne, *The Viceroy's Daughters: The Lives of the Curzon Sisters* (Weidenfeld and Nicolson, London, and William Morrow, New York, 2000).

Desmond, Ray, *Bibliography of British Gardens,* (St. Paul's Bibliographies, Winchester, 1988).

Donaldson, Frances, *Edward VIII: A Biography of the Duke of Windsor* (Weidenfeld and Nicolson, London, and J.B. Lippincott Company, Philadelphia, 1974).

Douglas-Home, Jessica, *Violet: The Life and Loves of Violet Gordon Woodhouse* (The Harvill Press, London, 1996).

du Colombier, Pierre *Le Château de France: son Histoire, Sa Vie, Ses Habitants* (Librairie Artheme Fayard, Paris, 1960).

Dwight, Eleanor, *Edith Wharton An Extraordinary Life* (Harry N. Abrams, Inc., New York, 1994).

Eden, Frederic, *A Garden in Venice* (London: Frances Lincoln, 2003).

Edwardes, Michael, *The Last Years of British India* (Cassell, London, and The World Publishing Company, Cleveland, OH, 1963).

Fielding, Daphne, *Mercury Presides* (Eyre and Spottiswoode, London, 1954).

Fielding, Daphne, *Those Remarkable Cunards: Emerald and Nancy* (Eyre and Spottiswoode, London, and Atheneum, New York, 1968).

Fleming, John *Spring and Winter Flower Gardening: The System of Floral Decoration as Practised at Cliveden, The Seat of Her Grace Harriet Duchess of Sutherland* (Journal of Horticulture and Cottage Gardener Office, London, 1864).

Fletcher, John, *Sutton Courtenay: The History of a Thames-Side Village* (The Friends of All Saints' Church, Sutton Courtenay, 1995).

Foreman, John, and Robbe Pierce Stimson *The Vanderbilts and the Gilded Age: Architectural Aspirations 1879–1901* (St. Martin's Press, New York, 1991).

Fowler, Marian, *In a Gilded Cage: From Heiress to Duchess* (Vintage Books, Toronto, 1993).

Fulford, Roger, *Samuel Whitbread 1764-1815 A Study in Opposition* (Macmillan, London, 1967).

Fullerton, Alice, *To Persia For Flowers* (Oxford University Press, Oxford, 1938).

Gardiner, Leslie, *The Making of John Menzies* (John Menzies plc., Edinburgh, 1983).

Gathorne-Hardy, Robert, ed. *Ottoline at Garsington: Memoirs of Lady Ottoline Morrell 1915–1918* (Faber and Faber, London, 1974, and Alfred A. Knopf, New York, 1975).

Girouard, Mark *Life in the English Country House* (Yale University Press, New Haven and London, 1978).

Gregory, Alexis, *Families of Fortune: Life in the Gilded Age* (The Vendome Press, New York, 1993).

Harrison, Rosina, *Rose: My Life in Service.* (Cassell, London, and The Viking Press, New York, 1975).

Hassall, Christopher, *Edward Marsh, Patron of the Arts* (Longman, London, 1959), *A Biography of Edward Marsh* (Harcourt, Brace and Company, New York,1959).

Heilbrun, Carolyn G., ed. *Lady Ottoline's Album.* (Michael Joseph, London, and Alfred A. Knopf, New York, 1976).

Hibbert, Christopher, *Edward The Uncrowned King* (MacDonald and Co., London, and St. Martin's Press, New York, 1972).

Horner, Frances, *Time Remembered* (William Heinemann Ltd., London, 1933).

Horsley, E. M., ed. *Lady Cynthia Asquith Diaries 1915–1918.* (Alfred A. Knopf, New York, 1969).

Howard de Walden, Margherita, *Pages From My Life*, (Sidgwick and Jackson, London, 1965).

Hussey, Christopher, *English Country Houses Open to the Public* (Country Life Limited, London, 1951).

Hussey, Christopher and John Cornforth, *English Country Houses: Open To The Public* (Country Life Ltd., London, 1964).

Hyams, Edward, *The English Garden* (Thames and Hudson, London: 1964).

Izzard, Molly, *Freya Stark: A Biography* (Hodder & Stoughton, London, 1993).

Jackson, Stanley, *The Sassoons* (William Heinemann, London, and E.P. Dutton & Co., Inc., New York, 1968).

James, Robert Rhodes, ed., *Chips: The Diaries of Sir Henry Channon* (Weidenfeld and Nicolson, London, 1967).

Jekyll, Gertrude *Wall and Water Gardens* (Antique Collector's Club, London, 1994, and Charles Scribner's Sons, New York, 1901).

Jekyll, Gertrude, *Wood and Garden* (Longmans, Green, and Co., London, 1899).

Jekyll, Gertrude, *Colour In The Flower Garden* (Country Life, Ltd., London, 1908).

Jekyll, Gertrude *Lilies For English Gardens* (Country Life, Ltd., London, 1903).

Jekyll, Gertrude, *Roses For English Gardens* (Country Life, Ltd., London, 1902).

Jekyll, Gertrude and Lawrence Weaver, *Gardens For Small Country Houses* (Country Life, Ltd., London, 1912).

Joliffe, John *Raymond Asquith Life and Letters* (Collins, London, 1980).

Jones, Louisa *Gardens of the French Riviera.* (Flammarion, Paris, 1994).

Jullian, Philippe, and John Phillips *Violet Trefusis: A Biography* (Harcourt Brace Jovanovich, Publishers, New York, 1976).

Kavaler, Lucy, *The Astors: A Family Chronicle of Pomp and Power.*(IUniverse.com, Lincoln, NE, 2000).

Keppel, Sonia, *Edwardian Daughter* (Hamish Hamilton, London, 1958).

Kingdon-Ward, Frank, *Plant Hunting on the Edge of the World* (Minerva, London, 1974).

Lambert, Angela, *Unquiet Souls: The Indian Summer of the British Aristocracy, 1880–1918* (Macmillan, London, 1984).

Langhorne, Elizabeth *Nancy Astor and Her Friends* (Praeger Publishers, New York, 1974).

Le Blond, Mrs. Aubrey, *The Old Gardens of Italy* (Dodd, Mead and Company, New York, 1926).

Lecomber, Tessa, *The Barker-Mill Story: A Hampshire family since the 16th century* (the Trustees of the Barker-Mill Family, Hampshire, 2000).

Le Lievre, Audrey, *Miss Wilmott of Warley Place: Her Life and Her Gardens* (Faber and Faber, London, 1980).

Le Moyne, Louis Valcoulon, *Country Residences in Europe and America* (Doubleday, Page & Company, New York, 1908).

Lees-Milne, James, *Ancestral Voices* (Chatto & Windus, London, 1975).

Lees-Milne, James, *Diaries 1942–1954,* abridged and introduced by Michael Bloch (John Murray, London, 2006).

Lovell, Mary S., *The Sisters: The Saga of the Mitford Family* (W. W. Norton & Company, New York, 2002).

Lewis, R.W.B., *Edith Wharton: A Biography* (Harper & Row, Publishers, New York, 1975).

Lindsay, W.A., *Q.C. The Royal Household 1837– 1897* (Kegan Paul, Trench, Trubner & Co., Ltd., London, 1898).

MacCarthy, Desmond *Lord Oxford's Letters to a Friend: Second Series. 1922–1927* (Geoffrey Bles, London, 1934).

MacMillan, Margaret, *Paris 1919* (Random House, New York, 2001).

Madsen, Axel, *The Marshall Fields* (John Wiley & Sons, Inc., New York, 2002).

Marsh, Edward, *A Number of People: A Book of Reminiscences* (Heinemann, London, and Harper & Brothers Publishers, New York, 1939).

Martineau, Mrs. Philip, *Gardening in Sunny Lands: The Riviera, California, Australia* (Richard Cobden-Sanderson, London, 1924).

Maxwell, Sir Herbert, *Scottish Gardens* (Edward Arnold, London, 1908).

McLeod, Kirsty, *A Passion for Friendship: Sibyl Colefax and Her Circle* (Michael Joseph, London, 1991).

Menzies, John & Co., Ltd., ed., *The House of Menzies* (John Menzies & Co., Ltd., Edinburgh, 1958).

Meyers, Jeffrey, *Somerset Maugham: A Life* (Alfred A. Knopf, New York, 2004).

Mosley, Nicholas, *Julian Grenfell: His Life and The Times of His Death 1888–1915* (Weidenfeld and Nicolson, London, 1976).

Murray, John, *Murray's Handbook for Travellers in Oxfordshire with Maps and Plans* (John Murray, London, 1894).

Murray, John, *Murray's Handbook for Travellers in Somerset with Maps and Plans* (John Murray, London, 1899).

Nicolson, Nigel, ed., *Harold Nicolson Diaries and Letters 1930–1939* (Collins, London, 1966).

Nicolson, Nigel, *Great Houses of Britain* (Weidenfeld & Nicolson, London, 1965).

Nicolson, Nigel, *The World of Jane Austen* (Weidenfeld & Nicolson, London, 1991).

Norwich, John Julius, *The Architecture of Southern England* (Macmillan, London, 1985).

Norwich, John Julius, ed., *The Duff Cooper Diaries* (Weidenfeld & Nicolson, London, 2005).

Page, Russell, *The Education of a Gardener* (William Collins Sons & Co., Ltd., London, 1962).

Patterson, Jerry E., *The Vanderbilts* (Harry N. Abrams, Inc., Publishers, New York, 1989).

Pearce, James, *Old Thunder: A Life of Hilaire Belloc* (Ignatius Press, London, 2002).

Pearson, John, *Façades: Edith, Osbert, and Sacheverell Sitwell,* (Macmillan London Limited, London, 1978).

Perouse de Montclos, Jean-Marie, *Vaux le Vicomte* (Editions Scala, Paris, 1997).

Phillips, John, Peter Quennell and Lorna Sage, eds. *The Last Edwardians: An Illustrated History of Violet Trefusis & Alice Keppel* (The Boston Athenaeum, Boston, 1985).

Racine, Michel, Ernest J-P. Boursier-Mougenot, and Francoise Binet, *The Gardens of Provence and the French Riviera* (The MIT Press, Cambridge, Massachusetts, 1987).

Ramsay, Alex and Attlee, Helena *Italian Gardens* (Robertson McCarta Limited, London, 1989).

Robinson, William, *The English Flower Garden* (John Murray, London, 1883).

Rockley, The Lady, *Historic Gardens of England* (Country Life Ltd., London: 1938).

Rohde, Eleanour Sinclair, *Oxford's College Gardens* (Herbert Jenkins, London, 1932).

Roper, Lanning, *The Gardens in the Royal Park at Windsor* (Chatto and Windus, London, and Doubleday & Company, Inc., New York, 1959).

Rowe, Rev. A.D. *Every-Day Life in India* (American Tract Society, New York, 1881).

Russell, Vivian, *Gardens of the Riviera* (Little, Brown and Company, Boston, 1993).

Sackville-West, Vita, *English Country Houses* (Collins, London, 1947).

Sassoon, Philip, *The Third Route* (Doubleday, Doran & Company, Inc., New York, 1929).

Scott, Geoffrey, *The Portrait of Zelide* (Constable & Co., London, 1925).

Seebohm, Caroline, *No Regrets: The Life of Marietta Tree* (Simon & Schuster, New York, 1997).

Shewell-Cooper, W.E., *The Royal Gardeners* (Cassell & Company Ltd., London, 1952).

Singer, Anne, *Paul Maze: The Lost Impressionist* (Arum Press, London, 1983).

Sitwell, Osbert, *Laughter in the Next Room* (Macmillan & Co. Ltd, London, 1949).

Speaight, Robert, *The Life of Hilaire Belloc: The Authorized Biography* (Farrar, Strauss & Cudahy, New York, 1957).

Stansky, Peter, *Sassoon: The Worlds of Philip and Sybil* (Yale University Press, New Haven and Lonon, 2003).

Stasz, Clarice, *The Vanderbilt Women* (iUniverse.com, Lincoln, NE, 1991).

Strong, Roy, *Royal Gardens* (Conran Octopus, London, and Pocket Books, New York, 1992).

Stuart, Amanda Mackenzie, *Consuelo and Alva Vanderbilt* (HarperCollins, London, 2005).

Sykes, Christopher, *Nancy: The Life of Lady Astor* (Collins, London, and Harper & Row, Publishers, New York, 1972).

Synge, Patrick M., ed., *The Royal Horticultural Society Supplement To The Dictionary of Gardening* (Oxford University Press, Oxford, 1969).

Thomas, Graham Stuart, *Cuttings from My Garden Notebooks* (John Murray, London, and Sagapress, Inc., New York, 1997).

Tilden, Philip, *True Remembrances: The Memoirs of an Architect* (Country Life Ltd., London, 1954).

Tree, Ronald, *When the Moon Was High: Memoirs of Peace and War 1897 – 1942* (Macmillan, London, 1975).

Trefusis, Violet, *Don't Look Round* (Hutchinson, London, 1952).

Tyack, Geoffrey, *Cliveden and the Astor Household Between the Wars* (Geoffrey Tyack, Henley-on-Thames, 1982).

Valery, Marie-Francoise, Angelika Taschen, Deidi von Schaewen, and Chris Miller, *Gardens of Provence and the Cote d'Azur* (Benedikt Taschen Verlag, Koln, 1998).

Vanderbilt, Arthur T., *Fortune's Children: The Fall of the House of Vanderbilt* (William Morrow, New York, 1989).

Von Arnim, Elizabeth, *The Enchanted April* (Doubleday, Page & Company, New York, 1924).

Wantage, Lady, *Lord Wantage, V.C., K.C.B.: A Memoir by His Wife* (Smith, Elder & Co., London, 1907).

Webber, Ronald, *Percy Cane Garden Designer* (John Bartholomew & Son Ltd., London, 1975).

Whistler, Laurence, *The Laughter and the Urn: The Life of Rex Whistler* (Weidenfeld and Nicolson, London, 1985).

Williamson, Mrs. Harcourt, ed., *The Book of Beauty: (Late Victorian Era) A Collection of Beautiful Portraits with Literary, Artistic, and Musical Contributions of the Men and Women of the Day.* (Hutchinson & Co, London, 1896).

Windsor, H.R.H. Edward, Duke of, *A King's Story: the Memoirs of The Duke of Windsor* (Cassell and Co., London, and G.P. Putnam's Sons, New York, 1947).

Wood, Martin, *Nancy Lancaster: English Country House Style* (Frances Lincoln, London, 2005).

Ziegler, Philip, *Osbert Sitwell* (Chatto and Windus, London, 1998, and Alfred A. Knopf, New York, 2000).

PERIODICALS AND BROCHURES

'The Gardens at Blickling, Norfolk.' *Country Life* (1910).

'A Riviera Garden, Lou Sueil.' *Country Life* 63 (1928): 900–903.

'The Borders At Trent Park.' *Country Life* 72 (1932): 65.

'The Hardy Flower Border. Flowers For Early Autumn Planting.' *Country Life* 74 (1933): 322–324.

'The Manor House, Sutton Courtenay, Berks. The Residence of Capt. H. Lindsay.' *Country Life* 15 (1904): 198–204.

'The Singularly Choice Freehold Residential Properties Comprising The Manor of Sutton Courtenay.' Hampton & Sons Real Estate Sales Circular (1920): 1–26.

Cox, E.H.M., 'Lou Sueil – I. Eze, A.M. the Residence of Colonel and Mme. Balsan.' *Country Life* 61 (1927): 208–214.

Cox, E.H.M., 'Lou Sueil – II. Eze, A.M. the Residence of Colonel and Mme. Balsan. *Country Life* 61 (1927): 244–252.

E.C., 'A Riviera Garden. Sainte-Claire Le Château, Hyères.' *Country Life* 64 (1928): 610–613.

Doree, Stephen, 'Trent Park. A Short History to 1939.' Dr. Stephen G. Doree, 1974.

Hussey, Christopher, 'A Bathing Pool in the Garden.' *Country Life* 74 (1933) 184–186.

Hussey, Christopher, 'Blickling Hall – I. Norfolk. A Seat of The Marquess of Lothian.' *Country Life* 67 (1930): 814–821.

Hussey, Christopher, 'Blickling Hall – II. Norfolk. A Seat of The Marquess of Lothian.' *Country Life* 67 (1930): 902–908.

Hussey, Christopher, 'Blickling Hall – III. Norfolk. A Seat of The Marquess of Lothian.' *Country Life* 67 (1930): 936–940.

Hussey, Christopher, 'Cliveden – I. Bucks. The Seat of Lord Astor.' *Country Life* 70 (1931): 38–44.

Hussey, Christopher, 'Godmersham Park, Kent – I. The Home of Mr. and Mrs. Robert Tritton.' *Country Life* 97 (1945): 288–291.

Hussey, Christopher, 'Godmersham Park, Kent – III. The Home of Mr. and Mrs. Robert Tritton.' *Country Life* 97 (1945): 376–379.

Hussey, Christopher, 'The Manor House – II. Sutton Courtenay, Berks. The Property of Col. Harry Lindsay.' *Country Life* 69 (1931): 646–652.

Hussey, Christopher, 'Mottisfont Abbey, Hampshire – I.' *Country Life* 115 (1954): 1310–1313.

Hussey, Christopher, 'Mottisfont Abbey, Hampshire – II.' *Country Life* 115 (1954): 1398–1401.

J.Y., 'Planning the Herbaceous Border.' *Country Life* 66 (1929): lix–lxi.

Landsberg, A.C., 'An Historic Italian Villa: Malcontenta – I Venice. The Residence of Mr. A.C. Landsberg.' *Country Life* 82 (1937): 396–401.

Landsberg, A. C., 'An Historic Italian Villa: Malcontenta – II Venice. The Residence of Mr. A. C. Landsberg.' *Country Life* 82 (1937): 420–425.

Lindsay, Norah, 'Planning The Spring Garden.' *Vogue House & Garden Book* (1929): 21, 48.

Lindsay, Norah, 'Where Is Spring?' *Country Life* 65 (1929): 387–390.

Lindsay, Norah, 'The Garden In July.' *Country Life* 66 (1929): 78–80.

Lindsay, Norah, 'The Manor House – I. Sutton Courtenay, Berks. The Residence of Mrs. Harry Lindsay.' *Country Life* 69 (1931): 610–616.

Oswald, Arthur, 'Bretton Park – I. Yorkshire. The Seat of Viscount Allendale.' *Country Life* 83 (1938): 530–535.

Oswald, Arthur, 'Great Swifts, Cranbrook, Kent. The Seat of Major Victor A. Cazalet, M.C., M.P.' *Country Life*, 86 (1939): 524–528.

Oswald, Arthur, 'Kelmarsh Hall, Northamptonshire. The Property of Capt. C.G. Lancaster.' *Country Life* 73 (1933): 198–203.

Simms, Barbara, 'Perfection of Their Kind: Notes on Sir Philip Sassoon's Gardens at Trent Park.' The London Gardener or The Gardener's Intelligencer For the Years 2000–01. *Journal of the London Historic Parks and Gardens Trust* 6 (70–77).

Taylor, G. C., 'Late Summer In The Garden.' *Country Life* 72 (1932): 285–287.

Taylor, G. Crosbie, 'The Garden at Port Lympne.' *Country Life* 66 (1929) 513–517.

Taylor, G.C., 'The Garden at Port Lympne. Hythe, Kent. A Residence of Sir Philip Sassoon, Bt.' *Country Life* 79 (1936): 276–282.

Tipping, H. Avray, 'Early Summer at Hidcote Manor.' *Country Life* 68 (1930): 231–233.

Tipping, H. Avray, 'Mells Manor House, Somerset. The Seat of Sir John Horner.' *Country Life* 42 (1917): 444–450.

Windsor, H.R.H. The Duke of, 'My Garden. By H.R.H. The Duke of Windsor.' *Life* Magazine. (1956): 62–78.

W. S., 'Balcarres, Fifeshire. The Seat of The Earl of Crawford.' *Country Life* 12 (1902): 176–186.

INDEX

AUTHOR'S ACKNOWLEDGMENTS

One of the benefits of writing this book was getting to know many members of Norah Lindsay's current extended family, all of whom I now consider to be among my own circle of friends. I wish to express my sincere thanks to these family members who so generously opened their homes and archives to me and without whose assistance this book would not have been possible: Sam and Jane Whitbread; David and Sarah Lindsay and their children Jack, Alice, and Charlie; and Penelope and George Dare.

To the owners of Norah's home at the Manor House of Sutton Courtenay, past and present, I am most grateful. Thanks to the past owner, the Hon. David Astor for his hospitality and his spellbinding memories of Norah –what she looked like, what she sounded like, and how her house and gardens appeared in her day. To the present owners, Anthony and Penelope Warne, thanks too for their continued hospitality and openness to share the history of the house and gardens at Sutton Courtenay. To the gardeners who have continued to till the soil at Sutton Courtenay, thanks to Keith Deane and Inara Gipsle. To those who have had an active administrative connection to the house, thanks to Kebede Berhanu and Pat Hepburn Porter. And across the street, to the Reverend Helen Kendrick, vicar at All Saints Church in Sutton Courtenay, who helped me in the search for Norah's grave.

To the descendants of those who assisted Norah in her everyday life, her maids and gardeners, I owe thanks for their memories and family stories: Joan Carter, Janet Barnard, and Elizabeth Hemingway.

I am indebted to the owners of the grand estates where Norah once worked who allowed me to roam their properties, ask them endless questions, and who offered up their archives for my research: The Earl of Oxford and Asquith, Mells Manor House, Somerset; The Marquess of Cholmondeley, Houghton Hall, Norfolk; Sir James and Judy Scott, Rotherfield Park, Hampshire; Mr. and Mrs. John B. Sunley, Godmersham Park, Kent; Mr. and Mrs. Charles Philipps, Dalham Hall, Suffolk; Sofka Zinovieff, Faringdon Hall, Oxfordshire; Mr. and Mrs. David Hamilton, St. Georges-Motel, France; Princess Elizabeth Karageorgevic, Bled Castle.

The history of these great estates was not only told to me by their owners, but also by dozens of archivists, gardeners, and administrators who shared their time and knowledge in helping me uncover the secrets of Norah Lindsay's past, especially James Collett-White, the archivist at Southill Park who spent weeks helping me sift through the letters and diaries of Norah and her siblings. Others who have been immensely helpful during this research include Michael McGarvie, archivist at Mells Manor House; David Yaxley, archivist at Houghton Hall who helped me with the Sassoon archives; Susan Cleever, administrator at Houghton Hall; Lou Elderton, archivist, for her hospitality and superb research at Rotherfield Park; Steve Barton and Jenny Cooper, head gardeners, and Vince Eastwood and Anita Robson, chauffeur and chef who transported me to and fro, and who fed me while at Godmersham Park; Mr. and Mrs. Frank Bilecki for their photographs and memories of the Trittons at Godmersham Park; Paul Underwood, head gardener, Anna Johns, house steward, and Richard Lee, marketing and events assistant at Blickling Hall; Lucy Scurfield who, while still a student in garden conservation at the Architectural Association in London, sent me invaluable information about the gardens at Blickling Hall; David Locke, head gardener, Chirk Castle; Katie Fretwell, garden historian, and Jane Clarke, administrator for the National Trust; Philip Cotton, head gardener, Cliveden; Keith Goodway, trustee, and Nick Burton, head gardener at Kelmarsh Hall; Trevor King, head gardener, Port Lympne; Michael Hughes, archivist and David Manktelow, head gardener, Rhodes House; Glyn Jones, head gardener, David Owen and Peter Dennis, assistant gardeners, Hidcote; Barry Futter, Mottisfont Abbey; John Knowles for his in-depth knowledge of Ned Lathom; Jonathan Leiserach for his findings on Fort Belvedere; Katharine Walsh at The Grove, and Simon Brown at Gleneagles; and Gordon McVinnie, archivist for the John Menzies Company. I wish to thank my friend, Roger Phillips, for his expertise in the difficult task of photographing an almost life sized painting by Harrington Mann of a very young and beautiful Norah Lindsay.

Staff members at several libraries were of considerable assistance and deserve thanks: David Rymill, archivist, Hampshire Record Office for putting all the pieces of the story together on Mottisfont Abbey; Michael Bott, archivist, Reading University Library, Papers of Nancy Astor; Alan Kucia, archivist, King's College London; Dr. Kate Harris, Librarian and Archivist to the Marquess of Bath, Longleat Library; Jennifer Quan and Carolyn Kennedy Schlosberg, John F. Kennedy Library Foundation; and Camilla Costello at Country Life Picture Library and her dedicated staff, especially Lara Platman and Paula Fahey. I am indebted to Roy Vickery and Susan Snell, archivists at the Natural History Museum, London for their assistance in my research on Nancy Lindsay's trips to Persia; John Grimshaw for his knowledge of plants found during Nancy Lindsay's trips to Persia; and to Dee Simmons, Elizabeth Parker-Jervis, Dr. and Mrs. P. F. Barwood, and Mr. and Mrs. Wrangy Kandiah for their memories of Nancy Lindsay.

Friends and fellow historians who offered up bits and traces of information and to whom I am indebted because they encouraged me to find the answers to Norah's life include: Judith Tankard, Barbara Simms, and Martin Wood. Thanks also to Charles Quest-Ritson and Kathryn Bradley-Hole for their help in my searches for information about Norah's gardens on the Continent.

While I was unaccompanied on most of my trips traversing the byways and backroads of England in search of Norah's various gardens, I am most appreciative for the assistance from my sister, Jeanne Morris, and from my friend, Debbie Thornton, who joined me on separate occasions to act as my research assistants, all the while guiding me with their map-reading skills and providing entertaining companionship along the way.

Thanks to the staff at Frances Lincoln, who have also been added to my circle of friends, especially, Jo Christian and Sarah Mitchell, my editors; and Anne Wilson, who so skilfully designed the book. And finally, to my husband, Patrick Kareiva, who remained strongly supportive throughout the quest for the truth about Norah Lindsay. He endured my long research trips away from home, endless hours reading draft after draft of the chapters, and throughout acted as my business manager for the entire process.

My research is continuing on the life and work of Norah Lindsay, and on her daughter, Nancy. If you know of any other sources of information about either of them or their work, including archival letters, diaries, or photographs, please email: infoexchange@norahlindsay.com.

You may also visit the website www.norahlindsay.com at which you can obtain more information about Norah, and access a forum for exchanging information about her life, her gardens, and her clients.

PICTURE ACKNOWLEDGMENTS

For permission to reproduce the images below, the Publishers would like to thank the following:

Alston Family Archives: 67 all, 248

Astor Family Archives: 71, 150

Author's Own Collection: 10, 33, 108 below right, 109 below, 118, 119 above left, 127 lower right, 127 lower left, 128 lower left, 141 below, 143 all, 144 below, 145 below, 148, 152–153, 157, 159 above left, 159 all, 162 above left, 162 all, 163, 165 below left, 165 below right, 175, 178, 180 all,198 bottom left, 204, 205 all, 206 below, 207 below, 227 below, 238, 244 below

Bilecki Family Archives: 206 above, 207 above

British Library: 12

Carter Family Archives: 94 all, 95 all

Country Life Picture Library: 35, 39, 57 above, 80–81, 86 below, 86–87, 88, 89, 90, 91 all, 92–93, 96, 97, 98, 99 all, 100–101, 121 upper right, 127 above, 128 above, 130, 131 above, 142, 144 above, 145 above, 156, 158 all, 160, 174

Penelope Dare Family Collection: 13, 14 upper left, 14 upper right, 14 lower left, 15, 16 lower right, 17 upper left, 17 lower left, 18 upper right, 18 lower right, 19 upper right, 19 lower right, 20 below, 21 all, 22 above left, 22 above right, 24 above left, 24 above right, 25 above left, 25 above middle, 25 above right, 27 all, 31, 38 below, 41 below right, 43 below, 45 lower right, 46 below, 49 above, 49 lower right, 53 above, 56, 60 above, 62, 63

The Dorchester Hotel: 234 left, 234 right

Faringdon Archives: 70

The Gleneagles Hotel: 149 all

The Grove: 61 all

Hampshire Record Office. Mottisfont Abbey Archives: 198 above left, 198 bottom right, 199

Hampshire Record Office. Woodcote Manor Archives: 165 above

Hertfordshire Archives: 9 above

The Marquess of Cholmondeley, Houghton Hall Archives. From the papers of Philip Sassoon: Title Page, 75, 83, 84–85, 103, 121 upper left, 121 lower left, 121 lower right, 122, 132, 133, 134 all, 135 all, 136 all, 137, 138–139, 139 all, 141 above

John F. Kennedy Library Foundation: 214

Life Magazine: 171, 176

David Lindsay Family Collection: Cover, Frontispiece, 19 lower left, 24 lower left, 24 lower right, 25 below, 28 all, 29 all, 37 upper right, 38 above, 41 above, 41 below left, 42, 44 below, 44 upper left, 46 above, 47 all, 48, 49 lower left, 52 below, 53 below, 54 all, 55 all, 57 below, 59, 66, 73 below, 82, 237, 249

National Portrait Gallery, London: 51 left, 76, 211, 224

National Trust Photo Library: 112, 119 below, 119 above right, 125, 128 lower right, 131 below, 147, 154, 155, 198 above right, 226

Private collection: 223, 233

The Earl of Oxford and Asquith, Mells Manor Archives: 37 upper left, 51 above right, 51 below right, 52 above, 72, 104 all, 105 all, 106–107, 106, 108 left, 108 above right, 109 above, 110

Roger Phillips: Photography for frontispiece and 237

Rotherfield Park Archives: 181 all

Smithsonian Institution, Archives of American Gardens, Garden club of America Collection: 167, 168–169

Southill Park Archives: Table of Contents, 9 below, 14 lower right, 16 left, 17 upper right, 17 lower right, 17 middle left, 18 left, 19 upper left, 20 above, 22 left below, 23, 32, 36, 37 below, 40, 43 above, 44 upper right, 45 lower left, 45 above, 58, 60 below, 69, 73 upper left, 73 upper right, 114, 115 all, 116 all, 117 all, 166 all, 170, 187, 191, 192, 193, 194 all, 209 all, 227 above, 230, 244 above, 246 all

State Protocol Services of the Republic of Slovenia: 184 all

Yale University Beinecke Rare Book Library, Yale Collection of American Literature, Edith Wharton Collection: 200, 201, 217, 218, 219, 220 all